Canadian Churches & Social Justice

The publication of this volume is sponsored by the Ecumenical Forum of Canada.

The Ecumenical Forum is a Canadian centre for dialogue, education and training on contemporary approaches to mission and ecumenism. Through its publications program, the Forum seeks to encourage ecumenical dialogue, in Canada and internationally, on current issues of mission, world development and social justice.

The books published, however, reflect the opinions of their authors and are not meant to represent the official position of the Forum.

Canadian & Social Churches & Justice

EDITED BY JOHN R. WILLIAMS

ANGLICAN BOOK CENTRE
and
JAMES LORIMER & COMPANY, PUBLISHERS

Toronto 1984

ISBN 0-919891-18-7 (Anglican Book Centre)
       0-88862-755-6 (James Lorimer & Company Limited)

Design: Nancy Ruth Jackson

Canadian Cataloguing in Publication Data

Main entry under title:

Canadian churches and social justice

1. Church and social problems — Canada. 2. Economics — Religious aspects — Christianity. 3. Christianity and politics. I. Williams, John R. (John Reynold), 1942-

HN39.C3C36 1984   261.8   C84-099617-9

Anglican Book Centre
600 Jarvis Street
Toronto, Ontario
M4Y 2J6

and

James Lorimer & Company Ltd., Publishers
Egerton Ryerson Memorial Building
35 Britain Street
Toronto, Ontario
M5A 1R7

Printed and bound in Canada
6 5 4 3 2 1   84 85 86 87 88 89

Contents

List of Contributors

Assemblée des évêques du Québec
The British Columbia Conference, United Church of Canada
Canadian Conference of Catholic Bishops
The Canadian Council of Churches
Inter-Church Committee on Human Rights in Latin America
Inter-Church Committee for Refugees
Inter-Church Project on Population
Lutheran Church in America, Eastern Canada Synod
Project North
Roman Catholic Bishops of Atlantic Canada
The Salvation Army
Taskforce on the Churches and Corporate Responsibility
The United Church of Canada

Acknowledgements

Assistance in the preparation of this book from the following individuals and agencies is gratefully acknowledged: Dr. Leslie Harris, President, Memorial University of Newfoundland, for a grant from the University Publications Fund; the Social Sciences and Humanities Research Council of Canada for research funding provided through its general grant to Memorial University of Newfoundland; Miss Nancy Dawe, for her expert wordprocessing of the manuscript; and all the church and inter-church agencies which provided me with their documents and oral histories.

This book is dedicated to my mother and late father, Patricia and Reynold Williams.

INTRODUCTION

In 1968 Pierre Trudeau led the federal Liberal Party to a decisive electoral victory using as a campaign slogan "The Just Society." The late 1960s was a period of moral idealism and economic growth in Canada, and Trudeau evidently felt that Canadians both wanted and could afford a greater measure of social justice. The Liberal government was to find out very quickly that there was considerable disagreement among Canadians with regard to both the meaning of social justice and the best way to attain it. And as the 1970s progressed, the worsening state of the economy resulted in increasing constraints on the federal government's ability to initiate programs of social concern. As a result, it may be said that Canada is no more of a "just society" today than it was in 1968.

Among the many Canadian organizations which have taken up the cause of a just society, few have worked harder for the realization of this goal than the Canadian churches. The documents that are contained in this book are evidence of the churches' strong concern to identify and combat injustices wherever they appear in society. Although not all of the Christian churches in Canada share this concern, and of those that do some are relatively recent converts, nevertheless there can be little doubt that these churches are now firmly committed to the cause of social justice.

The purpose of this introduction is to give, first of all, a brief historical account of the churches' recent involvement in social issues in Canada. Secondly, it will identify the issues which are of major concern and will describe how the churches deal with these issues. Finally, an overview and analysis of the churches' position on social justice will be given.

1

THE HISTORICAL BACKGROUND

Although social justice was not a major focus of church concern for the greater part of Canadian history, and indeed was sometimes conspicuously ignored,[1] there had never been a time when the churches neglected these issues entirely. The Social Gospel movement of the late nineteenth and early twentieth centuries, Christian Socialism in the 1930s, and the Antigonish Movement in Nova Scotia all testify to a recurring (if intermittent) concern with the relevance of Christianity for the social order.[2] As a general rule, though, Christian churches in this country have avoided criticism of the existing social order, and have often given positive support to the political and economic system and authorities.

In the 1960s, however, things began to change. The Roman Catholic Church, which had been one of the most conservative of the large Canadian churches, was gradually transformed as a result of the Second Vatican Council (1962-65). In addition to a new openness to internal changes, it began to work in close cooperation with other Christian churches and non-Christian organizations on a variety of social issues. The larger Protestant churches were also feeling the spirit of the 1960s, and began to reevaluate their role in society. A significant focus of this revival of interest in social action was the Conference on Christian Conscience and Poverty, May 16-19, 1968, in Montreal. In response to this conference, a joint committee of the Canadian Council of Churches and the Canadian Catholic Conference (later renamed the Canadian Conference of Catholic Bishops) prepared a report entitled, *Towards a Coalition for Development*, which recommended much greater inter-church involvement and cooperation on social issues.

Another catalyst for the involvement of the churches in social affairs was the review of certain sections of the Criminal Code carried on by the Canadian Parliament from 1966 to 1969. Although the primary concern of those Canadian churches which participated in this debate was the legalization of contraception, homosexuality, divorce and abortion (under certain circumstances), that is, issues of personal rather than social morality, the opportunity to formulate and publicly express moral views awakened many churches to the possibility of further ethical analysis and teaching in the public sphere.

A third impetus to greater social involvement by the Canadian churches has come from their contacts with progressive religious groups in the Third World. The World Council of Churches conferences on "The Christian in the Technical and Social Revolutions of Our Time" in Geneva (1966) and on "World Cooperation for Development" in Beirut (1968—co-sponsored by the Roman Catholic Church) and their General Assemblies in Uppsala (1968) and Nairobi (1975) resounded to the charges of Third World Christians that the churches in countries like Canada were contributing to world poverty by failing to work for better treatment of the poor countries by their own governments and multinational corporations. Canadian delegates to these meetings took this message back to their own churches, and it has not been ignored. Meanwhile, Roman Catholic church leaders in Canada were participating in meetings with Latin American bishops and in the Third Synod of Bishops at Rome in 1971, where the theme was "Justice in the World." Like their Anglican and Protestant counterparts, they returned from these meetings determined to direct Canadian Christians towards greater social justice.

STRUCTURES AND ISSUES

As a result of influences such as these, the Canadian churches turned their attention to the problems of the country as a whole and especially to its most disadvantaged members: the poor, Native People, prisoners, immigrants, etc. In order to deal more adequately with these issues, many of the churches introduced structural changes into their organizations. The Anglican Church, for example, established in 1973 its Unit on Public Social Responsibility with a wide-ranging mandate to conduct research, education and action on such social issues as pollution, racism, domestic and world poverty, disarmament and consumption. The Unit was authorized to consult with business, labour and political leaders, to represent the General Synod of the Anglican Church at shareholders meetings, to join with other groups in exploring joint research, strategy and action, and to take public stands on issues. Since its formation, the Unit has actively fulfilled this mandate, often to the considerable displeasure of some Anglican businessmen who feel that the church has no right to criticize their policies and actions.

Many of the functions performed by the Anglican Unit on Public Social Responsibility have been taken up by newly established or refurbished agencies of other Canadian churches: the Social Affairs Commission of the Canadian Conference of Catholic Bishops, the

Department of Church in Society of the United Church of Canada, the Commission on Moral and Social Standards and Issues of the Salvation Army in Canada, and the Social Action Committee of the Baptist Convention of Ontario and Quebec, to name just a few. Although there is certainly no unanimity of approach or conclusions among these churches, there does seem to be general agreement among them that the teachings of Christianity can and should be applied to the pressing social problems of today's world, and not just to those issues which affect Christians as individuals.

Another locus of concern for social change within the individual Canadian churches has been their agencies devoted to international affairs. Most of these were founded to facilitate the spread of Christianity in the so-called pagan countries of Asia, Africa and Latin America through the sending of missionaries. In time, these missionaries came to minister to the material as well as the spiritual needs of the people with whom they lived and worked, and the Canadian churches began to raise money for the relief of poverty and for socio-economic development in the Third World. As the United Nations "First Development Decade" (the 1960s) ended with no appreciable diminution of world poverty, the church development agencies were analyzing more closely the causes of this poverty. Challenged by the calls of Third World Christians for more just international economic relations, the Canadian churches authorized their development agencies to initiate research and public education programs on Canada's responsibility for world poverty. These programs have often coincided very closely with the domestic social affairs activities of the churches as described above.

In addition to the social justice activities of the individual Canadian churches, the past decade has seen the creation of a large number of inter-church organizations to deal with specific social issues. One of the first of these was the Inter-Church Committee for World Development Education, which has sponsored an annual "Ten Days for World Development" program each year since 1973. The five participating churches in this agency are the Anglican, Lutheran, Presbyterian, Roman Catholic and United, and the Ten Days program acts as a preliminary to their Lenten fundraising efforts for international development. Although based in Toronto, the national committee works through local Ten Days groups across the country, and these committees are encouraged to make the connection between poverty and exploitation overseas and in their own area.[3]

Another inter-church organization which deals with international development is GATT-Fly. It was established by the same five church sponsors of the Ten Days program, along with the Canadian Council of Churches, as a result of a visit by four Canadian observers to the Third United Nations Conference on Trade and Development (UNCTAD) in Santiago de Chile in 1972. The initial focus of the GATT-Fly project was on the international trade issues raised by GATT (the General Agreement on Tariffs and Trade) and UNCTAD, and the basic objective of the sponsoring churches in establishing GATT-Fly was to contribute to a deeper understanding of current international economic justice issues. The GATT-Fly staff have published a large number of research studies on various aspects of international trade and development and their significance for Canadians. In addition, they conduct educational seminars for various interest groups (unions, farmers, unemployed, etc.) in Canada to help them understand their role in the global economic system.[4] Thus, GATT-Fly's activities are directed towards a more specific constituency than are those of the Inter-Church Committee for World Development Education, but the concerns of the two agencies overlap to a considerable extent, and the broad network of local Ten Days committees serves a useful distribution function for GATT-Fly materials.

One of the most controversial of the inter-church agencies is the Taskforce on the Churches and Corporate Responsibility. Established in 1973 as the Taskforce on Dialogue with Corporations and renamed in 1975, this organization has the same six sponsors as GATT-Fly plus the Canadian Religious Conference of Ontario, the Jesuit Fathers, the Redemptorist Fathers, and the Sisterhood of St. John the Divine. The main concerns of the Taskforce have been the activities of Canadian corporations, especially the chartered banks and mining companies, in Chile and Southern Africa. Taskforce members have tried to discourage bank loans and corporate investment in these countries until the civil rights situation improves there. Their preferred tactics to date have been dialogue with board and executive members, raising their concerns at shareholders meetings, and lobbying government officials to enforce higher standards of business morality.

Project North is an inter-church agency devoted to support of Native Peoples in northern Canada. Founded in 1975 by the Anglican, Roman Catholic and United churches (later joined by the Lutherans, Mennonites and Presbyterians), Project North has provided direct and indirect support for the formulation and publicizing of Native claims to self-government and aboriginal land title over the territories they inhabit. As a result of their efforts, the sponsoring churches have joined in the Native organizations' demand for a moratorium on all large-scale northern development projects until the land claims disputes are settled.

Other inter-church agencies dealing with social justice issues include PLURA, a funding and public education organization dedicated to helping disadvantaged groups in Canada eliminate the causes of their poverty (through self-help and political action, if necessary); Project Ploughshares, which attempts through public education and lobbying to challenge Canada's large military spending and arms exports; The Church Council on Justice and Corrections, which deals with law reform, especially criminal justice and punishment; and the Inter-Church Project on Population, the National Inter-Faith Immigration Committee, the Inter-Church Committee for Refugees, and the Inter-Church Committee on Human Rights in Latin America, all of which deal with the problems of immigration and refugees in Canada.

Besides these ecumenical groups, there are two Christian social justice agencies based in Toronto which contribute greatly to the work of bringing about a more just society in Canada. Citizens for Public Justice (formerly known as the Committee for Justice and Liberty) has been working since 1963 on such issues as "closed shop" union contracts and government financial aid to independent schools. Beginning in 1972, they became heavily involved in the interrelated issues of national energy policy, northern development, and Native rights, and they have been one of the principal organizers of opposition to the Mackenzie Valley pipeline proposals (see Section IV below). The Jesuit Centre for Social Faith and Justice is active on a variety of social justice issues, including those related to health care, Native rights, and human rights in Central America. They cooperate closely with the inter-church agencies on matters of common concern.

This description of church involvement in social issues would be quite incomplete without a mention of the regional church and inter-church contributions. Some of the national agencies have regional and/or local committees, such as Ten Days for World Development, Project North, Project Ploughshares and PLURA. Other independent groups have been formed to deal with specific issues, such as the Inter-Church Uranium Committee of Saskatchewan, the Inter-Church Coalition on Resource Development in Manitoba, and the Inter-Church Commission on the Social Impact of Resource Development in Newfoundland. Working with very limited financial resources, these groups have played a major role in opposing certain large-scale resource development projects which they consider to be against the interests of social justice in their areas (cf. Section III below).

In addition to the activities of these coalitions, the leaders of certain Canadian churches have from time to time made public statements on social justice issues. During the Ten Days for World Development in March, 1973, the leaders of the five participating churches drew up a joint statement entitled *Development Demands Justice* (reprinted below, #18) for presentation to the federal Cabinet and subsequently to the people of Canada. This statement was a call for greater justice in Canada's dealings with Third World countries, including an increase in both the quantity and the quality of our foreign aid. Three years later, the church leaders presented a second brief to the government, entitled *Justice Demands Action*. This document dealt with five areas of social concern to Canadians: international development, trans-national corporations, northern development, income distribution, and immigration, population and refugees. A third brief was presented in March, 1978, this time dealing with Canada's economic outlook (#21 below). Although the theme of this brief is that little if any progress has been made towards greater social justice in Canada since 1973, the church leaders evidently feel that these lobbying efforts are worthwhile and will eventually bear fruit.

Not all church members have agreed with the social justice statements and activities of these church groups. Some of these dissidents have set up organizations to try and persuade the churches to alter their views on certain social issues. The first of these, established in 1977, is the Confederation of Church and Business People. This group is composed mainly of business executives and some high-ranking clergymen, although it has no official church support, and its stated objectives are to analyze relevant social issues, to provide a reliable medium for communicating basic information on such issues, and to guard against small groups trying to use a church to project their own ideologies. The members of this organization accuse the inter-church groups and some church leaders of many misdeeds, including an anti-business bias and a failure to reflect the average churchperson's view of political and economic issues when making statements on behalf of the churches. To date, however, the Confederation has failed to convince church bodies to withdraw support for the inter-church groups under attack.

Another extra-ecclesiastical opposition group is the Centre for the Study of Economics and Religion, part of the Vancouver-based Fraser Institute economic thinktank. Its first activities were a pair of conferences on religion and economics in the summer of 1982, to which were invited both critics and proponents of capitalism. The proceedings of these conferences are to be published and distributed in an attempt to wean Canadian churchpeople away from their anti-capitalistic biases.[5]

The documents which have been selected for this collection do not deal with all of the issues which the churches have been involved with, nor are all the churches and inter-church agencies mentioned above represented here. The purpose of this book is to give an indication of both the wide range of the churches' concern for social justice in Canada and the variety of methods by which they treat these issues.

A BRIEF EVALUATION

A full-scale analysis and evaluation of the Canadian churches' involvement in social justice issues since the 1960s remains to be written. What follows is a brief overview of the documents contained in this collection and an indication of their principal strengths and weaknesses.

One noteworthy characteristic of these documents is that they reflect the different organizational structures of the churches which produced them. Some of them carry the full authority of the national church, since they have been approved by the highest level of authority in that church (e.g., the Roman Catholic Bishops of Canada). Others have been produced by regional sectors of a church (e.g., the B.C. Conference of the United Church of Canada), and presumably do not necessarily represent the other regions of that church. Still others have been issued by certain church departments or sub-sections (e.g., the United Church Department of Church in Society), and do not have the same force as if proclaimed by the highest authority of that church. Then there are the statements of inter-church organizations and leaders of different churches, all of which represent indirectly the positions of the participating churches and yet have not been explicitly approved by them.

This variety of answers to the question—what authority do these documents possess?—is paralleled by the answers to the question—to whom are the documents addressed? Some are directed to the government: the prime minister and his Cabinet, parliamentary committees dealing with specific social issues, certain ambassadors, etc. Others have been presented to government-appointed regulatory or advisory bodies: e.g., the Mackenzie Valley Pipeline Inquiry. Finally, there are those which are written for the general membership of the churches and sometimes the general public. This latter group of documents are intended primarily to educate their readers, whereas the others have more specific goals—e.g., the immediate change of government policies on matters of social justice.

A third form of variety among these documents relates to how explicitly religious they are. There are several ways of presenting religious teachings on ethical issues: through stories (history, myth or fiction); by the explicit application of theological or scriptural principles to social issues; through the presentation of factual information in a certain setting which evokes a religious response to that information (e.g., in a church service). The story approach has not been characteristic of the Canadian churches to date. The other two approaches are both in evidence among the documents in this book. Some of them identify with precision the religious basis for both the churches' involvement with the issues in question and the solutions to the problems which they are proposing. Other documents simply present the relevant political and economic analysis of the issue with a minimum of explicit religious (or even ethical) input (e.g., the *Issue* sheets of the United Church). Often the only thing that distinguishes these from non-religious documents is the name of the church or inter-church group on the title page.

All this diversity among these documents has not been universally beneficial to their effectiveness. Even those written for the general membership of the church often do not reach many church people, either because of bottle-necks in the distribution system (e.g., unsympathetic pastors) or because they are not fully integrated into "normal" church functions (e.g., the worship services). The documents which are addressed to specific groups such as government agencies are even less known throughout the churches. The only hint of their existence might be a brief summary in a church newspaper. For reasons such as these, the social justice concerns of the churches are not wholeheartedly supported by the vast majority of the church membership. And so it is relatively easy for politicians and business leaders to reject the demands of the churches for greater social justice, since these people know that the church leaders and inter-church agencies do not fully represent the general membership of their churches. To overcome this difficulty, some of the churches are stepping up their general educational programs on social justice issues in an effort to extend the official concern for justice as widely as possible throughout the churches.[6]

Another important characteristic of the documents in this book is the great degree of unity in the positions of the different Christian churches which have produced them. Despite the major differences on points of doctrine and even ethics (e.g., on abortion) which continue to separate these churches, they have managed to work very closely together on social justice issues. This is not to say that all the Canadian churches are in accord on these matters. The majority of evangelical Protestant churches have said very little about these issues, continuing their traditional preoccupation with the salvation of individual Christians. And not all of the churches represented in this book have been equally outspoken in their denunciation of social injustices in Canada. Among the five largest Canadian churches, however—Roman Catholic, United, Anglican, Lutheran and Presbyterian—there has developed a very close working relationship, at least at the national level, and the Christian concern for social justice has been greatly strengthened by the common declarations of these churches.

What exactly is the position of these churches on social justice? First of all, they are agreed that religious morality should deal not just with the actions of individuals towards other individuals but also with the actions of groups of people towards other groups (e.g., politicians and voters, unions and management, corporations and consumers). And many actions which were formerly considered to be beyond the scope of religious morality, such as political and economic activities, are now regarded as matters of church concern just as much as lying, stealing and killing between individuals. According to this view of morality, many aspects of our political and economic system are intrinsically unjust because they are harmful to certain human beings, especially the poor and otherwise disadvantaged. No amount of individual moral rectitude can overcome these structural defects of our society.

A second feature of the churches' position on social justice is that it has concentrated on issues which are of particular concern to Canadians. None of these is exclusive to Canada, but there is a much greater emphasis on such issues as resource development and the limitations of capitalism than on such American preoccupations as race relations and conscientious objection to war, for example. The churches' documents often display an overtly nationalist approach in that foreign control of the Canadian economy and American support of Third World dictatorships are condemned as major causes of social injustice.

One other characteristic of the churches' position is worthy of note—its lack of an explicitly formulated concept of social justice. This term is used constantly in the documents of the churches and inter-church groups, but very rarely is there any discussion of its meaning. Those who use the term seem to have an intuitive understanding of its significance and consider themselves quite capable of recognizing it when they see it in action (or at least its opposite—injustice).

The churches' social activists may be excused for not dealing with the extensive philosophical literature on the nature of justice. However, a brief discussion of social justice here may help to assess the documents in this collection. Using the dictionary definition of justice as "giving each her/his due" one can proceed to specify what is this "due." The churches' position is based on an understanding of the equality of all human beings; therefore their "due" is basically the same. Nowadays it is described in terms of basic human needs: food, clothing, shelter, health care, education, emotional and spiritual support. In addition, one's "due" includes the recognition of her/his basic human rights, such as freedom of religion, speech, etc. Any deliberate action which either directly or indirectly prevents people from fulfilling these needs and rights is interfering with social justice. There may be extenuating circumstances, but the cause of social justice requires that obstacles to the exercise of these needs and rights be eliminated. These obstacles are often political and/or economic in nature, and so the quest for social justice involves critiques of the local, national and international structures of political and economic power which deprive millions of people of their basic needs and rights.

This concept of social justice is an ideal which will probably never be realized on earth. However, the churches feel that it is imperative to identify the worst forms of injustice and take whatever steps they can to improve the situation. The documents in this book are evidence of this concern. To date they have had relatively little success in making Canada a "just society." Whether greater success will come in the future remains to be seen.

A NOTE ON THE DOCUMENTS

Well over 100 documents were considered for this collection. Of these, 21 have been chosen and edited according to the following criteria: (1) a few documents dealing with each of a fairly broad range of issues are presented rather than a more in-depth treatment of a limited number of issues, since this is the first collection of its kind in Canada; (2) most of the documents are reproduced in their entirety or with relatively minor deletions, in order that the reader may judge them on both what is said and what is left unsaid; (3) a balance is maintained, though somewhat imperfectly depending on the issue, between the presentation of factual information on a topic and arguments for a particular evaluation of the facts. In each section, suggestions for further readings from readily available publications are given for those who wish to undertake a more intensive examination of the issue.

SECTION I
POVERTY IN CANADA

The Canadian churches have always been concerned about poverty. Until recently, however, they were mainly preoccupied with the effects of poverty — inadequate housing and clothing, hunger, absence of educational opportunities, etc. — rather than with its causes. Traditionally, the churches and other religious organizations were leaders in providing social services for the poor, and even today, despite massive government welfare programs, most churches provide at least emergency assistance for the poor at the local level.

This palliative approach to the problem of poverty, necessary as it is even in a nation as affluent as Canada, is now regarded by many churches as no longer sufficient. In recent times they have been concentrating more and more on the causes of poverty, especially its structural aspects. They no longer regard poverty as primarily the result of the laziness or irresponsibility of the poor themselves or as the will of God for certain blameless individuals. Instead, they have come to view poverty as a direct consequence of the exploitation of the poor by the rich—not as individuals but as classes within society. And this exploitation is not simply an accidental feature of our political and economic system which can be overcome by a few reforms (always "when the economy improves") but is rather an essential element of free-market capitalism. Thus, the continuing fact of widespread poverty in Canada has led even senior church leaders to call for radical changes to our capitalist economic system.

The three selections in this section display the progression of Christian analysis of the problem of poverty from during the 1970s. The Salvation Army has long been noted for their welfare services to the poor. In their *Brief to the Special Senate Committee on Poverty*

(1970), they deal primarily with the personal causes of poverty, such as family breakdown. However, they do realize that poverty is very much a social problem as well, and that there is much that governments can do to alleviate the problem. But they do not call for any changes in the economic system of the country, and they generally avoid any confrontation with governments even when they disagree with official policies.

The report of the Special Senate Committe on Poverty, *Poverty in Canada* (1971), and *The Real Poverty Report* by Ian Adams *et al* (also 1971) focussed a considerable amount of public attention on this issue. As a result, a number of Canadian churches set up poverty taskforces to examine this problem and made recommendations for action. In 1973 the Eastern Canada Synod of the Lutheran Church in America issued its *Report on Poverty and Christian Responsibility*. Intended primarily for church members as an educational resource, this document is much more critical of the Canadian economic system than is the Salvation Army brief, and it makes several recommendations regarding government redistribution of wealth from the rich to the poor through the taxation system. This report also discusses the theological basis for Christian action against poverty.

By the mid-1970s the centre of attention for the churches' poverty taskforces was the federal government proposal for a guaranteed annual income (GAI). The Anglican and United Churches of Canada both issued study documents on this topic in 1975, and the reports of their taskforces on poverty, published in 1977, dealt with the GAI as part of an overall attack on poverty. By that time, however, the federal proposal had been shelved because of the failure of the provincial and federal governments to agree on its implementation. The third selection in this section is taken from the United Church of Canada, Department of Church in Society, *Issue* series of educational newsheets on social issues, #10 entitled, *The Economics of Injustice: Income Distribution and the GAI*. Following an examination of the extent and causes of poverty in Canada which parallels the Lutheran document (this section is omitted here), the United Church paper describes the GAI and indicates why it or a similar proposal should be implemented.

1 · BRIEF TO THE SPECIAL SENATE COMMITTEE ON POVERTY

THE SALVATION ARMY, CANADA, COMMISSION ON MORAL AND SOCIAL STANDARDS AND ISSUES, 1970

WHAT IS POVERTY?

There has never been a society in any period of human history that has avoided the curse of poverty. The degree of poverty has waxed and waned with the rise and fall of nations and "civilizations," but always there have been those described by the words of the poet where "...cruel penury has chilled the genial current of the soul."

The Salvation Army, as a religious and social movement, came into being in response to the challenge of a new wave of mass poverty rising in the wake of the Industrial Revolution.

"Darkest England" was a phrase used to describe the submerged tenth making up the human flotsam and jetsam of the booming industrial cities. It was much the same group that Marx described as the proletariat: downtrodden, inarticulate, powerless, impoverished. Using this unlikely material our founder organized the first war on poverty in modern times by recruiting them into a Salvation Army.

The problem of poverty persists into the affluent and technocratic twentieth century. In underdeveloped lands we hear of the millions in dire need below the subsistence level, and in the affluent West we have become so concerned that governments have launched massive new wars on poverty. Meantime, as the Negro spiritual puts

15

it simply and effectively, "the rich get richer and the poor get poorer."

Obviously, poverty today is a relative term. It goes far beyond the usual economic and financial criteria. How can we compare the poverty level in some countries where thousands of our fellow humans are on the verge of starvation, with the standards of living at all levels in the wealthier nations? Elaborate welfare programs, transfer payments, health and education programs are gradually placing citizens of the favoured nations above the level of physical and material need. Yet the pall of poverty hangs over a favoured nation like Canada to such an extent as to persuade you distinguished senators to carry out this commendable investigation in depth.

Perhaps what we are really investigating is the feeling of impoverishment brought about by the revolution of "rising expectations" marked by the popular pursuit engaged in by so many of us today— "more and more for less and less." It is true we have pockets of poverty, slums, ethnic ghettos, and poverty pockmarks and pollution marring the Canadian social landscape everywhere. The irony and tragedy is that we have the know-how and technical skills to eliminate this social blight if only we had the will and social conscience to provide the motivation. This is where the Church with its emphasis on spiritual dimensions comes into the picture.

Above all else poverty concerns man: the whole man, body, mind and spirit, all of which must be served if he is to live the "life more abundant." Surely it is clear today that the "good life" does not consist in the abundance of goods we possess. We see our fine young people dropping out from affluent homes because of the atmosphere of moral and spiritual impoverishment. We see aged parents, minority groups, the physically and mentally handicapped neglected, deprived of human dignity, human opportunity, human freedom for the same reason.

It will require more than government action to break through these social, psychological and spiritual barriers. What is needed is a partnership of individuals and voluntary groups committed and dedicated to serving man. In the early, less sophisticated days, the Salvation Army endeavoured to encompass the whole man with the simple slogan, "soup, soap, salvation." It realized that people suffering from impoverishment could only break out into a more abundant life as they personally became involved in finding solutions. Hence, the battle cry of that early and continuing war on poverty:

"Saved to Serve"—for "Man's extremity is God's opportunity"—and God works through His people.

CAUSES OF POVERTY

It is not true that most poor people are lazy and would rather live on welfare than get work. The working poor comprise from 65 to 75 per cent of the poverty problem in Canada. Many of the working poor would be better off financially on welfare, but they prefer working. The Economic Council of Canada, in its sixth annual review, chapter 7, says as much, adding, "On the basis of careful investigations, it would appear that most of the poor are ready to seize appropriate jobs when these are available. Furthermore, some recent research suggests that the aspirations of the poor for economic opportunities and a middle class style of life may be very strong, and the desire to participate in a productive way in our society is more often frustrated than lacking." Poverty, in many cases, is the consequence of forces beyond the individual's control.

Insufficient Income: While money is not the complete answer to the problem of poverty, it is obvious that many are poor because they do not have sufficient income. Others with insufficient income include those living on Welfare, Family Benefits and Old Age Security pensions. The problem is more acute when people with small incomes have large families. The high cost of living, especially the cost of housing, makes it almost impossible for people with low incomes to maintain even a reasonable standard of living.

Poor Education and Lack of Skills: Many in this automated technological age simply cannot fit in because of poor education and lack of skills. Some are incapable of absorbing further education or training, but this is not true of the majority. In some cases they left school early because they did not realize the value of education, or dropped out because of the necessity of helping to support the family. It may be their parents did not encourage them to continue at school.

Addictions: These vices drain away resources which should be used for essentials such as food, clothing, housing. This is becoming a growing problem due to aggressive promotion of the sale of liquor, and increasing permissiveness with respect to gambling and drugs.

Mismanagement: Many are inefficient at budgeting and managing their affairs.

Abuse of Credit Buying: Credit buying can be a boon to those who are able to plan and allocate funds through proper budgeting, but it is a serious pitfall to those with small incomes who are not competent. In many instances such people owe large amounts to finance companies and department stores. Advertising makes many things seem desirable and even necessary, and poor people yield to the temptation to buy on credit.

Misfortune: The large majority of poor people are not criminals, addicts or "multi-problem" individuals, but folk who, because of circumstances beyond their control, have become poverty-stricken. They include the physically and emotionally handicapped, elderly people who have worked hard, own their little home, get along on their pension, then are suddenly impoverished by inflation or heavy nursing-home expenses. Some have lost their jobs because of closing down of factories, making it especially difficult for an older worker to secure another position. Some people are "not so much born into the world as damned into it." They come from poor families, live in substandard housing—receive little care or training—and are not encouraged to stay at school.

POVERTY AND THE AGED

When one reads that a family spends more than 70 per cent of its income on food, clothing and shelter, and that the income of hundreds of aged is below the stated amount required to live decently and above the poverty line, we are faced with a problem that needs urgent attention. Again it is not that they are lazy or indifferent, but, on the contrary, unskilled, crippled or ill with no hope of supplementing their income. Much is being done to prolong life, but people should not then be left to languish in loneliness and want.

After working hard to build up what they thought was a reserve, paying off the mortgages on a house, educating children, paying their share of taxes, the aged find their resources eaten up with inflationary costs. They are forced to sell their home, live in rooms, or, if fortunate, a lodge or institution where they are charged beyond their means.

Recommendations

1. *Senior Citizens' Residences* should be built near transportation and shopping so that the elderly are not isolated. Our senior citizens

have a special contribution to make in society, and every effort should be made to keep them in the mainstream of the community. In our impersonal urbanized society this may be an effective way of bridging the generation gap that threatens to become a chasm.

2. *Drop-In Centres*: In such places those who live alone could have fellowship, conversation and creative activity.

3. *Increased Financial Assistance*: Old Age Security and assistance programs have failed to keep pace with inflation. These should be geared to the actual cost-of-living index. Incentive should be provided by allowing senior citizens to retain any earnings.

4. *Medicare*: Such plans should be upgraded to provide for drug prescriptions, eye glasses, dentures and other paramedical services for senior citizens.

POVERTY AND CRIME

There is a connection between crime and poverty. The lack of the essentials of life may influence individuals towards breaking the law. This points up the need for the government to strengthen and enforce the Minimum Wage Act.

Sending the Bread-winner to Prison: Too often the male bread-winner is jailed, and the family deprived of his earning power. The mother is reduced to accepting inadequate welfare, or, if she works, cannot cope with the cost of basic needs.

Recommendations

1. *Personal Recognizance:* We urge an increased use of the summons, which would reduce serious loss of jobs, or of workdays, both of which drain the small family income. Release on personal recognizance on charges that are not too serious allows the accused to continue to support his anxious family.

2. *"Time-to-Pay the Fine":* This is a help to those who have no ready cash, but even so it still prolongs family distress. We suggest, on the basis of our experience, that a warning, suspended sentence and/or probation would often have the desired effect.

3. *The Young Offender* needs closer supervision on probation. Often he cannot return to his poverty-stricken home. The ideal place

for him is the beneficial environment of homes like the House of Concord, where he may continue his schooling or learn a trade.

4. *Free Legal Aid:* Indigent persons urgently need this guidance, but it should be instituted on a much wider scale—at the federal rather than provincial level.

5. *Psychiatric Treatment:* When this is ordered by the court, the full cooperation of the employer should be sought so the accused may be able to maintain his earning power while under treatment.

6. *Pay for Prisoners:* We feel this system should be made more profitable through the manufacture, by prisoners, of goods that are in demand. If prisoners were paid more, the inmate could better support his family, make reparation to his victims or budget his savings, all of which would play a vital part in his rehabilitation. Such accumulated credits could provide funds at the time of the prisoner's release for families, for job training or for transportation. Under certain schemes money has been made available for work-permits, licences, tools, union dues, etc., and should be expanded under supervision to ensure early employment for released prisoners.

7. *After-Care:* The Salvation Army urges extension of present efforts to unite inmate husbands with wives and recommends the extension of the present "work leave" program now operative.

POVERTY AND THE MULTI-PROBLEM FAMILY

The term "multi-problem family" has long been a part of the vocabulary of social theorists. It describes a family that is the victim of a deep-seated entanglement of many social problems of long duration. These families are often bypassed, or given only emergency assistance. The Salvation Army has a wide contact with this group, and is concerned because present social policies aggravate and perpetuate the problem.

Contributing Factors: Poverty in the multi-problem family is best understood by looking at the factors contributing to its existence— the basic cause being unemployment and/or unemployability. Lack of money and material comforts are at the root of this snowballing phenomenon, leading to inadequate housing, growing worse over a period of time. Continued lack of money and dependence on small government assistance lasting from generation to generation leads to an irreversible lethargy on the part of the parents, manifested in personal and family neglect, and increasing hopelessness.

A Psychological Look: These families possess immature personalities in terms of ego development. They act out their feelings and frustrations and show poor impulse control, seen in the continued pattern of alcoholism and unreliability, or the inability to manage what limited financial resources are available.

Dependent Factors: The dynamics of dependency operate here. These people, disillusioned and with no ability to look to the future, are captives of the present, and are dependent on their life-situation as it is now. Their deep-seated hostility toward those who want to help or change them, makes it almost impossible to alter their situation.

Recommendations

1. To break this cycle of poverty we might best concentrate much of our effort on the children. There should be educational and rehabilitation emphasis, and we feel this can best be initiated from community or neighbourhood-based agencies. The individual must be seen as a complete person, not divided into segments of welfare, public health, school, manpower and child-welfare as he is now. We must be willing to adapt to new techniques.

2. *Jobs and Income:* Poverty is caused by an inadequate family income. Thus an effective war on poverty should include two basic socio-economic measures: (1) a program to create jobs and (2) a program of income maintenance. Such a policy of job creation would need full action on the part of the government as an employer and coordinator, and a commitment by the business community. Associated with this plan of creating job opportunities is the whole area of employability programs. This plan should be expanded.

3. *Income Maintenance:* Because of personal inadequacy, work alone will not solve the problem. We should consider a negative income tax plan to maintain income at a suitable level, while at the same time providing rehabilitation programs to encourage personal incentive.

SINGLE PARENT FAMILIES

The absence of one parent through divorce, separation, illegitimate pregnancy or death results in a single-parent family whose many problems deserve our concern and demand our attention.

The Salvation Army has been aware of the special needs of the unmarried mother and continues to develop services through maternity homes and hospitals to meet such needs until after the birth of the child. Should the unmarried mother accept the responsibility of keeping her child, her needs become those of the single-parent family.

The breakdown of the family irrespective of cause creates an identity problem for its members and their role may become irreversibly distorted. Their circumstances are such that their problems are frequently perpetuated from generation to generation. Economic poverty is an additional burden to the unnatural circumstances which exist. The single parent who is left with adequate financial support has a far greater opportunity to maintain a stable family unit than the one who must depend on public support.

Single-Parent Families Need Help
with Poverty in Several Areas

Physical Poverty: The results of physical poverty are clearly evident. Families are forced to live in inadequate houses, eat inadequate food and wear inadequate clothes. Their financial income is further depleted by their lack of management skills and also their inability to improvise.

Emotional Poverty may in its early stages be hidden poverty. Relationships are likely to be superficial and defensive. The poor are unwilling to reveal their deeper needs and experience further rejection. Such needs continue unmet.

Social Poverty becomes evident as children grow and develop without the opportunity to learn social skills through exposure to, and participation in, the facilities of the affluent society.

As we look at the total needs of people we must become aware of:

(i)   the inequality of justice—that allows welfare recipients to live in condemned housing yet pays tax dollars to the affluent landlord;

(ii) the inequality of opportunity—that restricts the mother in the use of dental services, recreation and educational facilities;

(iii) the inequality of expenditure—that provides large sums of money to care for a child once he has been removed from his own home.

How much does it cost to care? If we believe that a child's needs can best be met in his own family, then our spending of the tax dollars does not reflect our thinking. Through Mother's Allowance a natural mother is paid approximately $500 per year to meet the needs of her child. Through foster home care a mother is paid approximately $1,000 a year to meet the needs of the child who has been removed from his own home. The Treatment Centre is paid approximately $10,000 per year to meet the needs of the child who is not able to make a suitable adjustment within his own or surrogate home.

Recommendations

1. The Salvation Army asks government officials to determine whether or not this kind of spending can be justified when we know that much emotional illness results from rejection and stress in early years, when we know that treatment of emotional ills is more successful when treated in the phase of development in which it occurs.

2. We ask that consideration be given to the feasibility of a more adequate income supplemented by a more adequate counselling service for the single-parent family at the point of need. Surely such a program is not only financially more sound but emotionally more human.

3. Day-care service for the pre-school child is a luxury for some, a strong emotional support for others and a financial impossibility for many who need this kind of care. Such a service may free the mother to return to the labour force, become more fulfilled as a person and thus become a more adequate parent to her child. We recommend such services should be recognized in all areas of our country as worthy of tax support, making it possible for voluntary groups, already active in this field to meet the growing need.

THE WORKING POOR

For the purposes of this study we are dealing only with the working poor in urban areas. In many cases the cost of accommodation amounts to more than fifty per cent of the "take-home pay." As housing must always take priority over all other expenses, the provision of food, clothing and other necessities must suffer.

We must also realize that there will always be certain types of employment that are at the bottom of the wage scale. These jobs are not highly productive, and it would be economically unsound to pay high salaries to those who undertake this type of work.

One of the tragedies of our society is that often the bread-winner of the families we are considering finds it necessary to cease work in order that his family might be provided for. In short, welfare payments come to more than his wages. This of course means a loss of self-respect and independence, and the family accepting such a situation suffers immeasurable harm.

Another problem that sometimes arises in these families is that the wife and mother often feels compelled to get a job to supplement the family income, when she is really needed at home. Again the family suffers, and the children are deprived of the guidance and influence of the mother when these are most needed.

Recommendations

Housing: We feel more vigorous measures must be taken to provide subsidized, low-dividend or public housing.

Minimum Wage: We recommend the raising of the minimum wage.

Work Training Opportunities: The adult retraining program should be broadened to make it possible for the working poor, who had insufficient formal schooling, to upgrade themselves to the required entrance level—especially those over 40.

POVERTY AND ADDICTION

Addictions that contribute most to poverty appear to be alcoholism and the misuse of drugs. There is ample proof such addictions compound personal and family problems, resulting in unemployability, loss of work hours, permanent unemployment and, consequently, poverty.

Alcoholism: The consumption of alcoholic beverages appears to be recognized as part of our way of life. Social drinking seems to be equated with gracious living. The Salvation Army deplores this accelerating trend and finds confirmation for its concern in information gathered from data provided by the American Medical Association indicating a preponderance of alcoholics come from homes where social drinking was part of the family pattern....

Recommendations

1. Advertising of all products leading to harmful addiction or the possible impairment of health should be restricted and rigidly controlled.

2. The use or unnecessary display of addictive products in media presentation should be curtailed, preferably through the cooperation of the industry and the media.

3. Laws governing the use or possession of addictives, particularly drugs, should give priority to the treatment and rehabilitation of the victim rather than punishment, while, at the same time, retaining and even accentuating such clauses that ensure the effective punishment of the trafficker.

POVERTY AND THE TRANSIENT

Alienated Youth—Immigrants

Transients: Man's story is one of restless searchings through every age—this one is no exception. For over a century, the Salvation Army has served the homeless wanderer, seeking to help those who strain for new horizons—those who flee responsibility in their current environment or seek work in the next city. Depression, war, immaturity produce drifters travelling from one breadline to another. It is difficult to do more than meet the surface needs of such men—feeding the hungry, clothing the ragged, sheltering the weary. However, counselling and understanding sometimes are effective in instilling a sense of responsibility, especially in the young. Many men, now well-established in society, were drifters during the 1930s depression.

Alienated Youth: Today the problem is accentuated by youthful graduates from permissive or broken homes crowding in "hippie havens"—restless "floaters" determined only to please themselves—learning nothing from previous generations and responsible to none. Society has shown them, through the mass media, the worst in life, leading them to experiment with all the evils of modern society.

Disillusioned, then disturbed, they resort to unconventional and antisocial action that makes its contribution towards continued poverty. And while frequently based in large cities these young people are transients in spirit.

Facing these facts, our society must ask itself, "What can be done to halt this bitter harvest of a permissive sowing?" Proof is evident that youthful inexperience, unguided and uncontrolled, leads to disaster!

A genuine empathy for such youth, in unstructured, yet controlled programs, provides the greatest opportunity for a meaningful partnership, a lessening of tensions and alienation, while floundering for a firm foothold in this cybernetic era. Whether at a "drop-in" centre or hostel, warm personal guidance for the "whole" person is clearly indicated as a shelter from what is considered an impersonal "establishment" personified in government or business. We urge continued support and speedy extension of such *proven* centres which will increasingly bring the greatest returns for our own, and for community, investment.

Immigrants: Having emerged from previous generations of immigrants to Canada, one must be constantly reminded of the dire need into which the newcomer may still fall. He and his children are the citizens of tomorrow—this is sufficient, in itself, for assuring equal rights and privileges for all, for this is the land that beckons with the promise of "human rights" in a "just society"!

Patterns of discrimination regularly appear in employment/ unemployment situations and may need local or federal government intervention if the migrant family is to become happily absorbed as Canadians. The immigrant can be trapped in "red-tape" problems found at all levels of business—industry—labour. Manpower agencies are often unaware of the serious plight of the new citizen within our borders—and who may well have professional qualifications.

Here again, it can become a struggle to survive, let alone plan for a family which can include those still waiting overseas. Into such settings, the Army seeks to supplement aid from kindly neighbours while struggling to allay fears of deportation and untangle the web of circumstances that lead to worthwhile citizenship in their new home.

We have studied and appreciate the immigration policy of our country which, when operated on the basis of human need and personal helpfulness, is most effective. It is admittedly difficult for officials governed by fixed policy to maintain an objective attitude. Those thus concerned would do well to make their appraisal warm and humane.

SUMMARY AND CONCLUSIONS

The many-sided attempts to understand the ramifications of poverty today suggest the *urgent* necessity for a new approach. It is becoming clear that we are not only discussing human development but also human *survival*. Faced with a crisis of growing hate, hostility, frustration, violence and alienation, lonely voices are crying in a wilderness of fear and hopelessness for a compassionate society.

Civilization has arrived at a moment in history when there is no margin for error. Some people in society get more and more while the majority get less and less. Whether the causes are economic, social, cultural or authoritarian, to ignore the ecology of the problem or man's total needs would add to the *disparity* and to the *despair*.

It is evident the problems of poverty and human misery have overridden moral and spiritual dimensions. For example, the root *cause* of poverty is the breakdown of the family. The modern family instead of being the healing place of the soul has become the breeding ground for delinquency, divorce and individual breakdown. The unrelated attempts to *alleviate* this impoverishment of the spirit and personality have largely ignored the rights, the dignity and the worth of the individual. The *results* are dehumanizing and demoralizing. It is not sufficient to eliminate the physical and material needs of the poor when, under the complex surface symptoms, there is complete spiritual disarray. A deep concern of the church is that this spiritual malnutrition is suffered by all—not only the impoverished.

To bring relevancy to these issues, the time for paternalism, superimposed programs, false optimism and hypocrisy is past. The need is to improve the quality of human relations. The human endeavour must involve people in decision making and self-help projects. This is a shift in emphasis to being of service rather than imposing servility. It will require new motivation, dedication and moral courage that, we believe, best come from man's reconciliation with God.

It is a sad side effect of the new morality that there are growing tensions between church and state just at a time when there should be greater cooperation. The latter tends to regard religious bodies as of little significance or even of nuisance value. The church has no unique wisdom or technical answers to administrative problems but it has a definite role to serve as conscience for society. In addition it has the traditional role to serve the whole man.

To meet the challenge of poverty, all levels of authority must create the climate, the motivation and cooperation plus the perseverance to transform and renew all areas of life. Only in this manner is it possible for mankind to carry on the never-ending task of being a co-worker with God in finishing Creation.

2 · REPORT ON POVERTY AND CHRISTIAN RESPONSIBILITY

THE EASTERN CANADA SYNOD OF THE LUTHERAN CHURCH IN AMERICA, 1973

THE PROBLEM OF POVERTY

The Need for Sharing

What does it mean to be poor?

According to the Economic Council of Canada "the poor" have insufficient access to certain goods and services and conditions of life available to everyone else and accepted as basic to a decent, minimum standard of living.

To be poor may mean:

— a small girl in Halifax who refuses to take gym because she is ashamed to be seen in socks full of holes.

— a young boy in Toronto who has learned to undervalue himself because he has constantly been reminded that his father is too stupid or shiftless to find a decent job.

— a teenager in Hamilton who goes from one menial job to another because he decided it was a waste of time to further his education, since his parents could not afford it anyway.

— a mother in Montreal who is starving herself so she can provide a better diet for her children.

— a father on a run-down farm having to suffer the indignity of begging extra money from welfare to cover the cost of needed medical care for his family.

— a toothless old man in a tar-paper shack a few miles from Fredericton who has to walk half a mile for water.

— fifteen people sharing a bathroom in a crowded boarding house, or nine children sharing the only bedroom in a house, using coats as blankets.

What do these people see around them? The small girl may see a classmate who has a special gym outfit and a brand new pair of sneakers in November to replace ones which she has already carelessly lost.

The under-privileged teenager may see a fellow student driving his own sports car to school.

The mother may see families regularly eating out in high-class restaurants, or taking expensive ski holidays on the week-end.

The man on welfare may see the stately homes of the well-to-do and visualize the elegant furnishings and automatic household equipment which these homes contain.

The Problem of Poverty

This is *The Poverty Wall* of Ian Adams, a wall "built of greed, racism and the misery of 6,000,000 Canadians." Read the story of the young Indian boy who died of exposure in Northern Ontario trying to walk home from his Indian residential school, or the forgotten fluorspar miners of Newfoundland, slowly dying of lung cancer. Adams is one of the four staff writers for the Special Senate Committee on Poverty who became disillusioned and left to publish their own *Real Poverty Report*, available in paperback. This should be read in conjunction with the government-published report, *Poverty in Canada* because it is an analysis of the economic system that keeps people poor.

One basic assumption is that "any family or individual spending more than 70 per cent of total income on food, clothing, and shelter is in a low-income situation and likely to be suffering from poverty." In economic terms it is very difficult to fix a poverty line. Ten years ago the level of income was set at $1,500 for a single person, $2,500 for a two-person family, and an additional $500 for every other member up to a maximum of $4,000, a figure which does not make allowances for families with more than five persons.

Statistics given for 1969 show 1,142,000 families plus 629,000 individuals living below the Senate Committee's poverty level. The total number involved was about 5.1 million, including 1.5 million children under 16 years of age. In all they accounted for one-quarter of the population of Canada.

A recent Economic Council of Canada study shows that, in 1969, the poorest 20 per cent of the population in Canada share 4 per cent of the total disposable income of the country, while the top 20 per cent share 44 per cent of total income. "At the extremes, the lowest 5 per cent of families receive much less than 1 per cent of total income ... whereas the highest 5 per cent receive more than 15 per cent." If 10 per cent of the income of the top 20 per cent were given to the bottom 20 per cent, their incomes would more than double!

One commonly held belief is that the poor pay relatively less in taxes than others. They do pay less in income tax, but the proportion of their income which they pay in other forms of taxation is greater than that paid by the average. According to the Economic Council, people earning below $3,000 pay up to 60 per cent of their income for taxes while people earning over $7,000 pay around 40 per cent. The prosperous are also more successful than the poor in gaining subsidies and economic benefits from public sources.

The economic problem of poverty is more severe in the Atlantic provinces where in 1961 45 per cent of all families were classified as low income, as opposed to 19 per cent of Ontario families. The Senate report, using 1967 statistics, indicates, however, that 17.2 per cent of the poor in Canada live in the Atlantic provinces, 31.9 per cent in Quebec, and 23.3 per cent in Ontario.

Poverty is much more than a set of economic statistics. It is a human problem, crippling people in many different ways.

The Poor and Education

At least two-thirds of the heads of low-income families have no more than elementary school education. Workers with little or no education lose their jobs faster and oftener than anyone else. Traditionally education is worth money in terms of expectation of job earnings.

The Economic Council of Canada in its *Fifth Annual Review* (1968) has stated that "the educational levels of family heads were very likely influenced by their income and related circumstances of their parents and their circumstances in turn are likely to influence the educational levels attained by their children." The children of the poor are tending to stay in school one or two years longer than their parents; but so are the children of the rich. Therefore the gap between the two groups is not closing.

The disparity is even greater as we consider that the educational system assumes that children will have books, study space, and incentives which usually cannot be provided on a poverty-level income. Teaching itself may be of a poorer quality, as teachers in a large school system are rewarded for good service by "promotion" to a school in a better neighbourhood, or "demoted" to a school in a run-down area where modern teaching facilities are often non-existent. Rural children may be worse off than children in the inner city in terms of qualified teachers, who are reluctant to stay in an area where traditional teaching methods may not be effective. Poor children then are not receiving a fair share of public investment in education. Finally, teachers tend to have a lower expectation of the performance of poor children and the children themselves not only accept this, but as a result often find the approach and purpose of education useless, stifling and boring. The combination of all these factors virtually excludes most children of the poor from benefitting from the educational system and condemns them to a marginal economic status.

The Poor and Health

The health of the poor is worse than the health of the affluent because they cannot afford the proper food, clothing and medical care. Social services are not adequate in the area of family planning, pre-natal and family nutrition. The public may point to a very fat person on welfare as being overfed, when the problem is often one of poor nutrition and the starchy diet which is basic to low-budget eating.

Physical and mental disorders are more prevalent among the poor, thus compounding the vicious circle of those who are not fit to work or to earn an adequate wage. An improper diet for pregnant women affects brain development in the unborn child which can lead to mental retardation and lowered intelligence later. Poor diet during infancy also affects the mental and physical development of the child. Thus a child raised in poverty is less likely to be able to function well in our educational system, and later, in the economic system. The poor may lack the appearance and the vitality to be eligible for better-paying jobs. Greater incidence of sickness among the poor will take a larger percentage in medical expenses from the income of the working poor, and increase the dependence of others on welfare services.

The Poor and Work

Perhaps one of the great myths is the belief that the poor don't work and don't want to work. Too often being poor and being on welfare are assumed to be the same thing. Of the 832,000 families who in 1967 fell below the Economic Council's poverty line, 525,000 (or 63 per cent) heads of families were in the labour force at some time during the year working for what can be called poverty wages. Almost 40 per cent worked for the entire year. In the 1961 census, 76 per cent of poor families had one or more earner in the family, and very often these people earned less than they would have received as welfare clients. Also according to 1970 figures, 84 per cent of the adults who depended on welfare were not capable of earning a living, the elderly, sick, disabled, and women in charge of families which required their presence at home. Three per cent required assistance because their jobs did not pay enough to live on, and the remainder, slightly more than one in ten, were prospective members of the labour force not currently working.

The Senate report on poverty gives the example of woodcutters in the Tracadie area of New Brunswick who live in deplorable conditions at camp from Monday to Friday. They earn a maximum of $105.00 per week, but room and board, purchase and upkeep of saws, and transportation reduced this to $61.00 or net hourly earnings of little more than $1.50. The men all knew that they would be better off on welfare, yet continued to live and work under very primitive conditions.

In seeking a job, the poor are also handicapped, as they lack contacts through social groups that might lead to information about available jobs, and the cost of transportation puts them at a disadvantage in seeking a job opening in another area.

Work gives self-fulfillment, as well as the monetary reward. In our society a job gives status, and there are few people who would not work if they had the opportunity.

The Poor as Consumers

The difficulties faced by poor families as consumers are not simply those of having less purchasing power. They have less information, and usually pay higher prices for groceries associated with smaller quantity purchases, neighbourhood buying because they lack transportation or because they must shop at a store which extends credit. They may be forced into making unwise purchases (e.g., a used car) because they fail to qualify for credit ratings which would enable them to borrow at reasonable rates.

It is also a myth that the poor are not careful shoppers, and that they spend more on tobacco and alcohol than their more affluent neighbours. In 1967 Canadians as a whole spent $330 million on food, $70 million on alcohol and $49 million on tobacco, and the cost of alcohol consumption is increasing at the rate of 3 per cent per year. It has been calculated that the poor spend about 70 per cent of the amount spent by the average family on food, and little more than 60 per cent as much as the average family spends on alcohol and tobacco. They spend only 50 per cent of the average on personal care, reading, and medical care, 40 per cent on education and clothing, and about 30 per cent of the average on furnishings, recreation and transportation.

The Poor and the Law

Justice is supposed to be impartial, but in a number of ways our legal system discriminates against the poor. If a poor man is convicted of a crime and offered the choice of a jail term or a fine, he is more likely than a rich man to go to jail. When a poor man has served a term in prison, he is less likely to find a job when he is released. The incidence of difficulty with the law is more prevalent among the poor, especially the Native poor. In Saskatchewan, for example, 10 per cent of the population of the province is Native, yet 50 per cent of those who are put in prison come from the Native population.

The Minority Groups

As we consider the plight of the poor, we must remember also the minority groups—the blacks, and the Indians, Métis and Eskimos who make up about 2.5 per cent of the population of Canada. Not all blacks and not all Native People are poor, but those who are can be described as the poorest of the poor. As we examine variations on the poverty theme, we must be constantly reminded of their special problems.

Because the media constantly projects an image of Canada as a middle-class country where there is widespread affluence and equality of opportunity, the implication is that all Canadians live and work in that world. As the poor lack the economic and other resources to present the real story, the myth that the system works for all is maintained. This myth is so strong that even the poor begin to believe that there is something wrong with them. They are bombarded with advertising that bases worth on the consumption of a set of goods which they have no hope of realizing but which they think everyone else enjoys. Insult is added to injury and frustration heightened by helplessness and depression.

These are the problems which confront us as Christians. It is obvious that we have the economic resources to overcome them. The real question is whether we have the Christian resolve to share our wealth.

HUMAN DEVELOPMENT IS A MATTER OF CHRISTIAN CONCERN

At first glance it seems that setting down a rationale for Christian social action is the same as entering a car in the morning, recalling the make, model, year and serial number, and then starting the engine and driving off; it seems so self-evident. But, there are two good reasons for actually setting down Christian reasons for engaging in social action:

1. to convince or remind oneself that Christian faith is a force capable of moving, and intended to work, bringing forth fruits; and

2. to enrich the quality of Christian Action.

We will look at social action from three viewpoints:

1. Old Testament
2. New Testament—Jesus
3. New Testament—Early Church

Old Testament

As a background for social action in Old Testament times, one must see the Creation story, which formed Jewish ideas, to see the people of God as stewards of God's Creation. God has set men and women into this world to have dominion over it and to use it responsibly. Man is the Image of God, is responsible for the world, and to its, and his, maker. The Jews saw this and made it, in their laws, work out in the quality of life together. Laws were provided which were to ensure the necessities of life for all.

At the time of the "Landnahme" (Exodus), the land was divided according to the needs of the tribes and the families which made them up. Land ownership was to be as inviolate as possible. The year of Redemption, and the year of Jubilee (every seventh and fiftieth year) provided for the return of sold land to the original owner, thus making sure that an economic base for self-fulfillment was given and maintained. The year of Redemption and Jubilee also made it mandatory that men or women sold into economic slavery would be set free and provided with a new start.

Responsibility for the powerless members of a family (widows, orphans, sick, maimed, etc.) lay directly with the members of the family and clan, failing this, with the whole community. The community was also responsible for sojourners and strangers in its midst.

Exploitation of a fellow member of the "people" was directly forbidden. No taking of interest or excessive profit from a fellow Jew. We must be aware that even then these idealistic laws were being perverted, broken and misused. One needs only to look at the challenge thrown out by the prophets. They tried to recall the people to their roots.

> Isaiah 3:14-15: The Lord enters into judgement with the Elders and Princes of the people. It is you who have devoured the vineyards, the spoil of the poor is in your house. What do you mean by crushing my people, by grinding the face of the poor?

> Or, Proverbs 31:8-9: Open your mouth on behalf of the powerless, for the right of all who are left desolate. Open your mouth, decree what is just, maintain the rights of the poor and needy.

New Testament

The inspiration of Christ's life is clear. The following points seem especially explanatory, in regard to Christian social responsibility for action in the arena of public life, the community.

1. John the Baptist, while in prison, sent some of his followers to question Christ and ask for his credentials, a statement of proof that he was the Messiah, the One chosen and sent by God to save the world.

> Christ's possible credentials could have been:

> his family background—Son of David

> his educational qualifications—rabbi

> outside approval—authority of God "this is my beloved Son..."

> personal piety—theological inerrancy

His actually stated credentials were related strictly to his ministry of love—"Go back and tell John what you are hearing and seeing":

> the blind can see, the lame can walk the lepers are made clean, the dead are raised to life and the good news is preached to the poor.
>
> (Matthew 11:4-5)

2. The healing ministry of Jesus speaks for itself. Especially eloquent are Christ's acts of love, which reached across accepted social barriers against children, foreigners, the insane, lepers and the enemy.

3. The entire life of Christ sets a scene which takes the Christian far from his isolated, insular church life, into the wider communities of life—politics, education, economics, psychosomatic health. In particular, see his birth—in the stable of an inn; his upbringing—small-town, provincial Galilee, carpenter's son; his friends—fishermen, tax collectors, prostitutes, little people; his personal status—self-made failure, a criminal's death.

4. Christ took values which are often restrictive—family, clan, tribe—and extended them universally. When his family once tried to interrupt his ministry, he used the occasion to declare the creation of a much bigger family. "Who are my mother and my brothers?" (the objects of my love and my concern) He looked over the crowd of people around him and said, "Look, here are my mother and my brethren. For the person who does what God wants him to do, is my brother, my sister, my mother" (Mark 3:34-35).

Read also the challenge issued by Jesus concerning the needs of others. Read Matthew 25:31ff. This is the parable of the Last Judgement, when all nations of earth shall be gathered before the judgement seat of God to be separated into the righteous and the unrighteous. Observe especially how service to those in need is equated to service of Christ, and vice versa. In this parable, Jesus identifies himself definitely with suffering humanity. So close to his heart are the needs of men and women that the ministry to the least important of them is seen and accepted as a direct service to his own person. This identification of the heart of Jesus with the needs of suffering men and women gives the most powerful motivating force for Christian social service. Not because good works can buy a way into heaven, but because of a definite identification of our life with the life of Jesus Christ and our fellow man.

Early Church

Early Christians established communities which were miniature expressions of the deep confidence and radical action called forth by Christ's life, death and living. (Acts 2:44-45) "All the believers continued together in close fellowship, and shared their belongings with one another." They would sell all their property and possessions, distributing the money among all, according to what each one needed. Even if this did not become the accepted pattern all across the early Church, it did lay the basis for a deep involvement with the needy in all the communities in which the members of the early Church found themselves.

CONCLUSION

Anyone who attempts to carry out an active social ministry is always brought up short by the thought, "yes, but aren't we losing sight of personal faith and only seeing social action as worthwhile?" Many theologians have attempted to demonstrate that Christian identity is not a sequence of acts, a progression—as if a person believed and then acted—as if a person becomes a better Christian because of loving acts—as if faith came first and then works.

Social ministry claims that a person discovers and knows himself, his belief and his salvation, only in convinced action. A person may hear the Word of God, celebrate its Good News (planting of the seed), but Christian faithfulness has to do with fruits (the harvest).

The rhythm of Christian life is to keep recognizing and to keep creating opportunities for faith/action. This encounter with the living Word is the basis for, and also the end product of, the Christian community—the congregation.

Although the Word of God is ever around us, and being proclaimed for us, we discover, encounter and relate to that Word only in incarnation—the spending of human thought and personhood for the accomplishment of someone else's particular good.

Faith Apart from Works Is Dead!

HUMAN DEVELOPMENT AND SHARING OUR WEALTH

Because of the vast differences in incomes in Canada, the need for significant income redistribution is obvious, if *all* Canadians are to have an opportunity to realize their full potential. There are three basic ways that the government can bring about income redistribution—through progressive taxation, through the provision of free or subsidized services, such as medical care, and through income supplements such as old age pensions, social assistance (welfare payments), and unemployment insurance. In the case of the latter two approaches, they will bring about a measure of the desired income redistribution to the extent that the poor receive benefits in excess of their contributions to the financing of these programs. Unfortunately, because of the funding methods (e.g., premiums and sales taxes to finance medical care programs, property taxes to finance education) and limited accessibility of some services to the poor, these approaches have not led to any meaningful income redistribution. To add to this problem, the tax system is not progressive; it does not place a relatively greater burden on the rich. Because of the importance of sales and property taxes, the system has placed its greatest burden on the very low-income earners....

In addition, the Economic Council of Canada predicts that the recognition of capital gains as a form of income and their taxation as such will not significantly change the regressive nature of our tax system.

In Canada as elsewhere, we have only two forms of progressive taxation, that is, taxes which take a greater proportion of the income of the rich than of the poor. The two progressive taxes are income taxes and succession duties. The former, including taxation on capital gains as they are realized, is a tax on the income of the individual as he earns it. Succession duties are a tax on wealth as it is passed to another individual. If the Christian Church is to be concerned with income redistribution, it must see that these progressive taxes are not only maintained but become increasingly important parts of our tax system. Otherwise, any attempts at adding to the income of the poor will be offset by increases in their taxes. Thus, while we must advocate significant income transfers through such programs as the guaranteed annual income, we must at the same time see that these programs are financed from the progressive parts of our tax system.

It is with this in mind that we focus attention on the need for active involvement in the area of support for succession duties as a necessary immediate step for income redistribution. When the federal government passed its tax reform of 1971, it withdrew its share (25 per cent) of succession duties but agreed to collect them for the provinces. The federal withdrawal appears to have been prompted by two factors—increases in revenues from other sources and pressure from people who, having successfully requested that some capital gains be allowed to escape income tax until the death of the receiver (a concession available to no other form of income), these interests then said that the payment of this income tax at the same time that succession duties would be levied would impose a great hardship and was "double taxation." Having postponed an income tax, they complained that they had to pay it at a time that their heirs would also be paying a wealth transfer tax!

When its revenues are rising faster than necessary, what the federal government should do is lower the federal sales tax or transfer more funds to the provinces and municipalities so that they could lower their regressive sales and property taxes. This would increase the relative importance of the progressive taxes and would aid the process of income redistribution. Instead, the policy adopted by the federal government hampers this process, and the current actions of the provincial governments threaten it further.

After the federal withdrawal from the succession duties field, every province except Alberta entered the field with legislation to maintain its income from succession duties around the level received from the former federal legislation. However, the provinces have been under considerable pressure, mounted by the small minority of people who will be affected by succession duties, to withdraw from this field of taxation. Prince Edward Island has done so and both Nova Scotia and New Brunswick have moved forward the expiration dates of their legislation to March 31, 1974, and December 31, 1973, respectively. Thus, the federal withdrawal from the gift tax and succession duties field has meant the very rapid destruction of this important form of progressive taxation in several provinces and probably in all very soon. If this equitable tax is to be maintained and applied uniformly in Canada, it must be returned to the federal field. If the federal government does not require the revenues obtained, they can be used to lower the federal sales tax or be returned to the provinces from which they were raised.

The need for succession duties goes beyond their role in income redistribution. They are important in preventing the unimpeded transfer of wealth between generations. Without succession duties, large blocks of wealth would be passed and concentrated. No information is available on the ownership of Canadian wealth. In the United States, it has been estimated that the top 1 per cent of the population owns one-third of all the wealth! Concentration of wealth also implies a concentration of opportunity and privilege which affects not only the distribution of income but also the operation of democracy, which requires a high degree of equality of opportunity to work. If we believe that democracy is the best political system for Canada, we must see that it is not undermined by maintaining the current differences in income and wealth.

The opponents of succession duties often cite individual examples of hardship imposed on small farmers and businessmen. To the extent that such hardships are real, they are not an argument for an end to succession duties. Rather, they are an argument for longer payment periods and/or higher exemptions for sons and daughters. To the majority of Canadians who will inherit only debts or estates too small to be affected by current legislation, further exemptions to those inheriting much more may appear generous to a fault. However, legislation must reflect the importance of small business and farm operations to the economic lives and the aspirations of their owners and their families. For the sake of fairness, succession duties should be applied against the full market value of all estates, regardless of any special capital gains privileges which may be granted for income tax purposes.

The other frequent argument against succession duties is the false link with capital gains taxation. As pointed out above, capital gains taxation is a tax on income which had, until 1972, been unfairly free of tax. The fact that some forms of capital gains may be postponed gives their earners an advantage which lowers the effective rate of tax, as does the fact that only 50 per cent of capital gains are taxed whereas 100 per cent of other forms of income are subject to tax. In addition, the postponement of capital gains taxes till death does not justify the claim that this imposes "double taxation." As capital gains taxes are levied on the recipient of a form of income and succession duties are levied on the heir to wealth, they are different types of taxes on different people and do not constitute double taxation.

However, many people argue that succession duties are really a tax on the deceased and, therefore, are double taxation. If this is accepted, then the concept must be divorced from the payment of capital gains at death. Regardless of the form of income, whether capital gains, wages, salaries, etc., if it is invested to form an estate, succession duties will apply. However, the opposition would have us believe that the common payment period with succession duties implies some sort of vicious "double taxation." If one is concerned about the viciousness of double taxation one should recognize that our income is subject to numerous taxes, and the income of the poor more so than others. After we have paid our income taxes and spent our disposable income, we pay provincial sales tax on top of federal sales tax on top of tariffs, property tax on top of land transfer taxes, etc. If one wishes to end "double taxation" then, there should be only income taxes so that the regressive tax forms could be done away with and all government revenues financed by a single, equitable income tax. Until such a major reform is instituted, however, anyone concerned with fair taxation, with democracy, and with income redistribution must be working for the preservation of succession duties and gift taxes—which implies a return to federal legislation.

Recommendations

As Christians, we are deeply disturbed by what we see:

An economic system in which rewards are grossly unequal and in which there is no effective mechanism for the correction of this situation.

A tax system which compounds the problems of the poor by taking away a greater portion of their incomes than of the incomes of those earning more.

We are, however, excited and encouraged by the possibilities we see:

The economic wealth of our country is so great that major improvements can be made immediately.

Christians are realizing that their faith requires action.

We therefore recommend that we, as individuals, as congregations, and in larger groups of Christians, provide a meaningful witness of Christ to his world by taking the following steps:

1. Endorse the principle of succession duties and gift taxes as important for income redistribution and the slowing down of the concentration of wealth.

2. Actively promote the re-entry of the federal government into this area with the funds so derived being returned to the provinces.

3. Recommend that the federal legislation include the following concepts:

(a) Provision to guarantee that no province may attempt to become a tax haven.

(b) Up to ten (10) years for payment of duties, with reasonable (prime rate) interest charges.

(c) A basic exemption, applicable to all estates, regardless of size and recipient, of $50,000.

(d) Tax rate based on the wealth of the recipient of the estate, as well as on the size of the estate.

4. Work to have the following changes made:

Income Tax: Personal exemptions for income tax should not be lower than the poverty line; that is, there should be no income tax deducted from anyone whose total income is below the poverty line.

Government Pensions and Allowances: (aged blind, disabled, etc.) that they be increased to meet the poverty line level where there is no other source of income. Where there are other sources of income, that these pensions be reduced, but not by the full amount of extra income from other sources. The higher taxes at the upper levels will guarantee that the increase will benefit only the needy.

Family Allowances: that they be increased substantially, and be included in the taxable income of the family.

Minimum Wage: that there be a standard rate for all Canadians; no area discriminations. No provincial minimum rate should be below that which is required to support a family of four at the poverty line.

3 · THE ECONOMICS OF INJUSTICE

THE UNITED CHURCH OF CANADA, DEPARTMENT OF CHURCH IN SOCIETY, 1975

SPRINGING THE POVERTY TRAP: GUARANTEED ANNUAL INCOME

And if your brother becomes poor, and cannot maintain himself with you, you shall maintain him; as a stranger and sojourner he shall live with you. Take no interest from him or increase, but fear your God; that your brother may live beside you. (Leviticus 25:35-38)

The ups and downs of our economy have been dutifully monitored by both the government and the press over the last two decades. Politicians, as they come and go, have steadfastly maintained their beliefs in full employment. Yet the economy hobbles along and unemployment worsens. Government mismanagement of the economy over the last decade has been particularly disastrous. Monetary and fiscal policies have continually put the needs of the economy ahead of the people. The traditional tools the government has used to reduce income inequality—the tax system, social security benefits, minimum wage laws—have had little effect.

Recently, the concept of a guaranteed annual income for Canadians has come to be accepted as a logical culmination of the current patchwork of government social security measures. The GAI will be one method of righting some of the basic economic injustices which divide our society. A GAI will ensure that all Canadians, not just those who find themselves unemployed, underpaid or unable to work, will have a secure economic floor to stand on. The GAI could be important in another sense in that it could eliminate the bureaucratic divisions between municipal, provincial and federal governments, all of whom help to administer the present unwieldy social security programs.

The GAI: What Does It Mean?

The concept of a guaranteed income is to most of us a relatively new idea. Yet the basic moral imperative in which the guaranteed income rests is an old one. Do we have an obligation of care and concern for our fellows?

> Should we or should we not guarantee the basic material conditions of human life as a social right of every man? Guaranteed income as a secure economic floor will make it possible for men to become what God intended them to become by free response. We need not feel that it is a risk which we take upon ourselves. We are relieved of the intolerable burden of having to decide which ones among us do and do not deserve an economic floor to stand upon. In one sense, none of us deserve this right. But in a deeper sense, this right to be is one which God has given to each of us regardless of our undeserving. Guaranteed income will be a recognition, in economic terms, of what God has done.

The idea of a guaranteed income is a call to sharing, but it is much more than that. It is a positive reinforcement to the Christian goal of communion and community. A guaranteed income means challenging the status quo which legitimizes the present unequal distribution of wealth and, naturally, it means challenging some of the values which enforce that inequality.

GAI and Work

It is important that some of the major fears of the GAI be dispelled. The GAI must not be seen as just another half-way social security measure for the so-called chronic welfare cases. It is an attack whose ultimate objective is the reduction of income disparities between all Canadian wage earners. A coherent GAI plan will benefit not only the poor but also those middle-income groups which pay substantial amounts of their income to the tax system but are excluded from social security policies because of stringent qualifications.

Many people fear that a guaranteed income might kill the incentive to work. A GAI test program in New Jersey has shown that this is an unduly harsh and pessimistic view of human nature. In the New Jersey experiment the GAI had no effect on the work incentive. People did not rush to quit their jobs because their income was guaranteed. The only noticeable change was that children tended to stay in school longer and since the need for a second income was reduced, women left their jobs to stay home with their children. On the bureaucratic side, administrative costs were cut from $300 per recipient under the previous welfare programs to $92 per recipient under the test GAI program.

Certainly there would be a scant few that might abuse such a system just as there are those who would prefer not to work in any circumstances. A good income security scheme would, as Health and Welfare Minister Marc Lalonde has said, maintain more effective monetary incentives to work than do most of the present social assistance programs. The vast majority of people want to work if they can. For proof, we have only to look at those working poor who continue to work despite the poverty-level wages. Any program would have to ensure that it would always be more profitable for the able-bodied person to work than to receive a government income supplement. When we talk about incentives to work we must discuss more than just financial incentives. The question of work incentives also raises the problems of adequate opportunities for meaningful work. The malaise and despondency created by unsatisfying jobs do much more to kill the incentive to work than the prospect of a guaranteed income.

The GAI: Where It's at Now

Marc Lalonde has stated repeatedly that it is his department's intention to bring in GAI legislation for both the work-handicapped (those unable to work or unable to find work) and the working poor within one or two years. The major political struggles now seem to be amongst Mr. Lalonde's cabinet colleagues and between the federal and provincial welfare departments. Former Finance Minister John Turner's recent budgetary restraints seem to have effectively scotched the plan for the immediate future.

Mr. Lalonde's proposed scheme is a two-tier system with an upper level to cover those people who cannot derive income from normal work (those who currently receive provincial welfare payments and would continue to do so on the new plan) and a lower level of income supplementation for the working poor. The administration of this lower tier has yet to be decided and is a major point of contention at the moment. In his address to the Federal and Provincial Welfare Ministers Conference in February, 1975, Mr. Lalonde said:

...there are two major steps to be taken in the reform of Canada's income security system. The transformation of Canada's social assistance plans into income and employment plans and the development of work incentives measures designed to reinforce the incentive to work both for those on social assistance and for those who are working at incomes which are below, or only slightly above, what they could receive on social assistance.

Some provinces balked at the plan. Before federal guidelines are endorsed they want a clear definition of provincial responsibilities and the division of financing between federal and provincial governments. The poorer provinces in particular want to make sure that both the rich provinces and Ottawa are pulling their weight in any proposed GAI program.

The Universal Demogrant

The United Church advocates a slightly different approach to the GAI—one which would eliminate any of the social stigma attached to being a welfare recipient. The "universal demogrant" scheme would mean that everyone would receive a flat cash payment whether working, unemployed, unable to work or between jobs. Through revamped taxation rates, the grant would be recovered from all those who did not need it. The payment would be coordinated by Ottawa, scaled to family size, issued monthly and revised according to cost-of-living increases. Much of the negative psychological impact of current welfare testing would be avoided by this method. There would be no testing of employability to determine what level of assistance an individual might receive.

The United Church Position

Rev. Robert Lindsey, associate secretary of the Division of Mission and the chief United Church spokesman for poverty issues, sees the universal demogrant plan as the ideal to be aimed for. He realizes, however, that this approach can only be arrived at by degrees and encourages the government in its efforts to institute a guaranteed income plan, emphasizing that Mr. Lalonde's scheme should avoid at all costs any of the stigma and categorization present in the existing welfare system. The following four recommendations have been drafted for consideration by all United Church members as guidelines for the implementation of the planned two-tier GAI.

1. A guaranteed income for work-handicapped persons should be administered without the arbitrariness or investigations that are associated with so much public welfare.

2. A guaranteed income for work-handicapped persons in any category should be characterized by a significant increase, in total dollars, over welfare rates. It should be a provincial and federal policy that guaranteed income will redistribute income so as to close the gap between the poorest fifth of Canadians and the top fifth. The public should be assured that the spending power of the poor, in relation to that of the non-poor, will gain ground in more than a token or minimal way.

3. The poor are the most harassed by inflation. In proportion to their income, they are more highly taxed than others. Therefore, it is vital that the federal and provincial governments introduce both the upper and lower tiers not later than January 1, 1977.

4. The federal and provincial governments are to be encouraged and supported in their every positive measure to widen job opportunities.

Beyond the GAI

In his concluding comments on the Nuffield Seminar on the GAI in 1972, Gerald Fortin, director of the Centre for Urban and Regional Research at the University of Quebec, made the point that the guaranteed annual income is more than just a different technique for distributing funds. It is, he said, "More than a technique: it is hope for a different kind of society." (*Guaranteed Annual Income: An Integrated Approach*, Canadian Council on Social Development, p. 270)

The alleviation of poverty must mean more than just equal access to the goods and services that our society has to offer. The GAI must be seen as a first and temporary step in attacking poverty. While a guaranteed annual income will afford minimal financial security for many Canadians, it will not, in the end, do a great deal to close the widening gap between rich and poor in this country.

A more comprehensive approach to the income security question must incorporate a cash payment into a combination of programs including health care, housing, education, mass transportation, recreational needs and other similar social services. Even at that, the poor are not likely to catch up quickly unless specialized programs are created, geared to the special needs of the poor: their inhibitions, fears and inabilities to deal with a society which stigmatizes and intimidates those who have failed to realize our middle-class goals.

The GAI is not the answer to poverty. It will still leave the basic questions of how wealth is created, and who decides how it is created and for what purposes. The real solutions to poverty will only emerge when Canadians start to challenge the structure of the present social, political and economic system, and the underlying causes of poverty which are the result of that system. The call for a more equitable distribution of wealth is a call for justice—justice which will remove the social and economic barriers to fuller participation in Canadian society and enable everyone to earn a decent living wage through personally meaningful work.

FURTHER READING

The Anglican Church of Canada, Task Force on the Economy. *A Position Paper on Guaranteed Annual Income*. Toronto: 1975.

The Anglican Church of Canada, Task Force on the Economy. *Poverty in Canada: A Christian Perspective*. Toronto: 1977.

The Canadian Conference of Catholic Bishops. *Unemployment: The Hidden Costs*. Ottawa: 1980.

Gabbert, Mark. "Anglicans and Social Justice." *Queen's Quarterly* 85 (1978-79): 191-202.

Ten Days for World Development. *Making a Living*. Toronto: 1980.

The United Church of Canada. *Income Security: Where Do We Go from Here?* Toronto: 1982.

The United Church of Canada. *Report of the National Poverty Task Force to General Council*. Toronto: 1977.

The United Church of Canada, Department of Church in Society. Issue #6, *Women Working* (1975).

The United Church of Canada, Working Unit on Social Issues and Justice. *The Control of the Canadian Economy and the Human Problem of Unemployment: A Christian Perspective*. Toronto: 1979.

SECTION II
CAPITALISM AND
CORPORATIONS

In developing their analysis of poverty as rooted in the capitalist economic system, the Canadian churches began to pay close attention to the operations of big business in this country and abroad. The Taskforce on the Churches and Corporate Responsibility has been the principal vehicle of the churches' activity in this area, although both GATT-Fly and Project North have also found the large corporations to be among the major obstacles to social justice in their respective realms. These inter-church coalitions offer two main criticisms of the corporations: (1) they wield an inordinate amount of power over the economic and political aspects of our society, and (2) they use this power to further their own objectives, which are often opposed to the general welfare of society, especially its weaker members.

The ecclesiastical critics of capitalism and the role of the corporations in this system are divided as to how to remedy the situation. Some feel that capitalism is inherently immoral and anti-Christian and must be replaced by an alternative system, perhaps a form of socialism. Others feel that it is quite unrealistic to expect and work for the demise of capitalism and that the best that can be accomplished are reforms of this system to alleviate its worst effects. All agree, however, that the present economic system is highly imperfect and that it is a religious duty of Canadians to change it for the better.

As with the poverty issue, the churches feel that the first step towards a solution to the problems of capitalism and the corporations is the education of churchpeople and other citizens to the facts of the matter. To this end the United Church of Canada devoted its *Issue #14* (1977), *Who's in Control? The Rise of the Giants: The Transnational Corporations,* to this topic. No explicit ethical or religious analysis is provided in this paper, but the problems caused by the large corporations are presented in a manner which calls for action in response by all concerned citizens.

Among the largest and most powerful of Canadian corporations are the major chartered banks. Since its formation, the Taskforce on the Churches and Corporate Responsibility has concentrated much of its attention on the activities of the banks, especially their loans to countries such as South Africa and Chile where gross violations of human rights are accepted government policy. At shareholders meetings and in briefs to the banks' executives, the Taskforce has tried to discourage such loans or, at the very least, obtain more information about them. The banks' usual response has been to deny such information on the basis of client/banker confidentiality and to refuse any moratorium on such loans as long as they do not violate Canadian law. In its *Brief to the House of Commons Standing Committe on Finance, Trade and Economic Affairs concerning the Decennial Revision of the Bank Act* (November, 1978), the Taskforce called on the Canadian government to change the Bank Act so as to require the disclosure of information regarding loans in other countries.

Just as the Canadian economic system is characterized by the concentration of power in a relatively small number of corporations, so also do we find economic prosperity very unequally distributed among the different regions of the country. The Atlantic provinces have long been the region with the lowest per capita income and highest unemployment rate, and in 1979 the Roman Catholic bishops of this region produced a critical analysis of this problem entitled, *To Establish a Kingdom of Justice.* The bishops see regional disparity as a product of the capitalist impulse towards concentration of wealth—a further indication of the inherent immorality of this system. They encourage Christians in the Atlantic provinces to become aware of unjust social structures and to work to change them in whatever way they can.

Of all the statements by church groups on social issues since 1970, none has generated more publicity and controversy than the document entitled *Ethical Reflections on the Economic Crisis* by the Episcopal Commission for Social Affairs of the Canadian Conference of Catholic Bishops (January, 1983). Although the main points of this statement had been set forth before by the bishops in their

1976 Labour Day message, *From Words to Action*, their 1977 pastoral message, *A Society to Be Transformed*, and their 1980 social message, *Unemployment: The Human Costs*, none of these received much attention either inside or outside the church. The vigorous critique of capitalism which is contained in the earlier documents is here applied to specific government policies such as the greater concern with inflation than with unemployment, the restriction of collective bargaining, and the widespread cutbacks in social services, especially those directed towards the poor. Despite the off-hand dismissal of their recommendations by the leaders of the Liberal government and Conservative opposition (many of whom are Roman Catholics), the Bishops' Statement, as it is now known, has established in the minds of many Canadians for the first time the legitimacy of the critique of capitalism on moral and religious grounds.

4 · WHO'S IN CONTROL? THE RISE OF THE GIANTS: THE TRANSNATIONAL CORPORATIONS

THE UNITED CHURCH OF CANADA, DEPARTMENT OF CHURCH IN SOCIETY, 1977

There has been a remarkable change in our economic system since World War II. We have accumulated mountains of consumer goods and expanded our Gross National Product, but have widened the gap between rich and poor. There are frequent reports of rebellion or "threat" from the poorer nations of the Third World, and in the more affluent nations of the West we are beginning to question traditional concepts of economic growth and "development." Insecurity is in the air. We ask if the growth we've experienced has been worth the costs in poisoned environment, spent resources and increased alienation, loss of self-worth and dislocation in our own lives. We know that poverty at home and around the world has not been eradicated, and instead seems to have grown worse. We sense that although we may have more choice over what colour of toothpaste to buy, we have less and less ability to choose and create the sort of society we want for ourselves and our children. Some of us retreat and attempt to defend a very small area of home and garden where we can exercise some control over destiny.

Feelings of individual powerlessness have increased at the same time as the actual centres of power and wealth have consolidated their strength and their grip on the economic decisions that shape our social and political life. The post-war years have seen a particular form of private enterprise—the global corporation—become the dominant influence in our market or capitalist economies. These global corporations—sometimes called multinationals or transnationals—are the primary organizers of the production and distribution of goods and services not only in the affluent West but in most Third World nations as well.

Because many corporations have internationalized both their production and their marketing, many observers have called them "multinational." They seem to have moved beyond the legal power and national bias of an individual country. These "stateless" corporations appear to be able to generate profits, move goods, and employ workers without heed to traditional national loyalties. Their managers have come to view the world as an integrated economic unit. They have unrivalled access to world capital markets. They have a virtual monopoly over up-to-date technology. They can shift a factory from Bradford to Taiwan and pay taxes in Bermuda....

But despite the fact that many corporations employ workers and managers from many countries, there are very few modern corporations which are controlled in reality by citizens of more than one country. The great Japanese, American, French or German firms have "globalized" their production, marketing and financing but still remain in the control of the groups or families back home. And these groups still need and use the power of their national governments wherever possible to protect and enlarge their interests overseas. The global corporation of today is an organization with a particular national base, capable of operating across national legal boundaries, a nationally based *transnational* corporation....

Canada Inc.

Canada has a two-sided relationship with the new corporate giants, but is very much in the centre of the game. On the one hand Canadian-based resource, banking and utility firms have ambitiously carved out a competing role on a world scale with the transnationals of the U.S. or Europe. On the other hand the corporate giants of other countries walk freely through Canada. The *Financial Post's* top 200 companies operating in Canada for 1975-76 lists "69 companies wholly owned by foreigners, 43 that are more than 50 per cent owned by foreigners and 18 in which there is a substantial, sometimes controlling interest."

The Canadian government has played a part on both sides of the question. Cabinet ministers and civil servants travel to Brazil,

Indonesia and Mexico to open doors for Canadian-based corporate sales and investment. Meanwhile supposed efforts to regulate the size and power of foreign investment in Canada, like the Foreign Investment Review Agency (FIRA), are now being used as much to encourage and channel takeovers as they are to stop them. On both the Canadian and foreign-controlled sides of our national corporate ledger the concentration of wealth and power continues. Many Canadians find it frightening and a danger to our democratic traditions. The Canadian government responded to these worries by setting up a Royal Commission on Corporate Concentration last year. Chaired by Robert Bryce, a career civil servant and economic advisor to successive governments, the commission has a mandate to examine the extent of corporate concentration and to determine if and when it has become detrimental to the public interest. Will the Bryce Commission help to counter corporate power or simply legitimize it? Critics, like former businessman and Cabinet minister Eric Kierans, see it as no more than a public relations exercise.

Men & Monopoly

In Canada, between 1900 and 1933 there were 374 mergers. In 1874 there were 51 banking companies in Canada; by 1925 there were only 11. By 1927 the three largest banks—the Bank of Montreal, the Royal Bank and the Bank of Commerce—accounted for about 70 per cent of total Canadian banking resources.[1] As Mackenzie King, future Canadian prime minister, wrote in 1918, the "countless competing units" of capitalism "began to coalesce." "Industry no longer resembles the innumerable stars of the sky by night, as it once did with its distribution of power in a multitude of hands."[2]

The consolidation of Canadian corporations has continued. Since 1970, as Eric Kierans has pointed out, corporations in Canada have achieved startling rates of growth. Kierans notes that the Royal Bank in the five years from 1970 to 1975 accumulated more in assets than it had in the previous 100 years. Its assets went from $11.4 billion in 1970 to $25.2 billion in 1975. The chartered banks as a whole increased their assets by 242 per cent from 1967 to 75. The CPR, from 1881 to 1970, accumulated $2.3 billion. Five years later, the CPR had assets of $6.2 billion, an increase of almost 300 per cent.

"What happens," Kierans continues, "if the assets of the Royal Bank double every five years (the current rate of growth) and in

1985 exceed $100 billion? Or the CPR reaches $25 billion by 1987?"[3] What happens is that private corporations gradually come to have ever-increasing control over larger amounts of the total wealth of society. The point that Kierans makes is a critical one. What does corporate growth mean for society when corporations have become ends in themselves? Who are corporations ultimately responsible to except themselves when their goals are defined as growth in assets and profits?

This drift towards monopoly has largely been accomplished. Corporations, as Kierans says, have become immortal. Unlike human beings, the corporation does not die. It continues with different managers and different workers. And so does its growth and accumulation of wealth. Having conquered time, the next step is space. This, too, has happened with the emergence of the global corporation. Some people, like the former U.S. under-secretary of state George Ball, would like to see it go further. They foresee the "stateless" corporation, free of any national government's jurisdiction. This would put corporations outside anyone's control but their own, with no assurances that their aims would coincide with the needs and goals of people. Corporate power has evolved to the point where it now presents a direct challenge to our political institutions; those same political structures through which a society is supposed to choose its goals, priorities and direction.

Who Rules the Corporation?

The vast majority of people have no say in the corporate decisions which so deeply and gravely affect them. This is the most serious problem of the corporation and the system of which it is a part. In keeping with the necessity of generating increasing profits, the corporate-run economy has produced an emphasis on consumption as the cure for all problems, and an emphasis on individualism, competition and personal gain which belie the basic human needs for community, for harmony with our environment, for meaningful work.

The Corporate-Action Guide, p. 7

It is said that one of the characteristics of those who have power is their denial of it. This is especially the case amongst corporate executive officers, men who have one kind of real power: the power to direct investment. Alfred Powis, the intense president of Noranda, insists that the whole issue of corporate power has been overblown. He wriggles around any mention of power, calmly deflecting the question to the abuses of government and its alleged control over business. "Everybody in the economy has a degree of power. The only power we have is the power to shut down and decide what and where to invest our economic surplus. Government is where the real power lies."

It is precisely this power to invest that is the directing force in the world economy. Giants like General Motors, ITT, Unilever, and the "seven sisters" of the petroleum industry make decisions that affect the lives and the standards of living of millions of people. These investment decisions define where many of us work, what kind of jobs we work at, what we can buy, where we buy it, how we get home with it, where home is, and whether we can safely breathe the air in between.

Corporate power has crept up on us, and many of us don't think about it until we're directly affected. Bob Carty, a researcher with the Toronto-based Latin American Working Group (LAWG), gives the following example of corporate behaviour which jolts people into an awareness of corporate power. "What happens," Carty asks, "when some corporation, let's say in suburban Toronto, decides to close a small plant, lay off 500 people and relocate in Brazil to take advantage of cheap labour? This actually happened. Well, for one thing, people in the area are immediately affected. They really know and feel that the corporation has a control over their lives that they can't do much about, by decisions which neither they nor the government can do anything about."

Corporations are *private* institutions with enormous impact on *public* life. But they are not faceless organizations; behind the glossy ads and towering high-rise headquarters are human beings who make decisions and bear responsibility. What can be said about the real focus of decision-making and the men who govern modern corporations?

Many businesses proclaim that their objective is to serve all people, that their interest is the public interest. They point to stock ownership as proof of their democratic nature. But who owns shares? Statistics Canada reported in 1970 that only one in ten Canadian income earners owned as much as one share.[4] Who owns enough shares to have a real say in corporate policy? One per cent of Canadian income earners owned 48 per cent of the shares in 1968. As Wallace Clement asks in *The Canadian Corporate Elite*, "Is, for example, a person who owns ten shares of Power Corporation the same as ... a Paul Desmarais or Jean Parisien who own 1,350,765 shares each?"[5] Should you take your ten shares to an annual general meeting of a corporation, you will find millions of dollars of business transacted in little more than an hour, and votes literally swamped by the proxies in the control of management....

Global Reach

The small-town companies of the past have become giant transnationals in part because they control four basic essentials for western-style industrial growth and the accumulation of capital. The transnationals have a monopoly on modern technology. Once a nation—rich or poor—has committed itself to western industrial development, it is dependent on the technology which has built that development and on those who control it, transnational corporations based in a few wealthy countries. The danger of this technological dependency to a country's ability to direct its own development is obvious. In Colombia, as of 1970, 10 per cent of all patent holders owned 60 per cent of all pharmaceutical, chemical and synthetic-fibre patents. This 10 per cent were all foreign-owned transnationals.[6] In Canada, between 1966 and 1970, only 5 per cent of all patents granted went to Canadians.[7] In the United States the top 30 industrial corporations own over 40 per cent of the patents in their respective industries. In their classic study of the transnationals, Barnett and Muller write, "Concentrated control of technology is a classic device for eliminating effective competition and thereby establishing oligopolistic control of the marketplace."[8] (Oligopoly: where a handful of large companies dominate a key economic sector to their mutual advantage.)

If you import technology, you import a lot of values from the society which developed the technology. It may be as simple as an imported gas-guzzling car in a country less affluent in petroleum than Canada or the U.S. It may be sophisticated but non-essential consumer goods useful for elites but not very helpful in meeting the basic needs of the poor. Most importantly the labour-saving expensive technology of transnational corporations imported into a poor country with masses of unemployed workers brings a few specialized jobs and a big debt. Development by transnationals may mean a great leap forward for a few trained workers and managers. It has little positive effect on the multitude who need jobs and homes.

Transnationals have control of *marketing*. That more than half of world trade goes on internally in these corporations is simple testimony of their power over supply and pricing. Experienced in the consumer markets of Europe and North America, the transnationals and their partners in advertising are able to export our consumer patterns to limited but important markets in countries like Brazil and India. There are few countries which have not been infiltrated by corporate logos and advertising hype. A study of U.S. food and drug firms in Latin America by Robert Ledogar concluded that "the most succssful U.S. food enterprise in Latin America were soft drinks and cornstarch. It seems to be the least nutritious products that have been most extensively—and successfully—promoted to the poor."[9]

Transnationals, because of their size, have special access in the money markets of the world. This *access to finance* or credit gives them the competitive edge time and again as they fight for markets and concessions with domestic firms whether in Canada or Argentina. A subsidiary of a large foreign firm in Canada or Brazil has the collateral of its parent transnational to place against the riskier local competitor as they seek funds from the domestic bank. As Canadians have discovered, most "foreign investment" is done right here in Canada by foreign firms with Canadian money borrowed from Canadian banks. A United Nations study by Brazilian economist Fernando Fajnzylber in 1970 showed that from 1957 to 1965 American corporatons in Latin America financed 83 per cent of their investments from local savings and earnings in Latin America. Between 1960 and 1968 American-owned corporations took 70 per cent of their net profits out of Latin America.[10] A profitable approach for the transnationals but a notable drain on the resources of a developing nation.

Finally, transnationals have a marvellous advantage over both governments and labour: they are *mobile* and have an effective international organization. Transnational manufacturing companies have the ability to shift their operations from one location to another when wages, taxes or regulations are deemed too expensive. This gives them a powerful threat to use with governments who want their job-creating investment. Corporations within the United States and Canada have moved from areas where labour is unionized to areas where it is not organized. For the most part union organizations have nothing which can compete with the ability of a firm to shift production from Canada to Puerto Rico, Korea or Hong Kong. No world agency exists which can effectively keep tabs on transnational shifts, and few Third World governments or trade unions have the resources and the information to parry corporate moves effectively.

The rise of Western corporations to transnational scope, their global reach for resources, markets, cheap labour and profits, have been built on their power over technology, finance, marketing and their mobility. It is, as George Ball, chairman of the Lehman Brothers International Investment Bank, put it, "working through great corporations that straddle the earth, men are able for the first time to utilize world resources with an *efficiency dictated by the objective logic of profit.*"[11]

Profit For Whom?

"Efficiency is all very well," Eric Kierans said recently, "but efficiency for what end? Efficiency in doing what is not needed is neither efficiency nor economics." The transnationals, he continued, "don't know what I need. They know what they can produce, and they know they can create a market for their output. How efficient they would be in giving us full employment, or clothing, or food that would meet the minimum requirements for much of our population is another question."

The transnationals have shown that they are quite efficient in using the wealth created by their employees—miners, factory workers and stenos—to accumulate more wealth and power. Kierans sees a clear conflict between corporate goals for the use of wealth and the goals of the society at large. "Economists, politicians, all of us, should be concerned with the problems of people who are living today; the one-third of mankind who are living below the poverty line. It is a problem of equitable distribution of wealth. Governments may define success in terms of the standards of living of their people. Corporations define success in terms of the growth of assets. The corporation which distributes to the people the least of its profits will have the greatest growth. The corporation which distributes nothing at all will do the most for itself and the least for society. This institution has become an end in itself".

The increased standard of living in Western countries is often used to justify the growth of corporate wealth. The transnationals say they have delivered the goods. Yet the real measure of a just society is equity in the distribution of that society's wealth. In Canada, the distribution of national income is just as inequitable as it was 30 years ago. The top 20 per cent of the population still gets nearly 45 per cent of the wealth, while the bottom 20 per cent gets less than 4 per cent. We have not eliminated inequality, we have just camouflaged it. The growth of corporate power has occurred in this context.[12] In those developing countries where corporate concentration is most evident, a more negative pattern has developed. In Brazil, where Canadian corporations have joined other foreign investors in the bonanza of the "Brazilian miracle" with its rapid growth of Gross National Product, U.S. government studies show the distribution of income actually worsened. During the 1960s the poorest 40 million Brazilians (roughly 40 per cent of the population) dropped from a share of 10.6 per cent of the national income to 8.1 per cent. At the same time the richest 5 per cent of Brazilians increased their share of the national income from 44 per cent to 50 per cent.[13]

Corporate spokesmen may agree that income distribution is a concern but will often say that it is their responsibility to *create* the wealth and the government's responsibility is to *distribute* it. The fact that they may both benefit from and fight to maintain an increasingly regressive tax system which burdens the poor and average Canadian[14] is often ignored. Some business spokesmen argue that inequity is good in itself. Robert H. Jobs, president of the Winnipeg-based Investors Group, states in a business-boosting pamphlet:

> ... to me the very success of the system justifies the [unequal income] distribution. Today, people at the base of the pyramid enjoy a much higher standard of living than they did thirty years ago. Their shares have not grown, but the pie has. Better, I say, to share a bigger pie than to put your efforts into re-arranging distribution of a smaller one.[15]

Church bodies in Canada, in poorer nations and at the international level have made it clear that this sort of approach is just not good enough. It is inappropriate to the real needs of humanity and simply obsolete. In recent years, the United Nations, bodies like the International Labour Organization and events like Habitat have stressed that we must reorient our economic structures towards the satisfaction of the *basic needs* of the majority of the world's citizens. "Basic needs" refers to material items like food, clothing and shelter, and access to pure drinking water, sanitation and public transportation. It means the availability of public health, educational and cultural facilities. Since basic human needs are not all material, a basic-needs strategy for the economy implies a healthy social environment where people have a sense of self-worth. They need to participate in the making of decisions which affect their lives, livelihood and individual freedom.[16]

Global Challenge: Global Response

The impact of the growth of transnational corporations has stimulated a variety of responses around the world. It has also collided with the autonomous development of a number of societies and nations. Canadians considering the corporate conundrum need to be full participants in this international debate in order that they may more fully understand the interests and options before Canada. Responses to the corporate challenge may be described in three broad approaches.

1. **Change the System:** The most dynamic and far-reaching critique of the transnationals has arisen from commentators and leaders of Third World nations and from socialist analysts in Third World and developed industrial countries. In general the transnational corporation is considered as merely the current phase of development of Western capitalism which for several hundred years has benefited the rich industrialized northern nations at the expense of the rest of humanity. Colonialism has been replaced by economic neo-colonialism. The economies of poorer nations, shaped by their colonial past, and dependent in many ways on developed nations, now struggle with difficulty against the sheer economic power of the West. Third World resources and primary products have been exported to industrial countries, processed there, and sold back to the poor nations, a process which has left them vulnerable, dependent and exploited, and which some economists have described as a process of active underdevelopment or regression.

The transnational corporation, it is charged, is the primary agent of this process. American economist Paul Sweezy comments, "Multinational corporations are concerned only to make the greatest profits, not to satisfy the needs of the masses. In pursuit of profits they have naturally oriented their production in response to effective demand, which means for export and/or for the market provided by the small local upper classes." Any attempt to undertake autonomous industrialization in a poor nation runs into the market, technological and financial power of the corporation. Sweezy characterizes the age as one of "monopoly capital," that is, the domination of the *world* economy by a few hundred giant corporations.[17]

Against this direction of development, some Third World nations have placed a model of autonomous and self-reliant development geared to the needs of their internal market and their society as a whole. Rather than orienting themselves to external markets and corporate consumers, they first have turned inwards. China has been the most effective spokesman for this approach, but other African, Asian and Latin American nations have taken up elements of this response. Whether this sort of autonomy from the world economy dominated by the corporate giants is possible without violent revolution or war is a question posed by dozens of countries from Angola and Mozambique to Chile and Peru.

A number of nations have attempted a non-revolutionary approach of gradual nationalization of foreign corporate interests in an attempt to gain control over their economies. "Chileanization" of the copper industry was well under way before the Allende government came into office in 1970, and was extended by Allende to banking, textiles and a number of other sectors. Jamaica and Guyana as well as Peru and Venezuela have made considerable moves toward reclaiming key industrial sectors of their economies from the transnationals. But the threat of "destabilization," symbolized in the death of Chilean President Allende in 1973, cannot be avoided. A recent issue of *Business Week* shows the doors of Latin American nations opening to foreign investment, coincident, critics would comment, with the rise of right-wing military dictatorships in a number of the countries concerned.[18]...

2. **Regulate, Regulate:** In the advanced capitalist countries, virtually every stage in the consolidation of corporate power has been accompanied by an attempt to regulate the corporations, to legislate socially beneficial behaviour. The age of the "robber barons" in the late nineteenth century yielded regulatory boards and commissions and anti-trust laws in the United States. A period of mergers and scandals yielded anti-combines regulations in Canada. Some commentators have argued that these regulatory moves opened up a creative role for public participation in economic planning, and eliminated the gross exercise of private power. Others have pointed out that the regulatory agencies themselves often fell under the influence of the corporations, becoming instruments by which large and flexible companies were able to reduce competition from small or less-resourceful enterprises.

The rise of consciousness regarding the social and economic impact of transnational corporations has brought a similiar response.

Some feel corporations must be recognized and accepted as a permanent part of the world economy, but they must be regulated. The prospect of controlling transnationals through national and international "codes of conduct" has become a major item on the agendas of a number of world organizations.

The same sort of discussion is taking place in several industrial nations. Several presentations to the Bryce Royal Commission on Corporate Concentration have called for regulatory laws and agencies in Canada. Discussion has developed regarding the brief history of the Canadian government's Foreign Investment Review Agency. FIRA was set up to screen applications for foreign corporate takeovers and to ensure significant Canadian benefit in each case. While corporate critics maintain that the agency is regulating foreign investment out of Canada, Canadian nationalists have contended that FIRA actually encourages and directs foreign intervention rather than reduces it.

As long as governments look upon private corporations as the key instruments of economic development, they cannot be expected to exert a heavy regulatory hand. "Governments," states Eric Kierans, "do not work against—they work with—the vested, the established, the giants. The two sectors have exactly the same interest, increase the pace of economic activity and the growth of assets." As long as this "community of interest between a powerful public sector and a rich and dominating industrial core" exists, the hope of curtailing the power of corporate giants remains only a hope.

Beyond the pros and cons of government regulation, movement to offset corporate power has begun on the part of both union and public interest groups. Some larger unions with international connections have acted to organize against corporate power in several nations at once. Lynn Williams, director of District 6 of the United Steelworkers, states that unions must be strong at the local level and at the same time develop international muscle. "The corporations will ultimately have no place to hide when international unions and working people pull together. We have to push standards and codes of behaviour. It's a way of saying to corporations that they can no longer get away with exploitation of that kind."

The mobility of transnational corporations has prompted unions to work across international lines on bargaining procedures and strike action. To date this cooperation has largely been confined to developed industrial countries. If it is to be effective, more support will have to be extended to Third World workers. This is greatly complicated by political repression in many Third World countries, preventing or restricting the rights of workers to form unions or bargain collectively.

In some industrialized countries, consumer, community and public interest groups have become involved in attempts to regulate or limit corporate power. The pressure to get corporations to regulate themselves has formed into a *corporate social responsibility* movement in North America. Corporations have been encouraged by church, university and public action groups to establish social benefit guidelines.

This self-regulation has in fact filtered through to some management groups. General Motors, for example, publishes a yearly social audit which summarizes the countries' social achievements and sets social goals and priorities. The United Church of Canada has undertaken a social audit of several of the major Canadian corporations in which it invests. Will the idea of social audits and the talk of "corporate social responsibility" have much concrete effect? Can corporations be realistically asked to act beyond their own self-interest as defined by the need for profit? Some participants in the social responsibility movement have concluded that it may yield nothing more than a new style of corporate public relations.

At the same time, when public interest organizations have combined with significant sectors of the working population, with large consumer groups or with groups who are feeling the impact of corporate plans—like many Native organizations in Canada—campaigns have ensued which have forced some modifications in corporate behaviour. The organization of such efforts has made American advocate Ralph Nader a household word in many North American homes. The organization of public interest coalitions in Canada around such issues as the Mackenzie Valley pipeline project, the Reed Paper forest concession in Northern Ontario, the Bell Canada rate increases, and a variety of other environmental, consumer and resource-use issues has given evidence of considerable potential for such action in Canada....

3. **Let's Free Enterprise:** Countering the advocates of systematic change and those of regulation, are those who see unregulated private enterprise, and its proudest achievement, the transnational corporation, as the ultimate salvation of mankind, the universal

panacea for human development. Those who subscribe to what Peter Newman has called "the theology of free enterprise"[19] hold a deep faith in the corporations which form the core of our economic structures. Believing that untrammelled individual initiative has been the source of these wealth-creating and accumulating machines, they are highly critical of any attempts to regulate or restructure their institutions. Some business spokesmen have undertaken campaigns to roll back the government interventions which have occurred, seeking fewer restrictions in a wide-open marketplace.

Critical observers wonder just how real is the idea of the self-regulating marketplace and the free play of private enterprise today. Instead of the classic liberal political economy characterized by many competing private companies and firms, today's economy tends to be characterized by *oligopoly*. Oligopoly—where a few companies dominate one industry or sector—is a recognized economic fact. Price leadership by a few dominant corporations rather than price competition is the general rule. The situation in Canada is summarized in the 1971 Statistics Canada figures on corporations. In 37 major industry groups there were 231,536 companies. Of those, only 291 firms—one-eighth of 1 per cent of the total—controlled 58 per cent of the assets, a total of $159 billion out of $275 billion. These 291 firms produced 30 per cent of the goods and services, and collected 39 per cent of the total profits in the corporate sector.

But it is not only the development of oligopoly along with corporate concentration which has made the idea of a "free market" obsolete. The extensive use of state funds and state intervention in favour of corporate objectives in Canada makes it highly unlikely that the business community itself would ever support fully a drive to return to nineteenth-century market conditions. Instead, talk of "freeing enterprise" has become a rhetorical ploy used to protect certain profitable fields from publicly owned corporations, or to reduce taxation or royalty charges by the state on current resource and manufacturing operations.

On the other hand, there are powerful spokesmen who sponsor the point of view that only the private global corporation has the technological capacity and the efficiency of decision-making and organization to meet the world's needs. They argue that it is traditional democratic power structures—our governments, our unions—which stand in the way. As the chairman of the Dow Chemical Company said in 1972, "I have long dreamed of buying an island owned by no nation and of establishing the World Headquarters of the Dow Company on truly neutral ground of such an island, beholden to no nation or society."[20]

But those members of the global community who have the liberty to do so much ask what purpose the granting of such freedom to private corporations would achieve? Are the means they employ the means which will bring humanity closer to a just economic order? What results warrant such corporate claims?

The Bottom Line

Global Reach authors Barnet and Muller argue that "the vision of a world without borders dominated by a few hundred corporations is a seriously flawed vision, because it violates three fundamental human notions—those of social balance, ecological balance, and psychological balance." Social balance is violated because the corporation accelerates the concentration of wealth, and diverts resources from poor areas where they are needed to rich markets. Ecological imbalance is aggravated by the tendency of the corporate economy towards ever-increasing energy consumption and the quantities of consumer and military throw-away products produced. Psychological imbalance is created not only by the imposition of the hierarchical organization of corporations on the needs and wills of millions of the world's inhabitants, but also out of the destruction of community, national and family values by the extension of the homogenizing consumer society.

"The way to accomplish a worldwide redistribution of economic power," Barnet and Muller point out, "is *not* to further concentrate it in the private hands of American companies."[21] They suggest that some local communities are questioning the wisdom of turning over the dynamic sectors of their economies to large corporations.

But if we want a just distribution of economic power and wealth, we must organize institutions which will accomplish that task. The first priority, whether we live in Kenya, Brazil or Manitoba, is to decide our own development priorities: *Who needs jobs and where can they be created? What sort of technology will serve our social and economic goals? For what needs will products be produced? At what rate should we utilize our resources?* As the authors of *Global Reach* point out, "If the local community is to develop the power to protect the interests of the people, it should seek greater self-sufficiency and self-reliance. Until the community knows what it wants and what it can do on its own, it is not in a position to bargain effectively with global corporations."

The purpose of *Issue* #14 is to assist some Canadians in asking these questions and in developing their answers. It is a small step in helping us shape our own future.

5 · DECENNIAL REVISION OF THE BANK ACT

TASKFORCE ON THE CHURCHES AND CORPORATE RESPONSIBILITY, 1978

INTRODUCTION

The Taskforce on the Churches and Corporate Responsibility is a coalition of the major Canadian churches. It addresses questions of corporate social responsibility based on church policies of the participating denominations. As such, we have brought specific concerns to the attention of a number of corporations and to the attention of the five major chartered banks. We have also on several occasions addressed government and committees of the House of Commons if and when it seems appropriate that matters concerning corporate responsibility become subject to legislative decisions.

The Taskforce does not presume special knowledge of complex and technical commercial arrangements. That is not our function. We do presume, however, to bring important and often under-represented social concerns to deliberations of aspects of economic life. Many of today's social concerns reach into the realm of political and economic institutions whose decisions deeply affect the lives of people in Canada and abroad. The churches, themselves major social institutions, are examining the human implications of these decisions and are seeking to encourage support for policies which are socially beneficial while attempting to correct policies which they view as socially harmful. This is the mandate of the Taskforce.

We are anxious to present our views to the Committee because we believe that several aspects of the decennial revision of the Bank Act are of importance in this regard. We also believe that the enormous growth experienced by Canadian banks over the last ten years concentrates in their hands unprecedented control over economic decisions which have far-reaching social implications in Canada and abroad. According to a *Globe and Mail* report (October 25, 1978), assets of chartered banks have grown more than 400 per cent in the past ten years, rising from $31.7 billion in December, 1968, to $162.4 billion in May, 1978; foreign currency assets rose from 20 per cent or $6.5 billion in 1968 to $54.2 billion or 33 per cent ten years later. The Bank Act under review has given recognition to the implicit dangers of such a high concentration of corporate power by restricting the nature of directorships bank executives may hold to limit the risk of conflicts of interest. We support this legislation.

The issue we wish to raise with this Committee relates to the extent to which the exercise of this economic power of Canadian banks is hidden from public view, obscured frequently by a misapplication of the principle of client/banker confidentiality or an unjustified extension of this principle. Our concern is for the need of greater disclosure requirements to permit the public and the shareholders to grasp the significance of decisions made by these large institutions and to allow a modicum of informed judgement about these decisions.

REASON FOR CONCERN

Our work has involved us in raising question with bank management about loan policies to foreign governments and their agencies and departments. We believe this to be important because in many ways such loans or the absence of such loans are as significant in Canada's foreign relations as are the foreign policy stands taken by the Canadian government (and they are sometimes more significant). In our view, this is particularly so when such loans are made to repressive governments who have incurred public censure from the Canadian government and the international community. Indeed, in some instances these governments may justifiably regard such credits as politically more significant than rhetorical condemnations by our government and others. As international operations of Canada's largest banks accelerate, particularly through participation in international bank consortia, the extent of private financial support for repressive regimes becomes increasingly blurred and responsibility for decisions diffuses.

We offer two concrete examples. The Canadian government has for over a decade joined international condemnation of the apartheid regime of South Africa. It has, in the early 1970s, as a demonstration of its resolve not to stay involved in the apartheid system, divested itself of its South African holdings of Polymer Corporation. Yet we also know that private Canadian financial assistance to the South African government (in addition to private sector trade and investment) amounted to approximately $684 million between 1972 and 1976, thus assisting in neutralizing international and our own government's pressure upon South Africa to initiate fundamental changes.

We say approximately $684 million because we cannot be sure; the figure comes from an established research institute in the United States. We have attempted to learn the level of individual Canadian loan involvement from the various banks,[1] but we have encountered in this area extreme reluctance on the part of bank management to disclose even limited information.

The measures announced in December, 1977, by the secretary of state for external affairs to withdraw all government support for commercial transactions with South Africa further underline our point. The implication of these measures is clear. The Canadian government regards economic support for the apartheid government as strengthening that regime's ability to uphold the *status quo*. Yet, continued and increasing Canadian private sector loans or bond purchases in practice guarantee the South African government continued support. It is able, at no risk to itself, to ignore the intended warning signals from the Canadian government.

The situation in regard to the military dictatorship in Chile is equally pertinent. The Canadian government has twice joined in a vote at the United Nations General Assembly to condemn the junta for its continued human rights violations. As international outrage about Chile's human rights violations increased, major multilateral and bilateral aid to Chile began to decline. Towards the end of 1975, donor governments began to attach human rights criteria to loans to the junta. It was at this stage that the junta turned successfully to private financial institutions. As a percentage of Chile's total borrowing, private bank loans and suppliers' credits increased from less than 25 per cent to over 59 per cent in 1976 and to more than 80 per cent in 1977. The five largest Canadian banks, with most frequent participation from the Royal Bank, the Bank of Nova Scotia and the Bank of Montreal, were involved in bilateral or consortium loans valued at over $734 million by April, 1978. It is estimated that the Canadian component of these loans is about $100 million.[2]

These figures come from published sources in the U.S. and Chile and from press reports in Canada. They present an alarming picture of growing Canadian economic alignment with a regime whose dismal human rights record prompted such strong Canadian censure. However, Canadian bankers, when asked about the extent and nature of their involvement in these transactions, are adamant in their refusal to divulge such information. Yet, we submit that the activities of the major Canadian banks, together with other international banks, in this case as in the case of South Africa, play a major role in sustaining a regime unacceptable for its political repression to our government and to a large number of concerned Canadians. Hence they limit in a very direct way the options for international and Canadian pressure to curb the excesses of those repressive governments.

NEED FOR DISCLOSURE REQUIREMENTS

In its submission to the Royal Commission on Corporate Concentration,[3] the Taskforce noted:

> that corporations—like other institutions and individuals—have the responsibility to see that their endeavours contribute to the alleviation of human misery and the redress of social injustices and do not cause or contribute to their continuation.
>
> It is increasingly recognized that as the concentration of corporate power increases so also do the risks that the pursuits of economic gain will be carried out in ways that cause social injury or contribute to its continuation. The countervailing influence of competition, the searching light of publicity, the effective overview by governments, all are lessened as power, wealth and control are further concentrated. That concentration in turn increases the likelihood that corporate power ... secures prominence in political decision making. The exercise of corporate power is then further removed from public awareness and the capacity of the public to grasp the significance of what is known is proportionately reduced.

Given the substantial economic growth of the relatively few large Canadian banks, we submit that these comments are as appropriate here.

Loans to foreign governments often amount to hundreds of millions of dollars, and the individual loans of the participating

Canadian banks and other financial institutions amount to significant sums requiring major policy decisions in regard to the creditworthiness of the client. They also should require a sensitive assessment of the social and political impact these loans have upon the recipient government and its people. Yet, under present circumstances, these far-reaching policy decisions of Canadian banks are made and implemented without the knowledge of Parliament, the public, the banks' depositors or their shareholders. We understand that the banks are obliged to file with the inspector general of banks, but since this information is also kept confidential it does not serve the need for disclosure, as we see it.

Canadian banks are under no obligation to disclose the fact that these major loans are being made, their amount or their duration, or whether they are of a bilateral or multilateral nature. It is left entirely to the discretion of the individual banks to respond in an informative way to enquiries in this regard, and wide variations in their willingness to do so exist.

Yet studies by Canadian bank analysts reveal that they and other researchers, after extensive and costly research, are able to document with some accuracy the extent of Canadian loans to foreign borrowers.[4] But even these expert institutions admit to problems in obtaining data from Canadian financial institutions and favour greater disclosure requirements. But what can be determined by a few interested financial analysts should also be made available by the banks upon request and as a matter of right to all interested parties: owners, users and politicians.

Without such information the public remains in ignorance about the extent to which Canadian financial institutions shape, through their loan policies, economic and political directions in Canada and abroad. Significant loans to foreign governments are an important, at times a crucial, element in the determination of some governments of their social, political and economic systems and in the formation of Canadian foreign policy responses to them.

It concerns us that these large-scale activities of Canadian banks are not subject to public disclosure and therefore disallow an informed judgement about them by shareholders and clients who provide the ultimate means for such transactions.

It is, for example, of concern to us that such loans should not have socially undesirable effects and that they provide for the amelioration of poverty and underdevelopment in the client country.

The absence of any information about actual loans, let alone an assessment about their ultimate social impact, deprives church shareholders and the concerned public of an opportunity to take their responsibility as shareholders and as citizens seriously.

The reluctance by management to answer requests for information is frequently explained by an adherence to the principle of client/banker confidentiality. We would like to emphasize that we regard this principle as entirely proper and desirable and do not wish to tamper with its reasonable application. However, we strongly believe that clients, depositors and shareholders not only have the legitimate right but also the responsibility to know about important loan policy decisions made by their bank in regard to foreign governments and their agencies involving substantial sums. Client/banker confidentiality is a valid principle, but it seems that, arbitrarily applied as it is at this point by our banks, it may serve to an unjustifiable degree to avoid public accountability and public scrutiny.

Loans to foreign governments at times have significant political implications both for Canadian citizens and those of other countries. They also have implications for those charged with developing and administering Canadian policies towards other nations.

POLICY RECOMMENDATIONS

In order that the Canadian public be in possession of information which permits it to form valid judgements about the foreign loan policies of Canadian banks and other financial institutions involved in international investment or underwriting and in order that clients and shareholders be given the legitimate choice of raising questions about these policy decisions, we submit the following recommendations for inclusion in the revised Bank Act:

1. That the Bank Act make provision for uniform and equitable public disclosure requirements of loans by Canadian banks, their subsidiaries and affiliates and by other financial institutions made directly or through consortia to foreign governments or agencies of foreign governments of amounts totalling more than $1 million.

2. That in the interest of public and shareholder accountability, Canadian banks and other financial institutions be required to disclose the amount and the dates of such loans and publish them as a matter of record.

3. That in order to preserve the principle of client/banker confidentiality and in order to safeguard the principle of competition, financial institutions should not be required to disclose such loans prior to 30 days following signed agreements.

6 · TO ESTABLISH A KINGDOM OF JUSTICE

ROMAN CATHOLIC BISHOPS OF THE ATLANTIC PROVINCES, 1979

As Catholic bishops of the Atlantic provinces committed to the care and service of the people of God, we must constantly renew and enliven our faith in a future which will outgrow present suffering and create a new social order based on justice and love. We call upon people of good will to take up the struggle for social justice. We offer the following document as a stimulus to the involvement of all people in a process of critical analysis of our social, economic and political systems.

Our desire is to stimulate thoughtful Christian responses to social injustices—at parochial, diocesan and regional levels. Our goal is to promote fundamental changes representing the determined aspiration of our people for a more hopeful future.

This call is in keeping with the Pastoral Message of the Canadian Bishops, December 1, 1977, *A Society to Be Transformed*, in which we stated:

> We invite you to get more involved in reshaping society, and we urge a particular form of involvement. First in the name of the Gospel, all Christians must involve themselves in transforming our ways of living and our social and economic structures. The Lord calls Christians to be present in every search for new or renewed ways—new or renewed techniques, plans, programmes, institutions or systems—to resolve today's difficulties. Secondly, we stress once again that Christians must be leaders in identifying and promoting the solutions that come only through new or renewed values, attitudes and relationships.[1]

INTRODUCTION

While unjust and inequitable distribution of goods and power exploits the majority of Canadians wherever they live, this burden of injustice is compounded in Atlantic Canada by the problem known as regional disparity, a problem we share with other dependent areas of this country.

As we export our talents and raw materials, we import transfer payments and high-cost consumer goods. Failing to mobilize our human and natural potential to meet our own considered needs, we fall into dependency on the wealth and power of others. Generations of Atlantic Canadians have experienced the consequences of this dependency.

Peripheral status within Canada and in North America brings us:

— higher unemployment
— more marginal jobs
— inability to develop indigenous industry
— greater insecurity
— greater danger of family breakdown
— inadequate housing
— uprooting of families
— greater strain on our physical and mental well-being
— higher percentage of below poverty-line incomes
— pessimism about the future and profound difficulty in achieving meaning and fulfillment in our lives.

On a naive level we too often identify such problems simply as products of human nature. ("Some people would rather drink than work." "There is nothing we can do but give them handouts.") Or we may say, "The region is simply lacking in resources and in ability."

Let us understand the struggle and identify the suffering that is daily imposed upon us, by identifying and agreeing upon the root causes of regional disparity.

OUR ECONOMIC SYSTEM

Basic to our society and economy is the concentration of wealth and power in the hands of a small percentage of the population who determine the kinds of goods and services to be produced and control the means of producing and distributing them. Surpluses gained in the process of converting nature's bounty and mankind's

skill into objects for human consumption accrue in alarming dispro-
portion to a minority of corporations and individuals—multiplying
corporate power and enhancing the personal wealth of a few.
Unequal distribution of social goods is inherent in such a system.
Present distribution of wealth is such that almost half of all income
goes to 20 per cent of the population, while over 40 per cent of
financial assets belong to only 12 per cent of the population. And
at the other end, the poorest 20 per cent in Canada receive less
than 4 per cent of the nation's wealth.[2]

In other words, those who actually produce the goods and
resources are shut out of ownership and decision-making and are
robbed of the dynamic value of their own work. Our economy
provides some people with the income to make them effective
consumers while leaving the others with only the aspirations of
consumers. But all lack control of their lives and power to produce
what they need. And more is involved than a question of wealth.
Control of the economy embraces and requires for its continuation
the power to determine social values: the capacity to set goals for
the system as a whole, and for each individual within it. Not only
the manufacture and sale of "goods" but the very concept of "good"
itself becomes the object of manipulation by those who would
purchase our creativity and harness our wants. In our society today
in the name of profit and power many irrational decisions are made.
Continuous growth in sales and the unnecessary diversification of
product lines, the unwarranted introduction of labour substitution
devices and the continuous reduction of the work process to mind-
less repetitive tasks, establishment or curtailment of governmental
and private services to the public, the global quest for cheaper raw
materials and low-cost adaptable labour, are dictated by demands
for profit rather than by the basic needs of producers and consumers.
Some of the consequences of a system that puts profits before people
are: inequitable taxation, high-cost transportation, price manipulation, subsidized job-creation, sexist exploitation, racial discrimination, and continuing inflation.

Such basic needs as love, self-esteem, sense of belonging, trust,
spiritual growth, and participation in decision-making are neglected
as material growth is emphasized. This condition is as destructive
to the apparent beneficiaries as it is to the oppressed because the
exclusive importance placed on the acquisition of material goods
and status fosters cut-throat competition and criminality,[3] reinforces man's inhumanity to man and woman, and undermines the

pride in craftsmanship and joy in work which are fundamental to a healthy society.

THE REGIONAL CHARACTER OF DISPARITY

The story of Atlantic region dependency is as old as the story of Confederation. For decades Maritimers have experienced an increasing domination of their economy, their culture, their communications networks by interests controlled outside the region working in collaboration with and serving as models for a small minority of Atlantic Canadians who have accumulated in their own hands more and more of the wealth and influence remaining to the region.

Excessive concentration of economic and cultural power in the metropolitan areas of Canada has robbed the region not only of crucial indigenous economic institutions but of human and natural resources (people, lumber, fish, food, minerals) which have been rendered cheap exportable factors in the services of a centralized North American capitalism. With the conversion of the regional economy into a resource and manpower hinterland, a paradise for the lending agency, and a dumping ground for the purveyors of gaudy commodities, has come the transformation of our economic, cultural and political elite from guardians of regional pride and prosperity to agents of continued and deepening dependency.[4]

The Maritime banks, the Maritime insurance companies, the locally owned industries of yesteryear, have given way to government office buildings, shopping malls and fast-food outlets, quickie subdivisions and shore-front cottage lots, finance companies and collection agencies, fly-by-night processors, corporate farms and branch-plant lumber companies.

Into the breach left by a faltering economic system, and a people rendered fatalistic by years of unequal exchange for their products, underemployment and low wages, step ever more paternalistic governments delivering ill-conceived programs which fail to diminish regional disparity and often aggravate it. "Create jobs" is the cry, "Get these people off unemployment and into the workforce." Certainly we can agree that a policy of perpetual handouts to individuals or communities in distress ignores their basic dilemmas, fosters idleness and lack of vocation, and creates new categories of dependency at taxpayers' expense. But we cannot agree that meaningful job creation or regional development will be achieved by paying corporations to set up operations whose profits rest on low-cost labour—women, minors, the unorganized—exploiting vulnerable resources, manipulating primary producers, conning the consumer into expenditures beyond his or her means.

In the absence of people-oriented development, life for many Atlantic Canadians remains a continuous struggle against overwhelming odds. When work can be found, it is often in the service sector or in the lowest-paid labouring jobs in Canada, jobs which rank among the least desirable employment on this continent. Since many of these jobs are seasonal or temporary, there are long stretches on unemployment insurance and there is always the possibility of not being rehired. Primary producers frequently fish, farm and cut lumber for returns below the cost of production. Small store keepers face ruthless competition from large chains willing to cut prices in the short run to secure a permanent market foothold. Travellers and shippers alike bear the high costs and inconveniences of a run-down railway system neglected in favour of a highways network which mainly services the commercial needs of the largest centres but leaves vast rural areas at serious disadvantage. Airlines and ferry services are geared principally to the needs of tourists and commercial travellers in their seasonality, in the destinations they make convenient and in their increasingly prohibitive prices.

In the day-to-day effort to make ends meet, the unemployed and the underpaid, the aged, the young and the handicapped are faced with the need to purchase imported goods, of limited quality, at inflated prices.

They suffer from high provincial sales tax, high interest rates, high transportation costs.

The dependency of Atlantic Canada leaves little more for the majority of its citizens than struggle to survive and consume; struggle for security and some kind of prestige; struggle to keep up with and hopefully a little ahead of one's neighbour.

Limited opportunity and repeated frustration breed preoccupation with triviality rather than broad social vision; pessimism or escapism become ready substitutes for constructive and critical action.

The Christian community, while maintaining high respect for the good will and the capacity of our educators, is saddened by our education system which has too often provided our people with a passport out of the region without stimulating reflection on our disparity problems.

And then there are lotteries, set up by governments, which become "magic" solutions to economic hardships. Far from being cure-alls, they are sugar-filled recipes for transferring the weight of supporting public programs from the shoulders of the well-to-do to the backs of the underprivileged.

When all else fails, there is always the choice of "going down the road" to Toronto or Calgary to try one's luck, but too often this means leaving the family behind.

The predicament we have outlined is all the more painful to contemplate when we recall that Atlantic Canadians are traditionally a proud people with a heritage of hard work and self-reliance.[5] Their present situation is no reflection of their historic willingness to fight back against the odds and to organize for transformation of institutions and attitudes in the name of social justice and the full and abundant life. Credit unions, cooperatives, fishermen's unions and associations, Maritime rights movements, trade unions, numerous farmer organizations, the Antigonish movement, are a few examples of the tenacious versatility of our people in the search for solutions to the economic and social dilemmas of dependency. Sadly, none of them nor all taken together could defeat the forces of big money and burgeoning bureaucracy which beset the region. And the struggle continues.

Yet there is hope. The Atlantic Region is rich in natural and human resources. The land and sea have been generous in the past, and still promise bountiful fishing, farming, forestry and minerals. The people traditionally have been inventive, productive and hard-working in many areas of industrial and commercial enterprise.

Pope John Paul II, in his encyclical *Redemptor Hominis*, reminds us that all progress must have as its goal the dignity of man. "Does this progress which has man for its author and promoter, make human life on earth 'more human' in every aspect of that life?"[6]

While recognizing the positive elements in modern development he continues, "But the question keeps coming back with regard to what is most essential—whether in the context of this progress man, as man, is becoming truly better, that is to say, more mature spiritually, more aware of the dignity of his humanity, more responsible, more open to others, especially the neediest and the weakest, and readier to give and to aid all."[7]

A new social and economic system which has as its goal the full development of man should demand new jobs based on our natural resources which provide scope for creativity and opportunity to share in ownership. This society should appeal to the Maritimer's closeness to land and sea. Labour should be given the dignity it deserves, and development should be organized for the benefit of all, especially the most oppressed. The greater good of the people should take precedence over individual greed. Control and money should no longer belong to a few who are rich and powerful. The hope of a new society where there is equality and justice leads us to ponder the great social love of Mary who in her obedience and love of the Father recognized where God stood in relation to human dignity. "He has pulled down princes from their thrones and exalted the lowly, the hungry he has filled with good things, the rich sent empty away" (Luke 1:52-53). This is a strong plea for equality.

Pope John Paul II reminds us that "such a task is not an impossible one. The principle of solidarity in a wide sense must inspire the effective search for appropriate institutions and mechanisms...."[8]

CHRISTIAN APPROACH

The living Lord came to earth to establish a kingdom of justice and love. He does not look kindly on those who stand in the way by oppressing the poor, denying basic rights such as a right to work. As we describe the problems of Atlantic Canada, we are mindful of the truly extraordinary inequality of distribution of goods and services on a global scale. Since we recognize that the same system which creates so much misery in the Third World is responsible for inequality in Canada as well, we see the task of transformation as immense and urgent. Our region is trapped like many Third World countries with wealth of resources and people whose potential is very much underutilized. For Christians, the transforming of society is part of the task of building the kingdom of Christ, a kingdom of justice, truth, hope and love.

THE ROLE OF THE CHURCH

Solutions to the disparity problem require a variety of measures in the social, economic, political and spiritual domains which should be decided upon by the community as a whole and by each individual. The Christian Church in the light of the Gospel must recognize the sinful, unjust social powers that marginalize and institutionally oppress the people. We must remember the powerful message of Christ in Matthew 25: "I was hungry and you gave me no food, naked and you did not clothe me ..." and apply it as Pope John Paul II reminds us "to man's history: it must always be made the 'measure' for human acts as an essential outline for an examination of conscience for each and every one."[9]

The Christian Church in the hope of the Gospel must provide a liberating vision of human life which enables us to believe that living conditions can be made better and motivates us to realize a new, more just, social order which: frees us from fear and from manipulation by propaganda (including advertising); enables us to proceed with a process which forges a creative culture true to our traditions; assures effective representation and assures authentic participation by all; restores to each person the essential dignity conferred on him or her by God.

The Catholic Bishops of Canada, recognizing the bondage of too many Canadians, have stated: "The riches of Canada are unequally shared. This inequality, which keeps so many people poor, is a social sin."[10]

Pope Paul VI reminds us that: "It is not licit to increase the wealth of the rich and the domination of the strong, while leaving the poor to their misery and adding to the servitude of the oppressed."[11]

Our duty as Christians demands that we be clearsighted and loudly announce our distress in an effort to alert those who have the capacity and the ability to "serve." Our mandate as Christians, to go forth and renew, obliges us to point out oppression even when it is presented as progress and to make known our dissatisfaction with halfway measures and cures even when proposed with good intentions. Disparity and marginalization promote a feeling of apathy and helplessness. People become discouraged and even too cynical to act. The will to act and to assume responsibility can only be generated and sustained by hope, a hope that points to trustworthy alternatives for personal and social growth. Above all, this hope which Christians possess is a hope based on faith. God's kingdom is an earthly kingdom but it is also eternal. This knowledge that God is with us gives us strength. It fills us with love for our fellow-men and calls us to leave selfish interests in pursuit of the greater good of all men and women.

The words of Isaiah give us a glimpse of what society should be: "My chosen shall enjoy the fruit of their labour because the fruit of their household shall not be taken from them."[12]

The Christian community as a whole and especially in Atlantic Canada, hoping to realize the fruit of their labour, should see a challenge and a possibility to develop a socio-economic order based on equity and love. However, the variety of ways in which many Christians have "bought into" the system producing and perpetuating disparity raises a serious question. Do we have the will, the commitment and the creativity to effect the necessary changes in our present styles of living, consistent with the potential and the needs of the people of the Atlantic Region?

In this task we call on the Holy Spirit to strengthen us that we may stand together as a people. "This is why," in the words of Pope John Paul II, "the Church of our time—a time particularly hungry for the Spirit, because it is hungry for justice, peace, love, goodness, fortitude, responsibility, and human dignity—must concentrate and gather around that Mystery, finding in it the light and the strength that are indispensable for her mission."[13]

We do not propose a concrete program for the solution of the disparity problem, because programs and measures must be developed by the people themselves. We believe in the principle that "only knowledge gained through participation is valid in this area of justice, true knowledge can be gained only through concern and solidarity."[14]

We remind our political leaders of the words of our supreme shepherd: "The common good that authority in the State serves is brought to full realization only when all the citizens are sure of their rights."[15]

We propose that the churches in Atlantic Canada continue to fight in a renewed way against the root causes of injustice of which too many are the victims. We call on our governments to set new priorities which favour the common good of the people.

Recommendations

Committed to Christ the Lord we are committed to his example of bringing the Good News with the promise of justice. Therefore we propose a program of involvement, reflection and action in each of our dioceses. We will commit our time and resources for the purpose of bringing people together at parish, deanery, diocesan, and regional levels to reflect critically and propose lines of action to overcome the problems of regional disparity. At the same time, we see these meetings as a fulfillment of our commitment to follow up the recommendations outlined in *A Society to Be Transformed*.

We will promote meetings to bring together representatives from the entire Atlantic Region to clarify and add vision to the work being done at the local levels and to formulate plans for further action and cooperation. We also make the following recommendations to our diocesan and parish communities:

1. Seek out and identify with the people and groups who are most victimized. This demands a change of attitude.

2. Invite and welcome them in church decision and policy-making bodies in order that the Church become truly the church also of the poor.

3. Study, analyze and discuss the reasons for their particular problems as they relate to the structures that cause disparity.

4. Work for the establishment of a more just society by choosing and becoming involved in a specific issue related to justice.

5. Associate ourselves with groups and organizations involved in fighting local manifestations of the suffering caused by disparity.

6. When it is necessary to take a stand on a particular matter concerning justice, organize and exert pressure on political representatives, and all other public leaders.

7. Reflect seriously on our attitudes and lifestyle with regard to the true fulfillment of our human vocation.

CONCLUSION

The covenant of justice and love that God has made with us in Jesus Christ and that we renew in our celebration of the Eucharist requires that we work together to realize that covenant in all forms of our social life. We believe that our exclusively profit-oriented system is incompatible with the creation of a just social order. We appeal to all people to join us in creating a new order.

Finally, we ask God's blessing for the many fine initiatives already taken in our region by church social-action and community-based groups. Work being done in housing, with Irish Moss harvesters, in education for development both regionally and globally. On the food question, with farmers, fishermen, lumbermen, the unemployed and those on social insurance are signs of the future we speak of. They are signs of the Father's love which favours brotherhood, equality and sharing while opposing injustice, privilege and oppression. May the efforts of those already engaged in creating new alternatives, especially for the most needy, the young and the struggling, increase and multiply before it is too late. "Otherwise," as Pope Paul VI stated in *Populorum Progressio*, "continued greed will certainly call down the judgement of God and the wrath of the poor, with consequences no one can foretell."[16]

Through our efforts may the Gospel be heard and practised in a new way in solidarity with the oppressed by Christians in this region and ultimately in our country and world.

7 • ETHICAL REFLECTIONS ON THE ECONOMIC CRISIS*

THE EPISCOPAL COMMISSION FOR SOCIAL AFFAIRS, CANADIAN CONFERENCE OF CATHOLIC BISHOPS, 1983

As the New Year begins, we wish to share some ethical reflections on the critical issues facing the Canadian economy.

In recent years, the Catholic Church has become increasingly concerned about the scourge of unemployment that plagues our society today and the corresponding struggles of workers in this country. A number of pastoral statements and social projects have been launched by Church groups in national, regional, and local communities as a response to various aspects of the emerging economic crisis.[1] On this occasion, we wish to make some brief comments on the immediate economic and social problems followed by some brief observations on the deeper social and ethical issues at stake in developing future economic strategies.

As pastors, our concerns about the economy are not based on any specific political options. Instead, they are inspired by the Gospel message of Jesus Christ. In particular, we cite two fundamental Gospel principles that underlie our concerns.

The first principle has to do with the preferential option for the poor, the afflicted and the oppressed. In the tradition of the prophets, Jesus dedicated his ministry to bringing "good news to the poor" and "liberty to the oppressed" (Luke 4:16-19, 7:22; Matthew 11:4-6). As Christians, we are called to follow Jesus by identifying with the victims of injustice, by analyzing the dominant attitudes and

---

* Copyright © Concacan Inc., 1983.

structures that cause human suffering, and by actively supporting the poor and oppressed in their struggles to transform society. For, as Jesus declared, "when you did it unto these, the least of my brethren, you did it unto me" (Matthew 25:40).

The second principle concerns the special value and dignity of human work in God's plan for Creation.[2] It is through the activity of work that people are able to exercise their creative spirit, realize their human dignity, and share in Creation. By interacting with fellow workers in a common task, men and women have an opportunity to further develop their personalities and sense of self-worth. In so doing, people participate in the development of their society and give meaning to their existence as human beings.[3] Indeed, the importance of human labour is illustrated in the life of Jesus who was himself a worker, "a craftsman like Joseph of Nazareth."[4]

It is from the perspective of these basic Gospel principles that we wish to share our reflections on the current economic crisis. Along with most people in Canada today, we realize that our economy is in serious trouble. In our own regions, we have seen the economic realities of plant shutdowns, massive layoffs of workers, wage restraint programs, and suspension of collective bargaining rights for public sector workers. At the same time, we have seen the social realities of abandoned one-industry towns, depleting unemployment insurance benefits, cutbacks in health and social services, and line-ups at local soup kitchens. And we have also witnessed, first hand, the results of a troubled economy: personal tragedies, emotional strain, loss of human dignity, family breakdown, and even suicide.

Indeed, we recognize that serious economic challenges lie ahead for this country. If our society is going to face up to these challenges, people must meet and work together as a "true community" with vision and courage. In developing strategies for economic recovery, we firmly believe that first priority must be given to the real victims of the current recession, namely—the unemployed, the welfare poor, the working poor—pensioners, native peoples, women, young people—and small farmers, fishermen, some factory workers, and some small business men and women. This option calls for economic policies which realize that the needs of the poor have priority over the wants of the rich; that the rights of workers are more important than the maximization of profits; that the participation of marginalized groups takes precedence over the preservation of a system which excludes them.

In response to current economic problems, we suggest that priority be given to the following short-term strategies by both government and business.

First, unemployment, rather than inflation, should be recognized as the number-one problem to be tackled in overcoming the present crisis. The fact that some 1.5 million people are jobless constitutes a serious moral as well as economic crisis in this country. While efforts should continually be made to curb wasteful spending, it is imperative that primary emphasis be placed on combatting unemployment.

Second, an industrial strategy should be developed to create permanent and meaningful jobs for people in local communities. To be effective, such a strategy should be designed at both national and regional levels. It should include emphasis on increased production, creation of new labour-intensive industries for basic needs, and measures to ensure job security for workers.

Third, a more balanced and equitable program should be developed for reducing and stemming the rate of inflation. This requires shifting the burden for wage controls to upper-income earners and introducing controls on prices and new forms of taxes on investment income (e.g., dividends, interest).

Fourth, greater emphasis should be given to the goal of social responsibility in the current recession. This means that every effort must be made to curtail cutbacks in social services, maintain adequate health care and social security benefits, and, above all, guarantee special assistance for the unemployed, welfare recipients, the working poor and one-industry towns suffering from plant shutdowns.

Fifth, labour unions should be asked to play a more decisive and responsible role in developing strategies for economic recovery and employment. This requires the restoration of collective bargaining rights where they have been suspended, collaboration between unions and the unemployed and unorganized workers, and assurances that labour unions will have an effective role in developing economic policies.

Furthermore, all peoples of goodwill in local and regional communities throughout the country must be encouraged to coordinate their efforts to develop and implement such strategies. As a step in this direction, we again call on local Christian communities to become actively involved in the six-point plan of action outlined in the message of the Canadian bishops on *Unemployment: The Human Costs*.

We recognize that these proposals run counter to some current policies or strategies advanced by both governments and corporations. We are also aware of the limited perspectives and excessive demands of some labour unions. To be certain, the issues are complex; there are no simple or magical solutions. Yet, from the standpoint of the Church's social teachings,[5] we firmly believe that present economic realities reveal a "moral disorder" in our society. As pastors, we have a responsibility to raise some of the fundamental social and ethical issues pertaining to the economic order. In so doing, we expect that there will be considerable discussion and debate within the Christian community itself on these issues. Indeed, we hope that the following reflections will help to explain our concerns and contribute to the current public debate about the economy.

Economic Crisis

The present recession appears to be symptomatic of a much larger structural crisis in the international system of capitalism. Observers point out that profound changes are taking place in the structure of both *capital* and *technology* which are bound to have serious social impacts on *labour*.[6] We are now in an age, for example, where transnational corporations and banks can move capital from one country to another in order to take advantage of cheaper labour conditions, lower taxes, and reduced environmental restrictions. We are also in an age of automation and computers where human work is rapidly being replaced by machines on the assembly line and in administrative centres. In effect, capital has become transnational and technology has become increasingly capital-intensive. The consequences are likely to be permanent or structural unemployment and increasing marginalization for a large segment of the population in Canada and other countries.[7] In this context, the increasing concentration of capital and technology in the production of military armaments further intensifies this economic crisis, rather than bringing about recovery.[8]

Indeed, these structural changes largely explain the nature of the current economic recession at home and throughout the world.[9] While there does not appear to be a global shortage of capital per se, large-scale banks and corporations continue to wait for a more profitable investment climate. Many companies are also experiencing a temporary shortage of investment funds required for the new technology, due largely to an overextension of production and related factors. In order to restore profit margins needed for new investment, companies are cutting back on production, laying off workers, and selling off their inventories. The result has been economic slowdown and soaring unemployment. To stimulate economic growth, governments are being called upon to provide a more favourable climate for private investments. Since capital tends to flow wherever the returns are greatest, reduced labour costs and lower taxes are required if countries are to remain competitive. As a result, most governments are introducing austerity measures such as wage restraint programs, cutbacks in social services and other reductions in social spending in order to attract more private investment. And to enforce such economic policies some countries have introduced repressive measures for restraining civil liberties and controlling social unrest.

Moral Crisis

The current structural changes in the global economy, in turn, reveal a deepening moral crisis. Through these structural changes, "capital" is reasserted as the dominant organizing principle of economic life. This orientation directly contradicts the ethical principle that labour, not capital, must be given priority in the development of an economy based on justice.[10] There is, in other words, an ethical order in which human labour, the subject of production, takes precedence over capital and technology. This is the *priority of labour principle*. By placing greater importance on the accumulation of profits and machines than on the people who work in a given economy, the value, meaning and dignity of human labour is violated. By creating conditions for permanent unemployment, an increasingly large segment of the population is threatened with the loss of human dignity. In effect, there is a tendency for people to be treated as an impersonal force having little or no significance beyond their economic purpose in the system.[11] As long as technology and capital are not harnessed by society to serve basic human needs, they are likely to become an enemy rather than an ally in the development of peoples.[12]

In addition, the renewed emphasis on the "survival of the fittest" as the supreme law of economics is likely to increase the domination of the weak by the strong, both at home and abroad. The survival-of-the-fittest theory has often been used to rationalize the increasing concentration of wealth and power in the hands of a few.[13] The strong survive, the weak are eliminated. Under conditions of "tough competition" in international markets for capital and trade, the poor majority of the world is especially vulnerable. With three-quarters of the world's population, for example, the poor nations of the South are already expected to survive on less than one-fifth of the world's income. Within Canada itself, the top 20 per cent receive 42.5 per cent of total personal income while the bottom 20 per cent receive 4.1 per cent.[14] These patterns of domination and inequality are likely to further intensify as the survival-of-the-fittest doctrine is applied more rigorously to the economic order. While these Darwinian theories partly explain the rules that govern the animal world, they are in our view morally unacceptable as a "rule of life" for the human community.

Present Strategies

There is a very real danger that these same structural and moral problems are present in Canada's strategies for economic recovery. As recent economic policy statements reveal, the primary objective is to restore profitability and competitiveness in certain Canadian industries and provide more favourable conditions for private investment in the country.[15] The private sector is to be the "engine" for economic recovery. To achieve these goals, inflation is put forth as the number-one problem. The causes of inflation are seen as workers' wages, government spending, and low productivity rather than monopoly control of prices. The means for curbing inflation are such austerity measures as the federal 6 and 5 wage restraint program and cutbacks in social spending (e.g., hospitals, medicare, public services, education and foreign aid), rather than controls on profits and prices.[16] These measures, in turn, have been strengthened by a series of corporate tax reductions and direct investment incentives for such sectors as the petroleum industry. In effect, the survival of capital takes priority over labour in present strategies for economic recovery.

At the same time, working people, the unemployed, young people and those on fixed incomes are increasingly called upon to make the most sacrifice for economic recovery. For it is these people who suffer most from layoffs, wage restraints, and cutbacks in social services. The recent tax changes, which have the effect of raising taxes for working people and lowering them for the wealthy, adds to this burden. And these conditions, in turn, are reinforced by the existence of large-scale unemployment which tends to generate a climate of social fear and passive acceptance. Moreover, the federal and provincial wage control programs are inequitable, imposing the same control rate on lower incomes as on upper incomes.[17] If successfully implemented, these programs could also have the effect of transferring income from wages to profits.[18] Yet, there are no clear reasons to believe that working people will ever really benefit from these and other sacrifices they are called to make. For even if companies recover and increase their profit margins, the additional revenues are likely to be reinvested in more labour-saving technology, exported to other countries, or spent on market speculation or luxury goods.

Alternative Approaches

An alternative approach calls for a reordering of values and priorities in our economic life. What is required first is a basic shift in values: the goal of serving the human needs of all people in our society must take precedence over the maximization of profits and growth, and priority must be given to the dignity of human labour, not machines.[19] From this perspective, economic policies that focus primary attention on inflation and treat soaring unemployment as an inevitable problem, clearly violate these basic ethical values and priorities. There is nothing "normal" or "natural" about present unemployment rates. Indeed, massive unemployment which deprives people of the dignity of human work and an adequate family income constitutes a social evil. It is also a major economic problem, since high unemployment rates are accompanied by lower productivity, lower consumption of products, reduced public revenues, and increasing social welfare costs. Thus, alternative strategies are required which place primary emphasis on the goals of combatting unemployment by stimulating production and permanent job creation in basic industries; developing a more balanced and equitable program for curbing inflation; and maintaining health care, social security, and special assistance programs.

An alternative approach also requires that serious attention be given to the development of new industrial strategies.[20] In recent years, people have begun to raise serious questions about the desirability of economic strategies based on megaprojects, wherein large amounts of capital are invested in high-technology resource developments (e.g., large-scale nuclear plants, pipelines, hydro-electric projects). Such megaprojects may increase economic growth and profits but they generally end up producing relatively few permanent jobs while adding to a large national debt. In our view, it is important to increase the self-sufficiency of Canada's industries, to strengthen manufacturing and construction industries, to create new job-producing industries in local communities, to redistribute capital for industrial development in underdeveloped regions, and to provide relevant job training programs.[21] It is imperative that such strategies, wherever possible, be developed on a regional basis and that labour unions and community organizations be effectively involved in their design and implementation.

New Directions

In order to implement these alternatives there is a need for people to take a closer look at the industrial vision and economic model that govern our society.[22] Indeed, it is becoming more evident that an industrial future is already being planned by governments and corporations. According to this industrial vision, we are now preparing to move into the high-technology computer age of the 1990s.[23] In order to become more competitive in world markets, the strategy for the 1980s is to re-tool Canadian industries with new technologies, create new forms of high-tech industries (e.g., micro-electronic, petro-chemical, nuclear industries), and phase out many labour-intensive industries (e.g., textile, clothing and footwear industries). This industrial vision, in turn, is to be realized through an economic model of development that is primarily: capital-intensive (using less and less human labour); energy-intensive (requiring more non-renewable energy sources); foreign controlled (orienting development priorities to external interests); and export-oriented (providing resources or products for markets elsewhere rather than serving basic needs of people in this country).

There are, of course, alternative ways of looking at our industrial future and organizing our economy. This does not imply a halt to technological progress but rather a fundamental reordering of the basic values and priorities of economic development. An alternative economic vision, for example, could place priority on serving the basic needs of all people in this country, on the value of human labour, and on an equitable distribution of wealth and power among people and regions. What would it mean to develop an alternative economic model that would place emphasis on socially useful forms of production, labour-intensive industries, the use of appropriate forms of technology, self-reliant models of economic development, community ownership and control of industries, new forms of worker management and ownership, and greater use of the renewable energy sources in industrial production? As a country, we have the resources, the capital, the technology and, above all else, the aspirations and skills of working men and women required to build an alternative economic future. Yet, the people of this country have seldom been challenged to envision and develop alternatives to the dominant economic model that governs our society.

At the outset, we agreed that people must indeed meet and work together as a "true community" in the face of the current economic crisis.[24] Yet, in order to forge a true community out of the present crisis, people must have a chance to choose their economic future rather than have one forced upon them. What is required, in our judgement, is a real public debate about economic visions and industrial strategies involving choices about values and priorities for the future direction of this country. Across our society, there are working and non-working people in communities—factory workers, farmers, forestry workers, miners, people on welfare, fishermen, Native Peoples, public service workers, and many others— who have a creative and dynamic contribution to make in shaping the economic future of our society. It is essential that serious attention be given to their concerns and proposals if the seeds of trust are to be sown for the development of a true community and a new economic order.

For our part, we will do whatever we can to stimulate public dialogue about alternative visions and strategies. More specifically, we urge local parishes or Christian communities, wherever possible, to organize public forums for discussion and debate on major issues of economic justice. Such events could provide a significant opportunity for people to discuss: (a) specific struggles of workers, the poor and the unemployed in local communities; (b) analysis of local and regional economic problems and structures; (c) major ethical principles of economic life in the Church's recent social teachings; (d) suggestions for alternative economic visions; (e) new proposals for industrial strategies that reflect basic ethical principles. In some communities and regions, Christian groups in collaboration with other concerned groups have already launched similar events or activities for economic justice. And we encourage them to continue doing so.

Indeed, we hope and pray that more people will join in this search for alternative economic visions and strategies. For the present economic crisis, as we have seen, reveals a deepening moral disorder in the values and priorities of our society. We believe that the cries of the poor and the powerless are the voice of Christ, the Lord of History, in our midst. As Christians, we are called to become involved in struggles for economic justice and participate in the building up of a new society based on Gospel principles. In so doing, we fulfill our vocation as a pilgrim people on earth, participating in Creation and preparing for the coming Kingdom.

FURTHER READING

Baum, Gregory, ed. "The Maritime Bishops: Social Criticism." *The Ecumenist*, March/April, 1980, pp. 35-41.

Baum, Gregory. "Theology and Canadian Business." *Queen's Quarterly* 85 (1978-79): 650-53.

Baum, Gregory, and Cameron, Duncan, *Ethics and Economics*. Toronto: James Lorimer & Co., 1984.

Canadian Centre for Policy Alternatives. *Policy Alternatives*, Spring-Summer, 1983. Special issue on the Bishops' Statement.

Canadian Conference of Catholic Bishops. *Sharing Daily Bread*. Ottawa: 1974.

Canadian Conference of Catholic Bishops. *A Society to Be Transformed*. Ottawa: 1977.

GATT-Fly. *Paying the Piper: How Working People Are Saddled with the Debt from Huge Resource Projects While the Banks and Corporate "Pipers" Call the Tune*. Toronto: 1977.

GATT-Fly. *Power to Choose: Canada's Energy Options*. Toronto: Between the Lines, 1981.

Hutchinson, Roger. "Inflation: Moral Implications." *The Chelsea Journal*, May/June, 1976, pp. 113-16.

Smillie, Benjamin J. "Canada: A Silly, Senseless Pigeon or a Holy Nation?" In *More Than Survival*, ed. by Graham Scott. Don Mills, Ont.: CANEC, 1980.

The Social Action Commission, Catholic Diocese of Charlottetown. *Background Document on Atlantic Region Disparity*. Charlottetown: 1977.

Taskforce on the Churches and Corporate Responsibility. *Brief to the Standing Committee on the Administration of Justice of the Legislature of Ontario, in response to Bill 6, An Act to Revise the Business Corporation Act.* Toronto: 1981.

The United Church of Canada, Department of Church in Society. Issue #26, *This Land Is Whose Land? The Housing Squeeze*, 1982.

SECTION III
NUCLEAR ENERGY

The churches' critical analysis of capitalism quite logically entailed a study of the Canadian energy industry, since the energy corporations are the banks' only serious rivals as the most powerful agents in the economy of this country. With the promulgation of its 1980 National Energy Program, the federal government has placed its trust in energy megaprojects as the primary engine of economic development for the next two decades. The chief beneficiaries of this program, besides the federal and provincial governments, will be the multinational and some Canadian oil and gas corporations, certain energy crown corporations such as Petrocan, and the provincial electrical utilities.

The first major involvement of the churches in energy matters was in opposition to the Mackenzie Valley gas pipeline proposal (see below, section IV). More recently, they have developed a considerable interest in nuclear energy, and a number of church and inter-church groups have been formed to examine various phases of nuclear power generation, from the mining and refining of uranium to the disposal of radioactive wastes. Provincial hearings on whether and under what conditions uranium mining should be permitted were held in Labrador, Saskatchewan and B.C. in 1979-80; in each case churches presented submissions stressing the importance of social and environmental factors. And as the Atomic Energy Control Board of Canada began its consideration of how to deal with reactor wastes, the Taskforce on the Churches and Corporate Responsibility formed an energy and environment subgroup which, among other activities, submitted a brief to the AECB which called for a national public inquiry into the future of nuclear energy in Canada.

The generation of electricity by nuclear fission is an extremely complex process, and nuclear industry spokespersons often dismiss concerns for its safety on the grounds that critics do not understand its technical aspects. To counteract this unilateral invocation of expertise, the United Church of Canada devoted its *Issue* #5, *Nuclear Power: Blessing or Blight?* (1977), to an explanation of how nuclear power works and what are its potential hazards. As in most other *Issue* editions, the focus here is on factual information rather than religious or ethical analysis.

The following document, also from the United Church (British Columbia Conference), does concentrate on the ethical implications of the nuclear debate. Entitled *Ethics and Uranium Mining* (1980), it was produced for submission to the Royal Commission of Inquiry into Uranium Mining and Milling in B.C., which was established in January, 1979, and terminated abruptly in March, 1980. Unlike most such inquiries, which deal primarily with the technical and economic feasibility of proposed developments, this one was prepared to give considerable weight to ethical considerations. At the suggestion and with the assistance of the Uranium Working Group of the B.C. Conference of the United Church, the Commission held an ethics workshop in September, 1979, and it had agreed to include a four-day ethics phase of the inquiry; this was affected by the premature termination of the Commission's mandate. The sections of the United Church report which are included here convey the church's viewpoints on both the substantive issues of uranium mining and the procedural issues of how decisions should be made about whether such developments are or are not in the public interest.

8 • NUCLEAR POWER: BLESSING OR BLIGHT?

THE UNITED CHURCH OF CANADA, DEPARTMENT OF CHURCH IN SOCIETY, 1977

Vociferous critics and supporters agree the nuclear energy debate is more than a squabble over the dangers of radioactivity. Gordon Edwards, a mathematics professor and co-founder of the Canadian Coalition for Nuclear Responsibility—an active public-interest group opposed to nuclear power—has written:

> ... the nuclear controversy [is] one of the most crucial questions of our time. This question goes far beyond the dispute over whether or not nuclear energy is an acceptable technology for generating electricity. The question is: given the incredible power of modern technology, who should make the decisions in our society, and in what manner, and for what purposes? (*Alternatives*, vol. 5, no. 2, p. 30)

Dr. Margaret Maxey, a professor of bioethics at the University of Detroit, wrote recently in *The Christian Century*:

> The conflict underlying nuclear debates centres on the concept of human survival. How necessary to human survival are nuclear energy sources? What level of survival should be taken as a standard when we weight the risks against the benefits?...The way we perceive our survival both as individuals and as a society determines our assessment of nuclear energy. It is superficial to engage in debate over the alleged hazards of nuclear power. The real debate is about the kind and/or quality of life that make survival worth having. (*The Christian Century*, 21/7/77, pp. 658-9)

Sheila Collins, a Christian social action worker in the US, asks:

> Just think about the power to be gained through the control of access to nuclear material.

Think about the wealth that can be made by a few people who not only own a substance that could devastate the planet but also control the extraction, shipping and processing facilities needed to make use of that substance and the police system required to guard it....

Who should own what is necessary to human survival—namely energy?

Who really holds the power to make energy-related decisions, and who really bears the consequences?

Questions like these are crucial to any kind of informed ethical response to the dilemma of nuclear power. (*Christianity and Crisis*, vol. 36, no. 4, p. 51)

There are now 8 nuclear power reactors operating in Canada, all but one in Ontario. In less than 25 years, there may be 100 scattered across the nation. John J. Shepherd, executive director of the Science Council of Canada, estimates a low target of 70 reactors by the year 2000.

Canada, he says, will have to spend about $1.5 billion a year to maintain a nuclear commitment of that magnitude. (*Financial Post*, September 18, 1977, p. 7) When all energy-related projects are taken into account, Canadians may be facing a total energy bill of $180 billion over the next 15 years according to Energy, Mines and Resources. Given inflationary pressures and other cost factors, that estimate could climb. Yet nuclear power stations are considered more and more essential by energy-hungry industries and the utilities themselves.

Critics of nuclear power call it an unwise and potentially destructive choice for our long-term energy future. Opting for a nuclear future, they say, will create an enormous financial burden leading to an overall deterioration of our quality of life. A nuclear future would pre-empt more benign alternative energy sources and leave us open to unique social, political and environmental dangers. Hazards include how to keep radioactive wastes safely stored for hundreds of thousands of years and the potential arming of foreign nations with nuclear weapons produced from the spent fuel of Canadian-made Candu reactors.

On the other hand, not proceeding with an all-out nuclear push may put us at the mercy of untried and largely undeveloped alternative technologies. Nuclear advocates say we must look not only at the risks of going ahead but at the risks of not going ahead.

The nuclear power debate has come farther along the road to confrontation elsewhere. West German demonstrators recently occupied a nuclear power station and were routed by riot police. In France, marches and demonstrations of thousands have protested against the vigorous French nuclear program. In Sweden, nuclear power was a central election issue contributing to the defeat of the party in power. In the U.S., hundreds of anti-nuclear power groups have mobilized. In a state-wide vote in California, nuclear power was accepted two to one amidst heavy pro-nuclear publicity bankrolled by the industry.

In Canada, concerned groups have formed and are slowly gathering support. Citizens in the communities of Port Granby and Port Hope came together to form SEAP (Save the Environment from Atomic Pollution), when it was announced that Atomic Energy of Canada Ltd. (AECL) planned a new uranium processing plant in the area and an enlarged dump for radioactive waste products.

Hidden in the nuclear energy debate are questions of democracy and power. To "go nuclear" without examining the implications of that decision would be not only shortsighted, it would leave a decision of monumental impact on our future in the firm grip of a handful of politicians, senior civil servants and scientists.

Here we look at the pros and cons of a major Canadian commitment to nuclear power. What are the costs? Benefits? Advantages? Who makes the decisions and for what ends? What kinds of options are available for the future?...

Nuclear Wastes: Radioactivity and Storage

Like conventional generating stations, nuclear power stations produce waste products. With coal and oil, vast amounts of ash, smoke and noxious gases are released into the atmosphere. Adding effective but costly pollution-control devices can drastically reduce this waste. Nuclear reactors produce a different kind of waste, much less in volume, but radioactive. Although radioactive substances, like cobalt and iodine, have been used for great benefit—to irradiate cancerous cells and monitor certain physical malfunctions—radioactive materials can also present a distinct threat to human health.

Radioactive substances vary in strength, according to the stage they have reached in their disintegration to a stable non-radioactive substance. While some radioactive substances last no more than the blink of an eye, others have been around for millions of years. The intensity of radioactivity decreases over time. Alpha, beta and gamma rays released by radioactive atoms are all dangerous to the human body, but in different ways.

Radiation transfers energy into the atoms and molecules of matter with which it comes into contact. In the human body, this energy transfer can cause chemical changes which may produce leukemia (cancer of the blood), cancer of the thyroid, lungs, stomach, ovaries and cervix. It can also cause cataracts and other kinds of eye diseases, disorders of the endocrine system, skin diseases, severe anemia and sexual dysfunction. Beyond the immediate effects are more long-term, subtle results of radiation poisoning—genetic mutations. The germ cells may suffer chromosomal damage from exposure to radiation leading to physical malformations and mental retardation. These malformations may not show up for generations as the mutant cells are passed on from parent to child.

The dangers depend on how quickly the material decays, the intensity of the radiation, whether the material is inside or outside the body and the type of rays being emitted.

Alpha rays, for instance, consist of a thick path of excited electrons which travel very short distances. They can be stopped by a single sheaf of paper and will not penetrate human skin. But, once inside the body, they are extremely dangerous. An invisible speck of alpha-emitting plutonium lodged in a lung or stomach may cause the growth of a cancer.

The Candu produces numerous radioactive wastes, almost all of which are contained in the metal-encased fuel bundle. Less than 0.1 per cent of the waste is lost to the environment. Spent fuel is not seen as waste, since it may be reprocessed at a later date to extract plutonium for more fuel. But, once removed from the reactor core, it is radioactive and must be shielded from human contact.

Atomic Energy of Canada and Ontario Hydro have explored various methods of long-term permanent disposal. No radioactive material has yet been stored irretrievably. Meanwhile, the spent fuel, composed of radioactive fission fragments, is stored in vast pools of water at the reactor site. The water and the thick concrete walls shield the radioactivity from escaping. Power plants are built with about ten years of storage facilities. After that, the spent fuel must be removed and stored elsewhere.

Nuclear experts have proposed different kinds of long-term storage, but appear to favour incorporating radioactive wastes in non-leachable materials like glass or ceramics. AECL experimented with this method at the Chalk River Labs north-west of Ottawa as early as 1958. The wastes would eventually be buried deep in the ground in a stable, geological formation. Although no final site selection has been made yet, Geological Survey of Canada field teams are investigating probable locations. According to AECL, the most promising site so far is in south-central Ontario, near Madoc, about 75 miles north of Belleville. Sites are also being considered in northwestern Ontario. There could be a nuclear waste disposal plant operating in the region by the mid-1980s according to a spokesman for the Whiteshell Nuclear Research Station in Pinawa, Manitoba. (*Globe and Mail*, January 6, 1977, p. 8)

In the U.S. the question of underground storage is further advanced. The Energy Research and Development Administration (ERDA) recently announced plans to spend about $2 billion excavating old mine sites to store wastes from nuclear power plants. (*GM*, December 8, 1976, p. 12) However, public outcry has been so tremendous that few states are willing to become an atomic burial ground.

The most disquieting aspect of future nuclear waste storage is that pro-nuclear scientists, despite their faith in science and technology to solve societal problems, have not conclusively cracked the waste storage puzzle. George Wall, a Harvard University biology professor and 1968 Nobel Prize winner, comments:

> ... no one knows how to store the waste products, which will remain dangerous, for half a million years. The whole of human civilization is perhaps 10,000 years old, and we are producing material that will represent a lethal liability for man and for life on Earth for hundreds of thousands of years to come. At present this stuff is being stockpiled just about where it is produced, while we try to figure out what to do with it. (*The Progressive*, December, 1975)

Amory Lovins, a noted nuclear critic and respected physicist, contends that the safe storage of nuclear wastes will contribute to the formation of rigidly anti-democratic social tendencies. In an article written for the Habitat Conference in Vancouver, he says:

> ... if we want to protect nuclear wastes from geological, or rather theological, periods (hundreds of thousands of years, so that no responsible geologist can guarantee the storage site), we shall need hierarchal social rigidity or homogeneity so that the technological priesthood can go about its business undisturbed by social unrest. (*Habitat Guide*, May 31, 1976, p. 20)

Energy Probe, a Toronto-based public interest group concerned with a wide range of energy questions, underlines that even the experts are not sure of the methods of ultimate disposal. They quote P.J. Dyne, coordinator of AECL's program on waste management. "We cannot," Mr. Dyne says, "from the nature of the problem, give an absolute guarantee that none of the material will ever escape" (*CANDU: An Analysis of the Canadian Nuclear Programme*, part 1, p. 71)....

Nuclear Blackmail

In Canada and abroad, the shuttling to and fro of spent and reprocessed fuels will increase the possibility of theft and accident.

Those in the industry consistently downplay the idea of plutonium hijacking. Alan Wyatt, vice-president of Canatom Ltd., a firm of consulting nuclear engineers, says there are many more easy and effective ways to blackmail than with spent reactor fuel. "I can't get excited about terrorists stealing plutonium from Pickering and then having to go the whole reprocesing route before they could do something with it," he says.

In describing the central processing and storage complex, Dr. Foster says, "The irradiated fuel itself is protected against theft by its own radioactivity." He also notes that by associating fuel refabrication and fuel reprocessing in the same plant, there need never be large quantities of dangerous materials in relatively pure solutions. Ontario Hydro says it would take about 168 fuel bundles weighing about 23 tons to make a small atomic device. They insist that a specialized theft of that order would be unlikely to succeed.

But, no matter how unlikely a theft may be, it is still a possibility. In other nations touched by internal civil strife or wars with neighbouring states, where terrorism is seen as a justifiable political act, and safeguards may be less stringent, plutonium theft for an atomic device may be far less hypothetical than the experts allow.

Sabotage by a madman with no motive but wanton destruction could also occur by smuggling a small bomb into a nuclear station and lobbing it into the spent fuel bays. Such an act could, with minimum damage, contaminate the entire reactor area. With proper weather conditions and a powerful enough explosive, clouds of escaping radioactive particles could cover an area 20-30 miles from the reactor site. (Most of metropolitan Toronto is within this distance of the Pickering nuclear station). Even though odds are extremely low against this kind of occurrence, one cannot simply wave away the possibility as unfounded or illogical or gloss over it as nuclear supporters are prone to do.

Low-level Radiation

All nuclear reactors release minute amounts of radioactivity into the atmosphere as part of their normal operations. This low-level radiation escapes through the coolant and heat-transfer system and gradually seeps into the environment. In general people within the nuclear industry argue that low-level radioactivity is not a significant problem. Bill Morison, director of design and development for Ontario Hydro, says "there is no significant change in the natural background near a nuclear plant; 99.9 per cent stays inside the fuel bundle." He is certain that "if radioactive levels have to go even lower, then we could do more. The CANDU is designed to operate without any *significant* release."

Compared to the normal amount of radioactivity our bodies absorb daily, releases from nuclear reactors are very small indeed. People live in a sea of constant radioactive bombardment; from the earth's crust, cosmic radiation and manmade sources like X-rays and fallout from nuclear explosions. So, the Canadian Nuclear Association contends,

> a person living continuously at the boundary of Pickering station would receive less than 5 millirems per year due to the operation of the station. The effects of this would be indistinguishable from those due to the natural background radiation of 100 millirems. (*Questions and Answers*, p. 40)

The amount of natural radiation varies according to geology and elevation. Over the last forty years, enormous quantities of radiation have been artificially added to the earth over, what is in evolutionary terms, scarcely a thread in the fabric of time. Human beings have adapted biologically and genetically to natural background radiation over a time span of several hundred-thousand years. In this light, it would be imprudent to assume that we can determine the future effects of this relatively sudden onslaught of massive doses of radioactivity. It is impossible to prevent the background of radioactivity in the area surrounding a nuclear reactor from exceeding the background levels to which people are normally exposed.

Mining and Processing Uranium

Radioactivity is released at every point along the nuclear fuel cycle, from mining the uranium ore to ultimately disposing the final waste products. Like the fluorspar mines of Newfoundland and the asbestos mines in the southern townships of Quebec, uranium mines have taken their toll on miners' lives. Over the years, workers have breathed radioactive dust and inhaled radioactive gas (radon) which seeps from the decaying natural uranium. It took the Ontario government and the corporations operating the mines 16 years to implement internationally accepted safe levels of radiation exposure. It's still too early to measure the full cost in human lives of what might be termed willful negligence. Many miners have died lingering, gruesome deaths from cancer and silicosis.

An Ontario government study showed miners between 40 and 57 were four times as likely to die from lung cancer as an ordinary person.

The most visible scandal of the past few years has been Port Hope on the shore of Lake Ontario about 60 miles east of Toronto. Port Hope is the home of Eldorado Nuclear Ltd., a federal crown corporation involved in mining and processing uranium. Canada's only processing plant in Port Hope has been plagued with difficulties in disposing of the radioactive wastes and impurities left over after processing.

In 1975, it was discovered that radioactive wastes twenty years earlier had been used as landfill under some houses and one school in the town. AECL remained close-mouthed and unflappable as information had to be pried out of them by an inquisitive press. Under fire for underestimating the gravity of the situation, AECL supervised clean-up operations. Eight thousand tons of material have been hauled the 200 miles to Chalk River for burial, and officials say 70,000 more tons may have to be removed. (See *GM*, January 8, 1977, p. 12.)

Although the final effects of the Port Hope radioactivity exposure remain hypothetical, the incident has emphasized the *fallibility* of our institutions. Despite an outward air of self-assurance, AECL *has made* critical errors in judgement. It may do so again....

The Energy Race

In the post-war years, and particularly since the mid-1950s, there have been enormous spurts in energy consumption. Power companies, public utilities and industry all combined to push the equation of more energy use = greater standard of living. "Live Better Electrically" was an advertising slogan that captured the prevailing spirit right up to the sobering acceleration of oil, gas and electricity prices which began in 1973.

We are now beginning to feel the consequences of our squandering. To meet the demand which they in part created, public and private utilities have begun to ram through the first of many increases in the price of electricity. Indignant consumers in all provinces are absorbing double-digit rate increases. Nova Scotia rates, up 34 per cent in April, 1976, are going up another 67 per cent; B.C. rates went up 20 per cent last summer; N.W.T. customers are faced with an 89 per cent increase; Ontario residents experienced a 30 per cent jump and are expecting another of 12 per cent this year.

These rate increases have a twofold function: to cover the increased cost of oil, gas and coal for fossil-fuel generating stations and to provide extra cash to invest in additional generating capacity in future. These demand projections are based on population increase and location; a shift from oil and gas to electricity and an extrapolation of past demand increases. Ontario, for example, has planned for a 6.7 per cent yearly increase in electrical generating capacity up to the year 1995. But, while the population of Ontario is predicted to increase by about 50 per cent (from 8 to 12 million), per capita energy consumption is projected to grow by 250 per cent. Of the $180 billion energy expenditure projected over the next 15 years, almost 50 per cent will be directed towards nuclear energy.

Nuclear power is even more capital-intensive than large fossil-fueled generating stations. In its hurry to provide electrical power to industries, stores and citizens of Ontario, Ontario Hydro will spend $45 billion between 1983 and 1995. That does not include factors like cost of land, transmission lines or the costs of pollution abatement equipment. An issue paper of the Porter Royal Commission says funds required for the nuclear component of Ontario Hydro's development program may "exceed $30 billion by the end of the century" (p. 11). By 1985, Ontario will have spent $6.5 billion on the Bruce reactor heavy-water complex alone. Whether our public utilities raise the investment funds they need by loans or by increased rate hikes or both, it's the consumer who pays the shot.

In addition, as more of the country's available resources are channelled into the energy sector, there will be less available for investment in those areas which have been hardest hit by government cutbacks, production cuts and unemployment: schools, hospitals, roads, public transportation, unemployment insurance, public health care, income support schemes and other public spending areas.

The Energy Debt

Public utilities are amongst the largest Canadian borrowers on international money markets. Ontario Hydro, for example, has an outstanding debt of $6.3 billion. The enormity of these borrowings and the debt service payments that must be made on them contribute greatly to Canada's national balance-of-payments deficit. We paid out about $5 billion in 1976 to service our foreign debt. When external debt is compared to Gross National Product (GNP), Canada had the highest rate of borrowing in the world in 1976—even greater than the mendicants of the international community, Britain and Italy.

Continued heavy borrowing by public utilities for increased electrical expansion could spell severe economic dislocation. Inflationary pressures are stimulated by increasing the money supply without a corresponding flow of goods and services. Too much money chasing too few goods forces prices up. Any short-term flurry of economic activity is offset in the long run by a massive debt load.

Large inflows of foreign capital help to keep the value of the Canadian dollar artificially high. This means Canadian goods are high priced on world markets. Our exports become harder to sell. Ontario Hydro's Bill Morison admits offshore borrowing "keeps our dollar high and makes our manufactured goods more difficult to export." But, he denies that Ontario Hydro, a publicly owned, government-run corporation, has any responsibility for the effects of its borrowing on the national economy. "We don't run the country," he says, "and so far as I know it's still a free country, so we borrow where it's best for us and our customers." But the size of the debt load remains a growing worry.

The Face of The Future

The production of nuclear energy, by its very nature, requires a concentration of wealth and power, possible only to a government or a major corporation.... These technological achievements that concentrate great power, when incorporated into social systems that are already inadequate, require us to ask social and ethical questions. Ideally, the intricacy and scale of nuclear fission might contribute to a heightened sense of the interdependence of humanity, thereby raising human ethical sensibility. But it might equally well contribute to a heightened authoritarianism that bears down unduly on the weak. (*Facing Up to Nuclear Power*, p. 150-52)

In the next few decades we are going to be facing social and political questions of extreme consequence. We can drift through those years letting others determine the face of the future or we can insist that the questions be given wide public discussion. The energy question and nuclear energy in particular may be a decision of far-reaching implications. The important thing is to get the discussion into the open now, otherwise we may open our eyes in 30 years and find all other choices have vanished.

Amory Lovins, in a probing and prophetic article in the international journal *Foreign Affairs* (October, 1976), outlines a pathway to a non-nuclear future by switching to "soft-technology" energy options. Lovins argues that an all-stops-open commitment to nuclear power would create a high-technology, highly centralized, electrified society that would pose threats to democratic rights and personal liberties.

Fission technology has unique socio-political side-effects arising from the impact of human fallibility and malice on the persistently toxic and explosive materials in the fuel cycle. For example, discouraging nuclear violence and coercion requires some *abrogation of civil liberties;* guarding long-lived wastes against geological or social contingencies implies some form of *hierarchical social rigidity* or homogeneity to insulate the technological priesthood from social turbulence; and making political decisions about nuclear hazards which are compulsory, remote from social experience, disputed, unknown, or unknowable may tempt governments to bypass democratic decisions in favour of *elitist technocracy.* (p. 93)

Lovins also notes that "few have considered the economic or political implications of putting at risk such a large fraction of societal capital. How far would governments go to protect against a threat—even a purely political threat—a basket full of such delicate, costly and essential eggs?"

Would a full-scale nuclear program lock us permanently into some sort of controlled, elitist, totalitarian state? How do we test the proof of these predictions? The most unreliable element in the whole nuclear system is human behaviour. If the system is to be made as foolproof as possible, is it not likely that the tourniquet of control and regulation would be applied at that crucial weak spot?

People within the nuclear game tend to credit critics like Amory Lovins with opening the debate to wider issues but they are unwilling to agree with his conclusions.

In most cases, industry spokesmen keep the argument on the same axis of electricity need. Other ways of producing electricity would create even greater hazards than nuclear, Alan Wyatt says, although "it is difficult to quantify the effects of not going nuclear." The main effect of not going nuclear, Lovins and others would argue, would be having to make do with less electricity. Lovins contends that with proper planning the threat less electrical power would pose to our way of life would be almost imperceptible.

Sweden and West Germany have per capita energy consumption almost half of that of North Americans. Yet their standards of living are at least equal to ours. Fred Knelman, a leading Canadian antinuclear critic, in a study for the Science Council of Canada, estimates reasonable conservation measures could save 15 per cent of projected energy demand by 1995 and perhaps as much as 30 per cent. With intensive conservation measures like insulation of commercial and residential buildings and efficient use of waste heat combined with a major effort from power and industrial plants in the development of alternate sources (solar, biomass, etc.), nuclear critics like Sean Casey of Energy Probe believe we can safely abandon the pathway to nuclear nirvana.

A shift to "small-scale, energy-income technologies" with the emphasis on solar heating and organic conversion (methanol from plant matter), critics like Casey and Lovins contend, would put us in touch with a more human world, avoiding the anti-democratic tendencies of a centralized, high-technology nuclear energy sector.

A recent British report by the U.K. Royal Commission on Environmental Pollution—*Nuclear Power and the Environment*—concluded that alternate sources of energy should be pursued immediately with the fullest effort possible. "Our basic concern," the report states, "is that a major commitment to fission power and the plutonium economy should be postponed as long as possible, in the hope that it might be avoided altogether, by gaining the maximum time for the development of alternative approaches which will not involve such grave potential implications for mankind" (*Anticipation*, November, 1976, p. 16).

Nuclear Power and the Developing Nations

The recent scandal around AECL and the sale of nuclear reactor technology to Argentina and South Korea has done more to obscure than clarify the deeper issues in the export of nuclear power to Third World nations.

The problem of the overwhelming majority of the Third World is poverty and its consequences: hunger and lack of shelter, clothing and productive employment. These people need energy as we in the West do. But, they need energy in a form which will be appropriate to their most basic needs.

What about nuclear energy? It offers the Third World exactly the same thing it offers the West. A centralized, high-technology, capital-intensive source of electricity suited to the industrial patterns of the West. Nuclear technology, says A.K.N. Reddy, an Indian scientist working with the U.N. Environmental Programme, is a product of Western technique and Western values. "Scratch any piece of technology and you will find the values and aims of the society it was designed to serve" (*Anticipation*, November, 1976, p. 27).

The choice of what kind of technology to enlist in the development struggle should be based on whether it meets the simple, basic needs of the people whose interest it's supposed to serve. Nuclear power stations are designed to plug into Western industrial-style development. Yet, most people in the nuclear industry support the export of reactor technology to developing nations. E.C.W. Perryman, director of applied research and development at AECL's Chalk River nuclear labs, believes the CANDU is "ideally suited to underdeveloped countries." "How," he asks, "can we play God and say this or that country should not have this technology?"

But the Canadian government is not neutral. We have played God by pushing reactor sales for our own economic self-interest. Whether or not we decide to help a country acquire nuclear reactors, we are making a decision of some consequence. To claim that if we don't sell our reactors to a prospective buyer that another country will, is irrelevant.

Reddy notes that the real search should be for "alternative technology...in harmony with the environment and with genuine development...to reduce inequalities, to meet real needs instead of artificial demands, and to increase self-reliance and participation by people in the decisions which affect their lives."

In China, for example, the last 20 years have seen amazing progress in intermediate technologies. Tens of thousands of small, rural hydro generating stations have been built and operated by Chinese peasants, supplying electricity for individual villages and communes. Electricity is used in ways most immediately beneficial to the people: for local fertilizer production, irrigation and drainage, grain threshing and milling, fodder crushing and timber sawing.

In addition, the Chinese have promoted family-scale production of biogas from decomposing organic matter. Simple insulated containers dug into the ground break down various organic materials into a gas suitable for cooking and lighting. A high-quality organic fertilizer is also produced. Millions of Chinese already use biogas and the government is encouraging more use in areas that are climatically suitable. Larger village-size "digesters" are being built collectively to fuel water pumps, farm machinery and small-scale power generation. (See *The Bulletin of the Atomic Scientists*, February, 1977.)

Perhaps this type of decentralized technology is what Canada should be helping to provide to the Third World. Expensive, centralized power sources like nuclear power will do little to ease the problems of urban growth. Power reactors must be built close to the largest consumer base—urban, industrial centres—for economic reasons, since electricity becomes more expensive the farther it is transmitted. Thus, rural regions are penalized.

At a time when developing nations are seeking self-reliant, autonomous development, nuclear power weaves new threads of technological dependence. Third World nations who opt for nuclear energy will depend on Western-based transnational corporations for most materials and components. And they will depend on the governments of the developed nations for technical and financial assistance. Three industrial nations, Canada, Australia and the U.S., have a virtual monopoly on global uranium supplies.

Will nuclear power increase the standard of living of the poor? Its proponents believe it will. But, careful analysis shows it to be a singularly inappropriate development tool, which contributes nothing to the most pressing basic needs of physical survival.

Reactor Exports and Nuclear Proliferation

There are close to 500 nuclear reactors now in operation, being built or on order around the world. Thirty countries have already opted for nuclear energy. They include major industrial powers like France, Japan, Britain, the U.S., the USSR, and West Germany. They also include Third World nations like Argentina, Brazil, Korea, Taiwan, Pakistan, India, Iraq and Iran. Israel, at the centre of the Middle East powder keg, and South Africa, the white tip of black Africa, have also opted for nuclear power.

Nuclear power reactors are becoming an increasingly important priority on the shopping lists of developing nations. Critics of nuclear sales are wondering whether it will be possible to stop the use of such technology for the manufacture of nuclear bombs. They have good reason. It was only May, 1974, that India became the newest member of the nuclear club by detonating a nuclear device using Canadian and American technology. How many other countries will acquire the Bomb through this back-door method is still a matter of conjecture. Both Israel and South Africa are reputed to have nuclear devices at the ready.

Canadian nuclear spokesmen downplay the possibility of reactor hardware being used for nuclear explosives. The Indian explosion scarcely seems to have ruffled the industry's confidence. They say there are easier methods of obtaining nuclear weapons than through reactor technology. None the less, new and more stringent safeguards have been recently imposed by Ottawa. These safeguards, which have to be accepted by Canada's nuclear partners, require thorough inspection by the International Atomic Energy Agency (IAEA), the Geneva-based, international agency that monitors stocks of new and spent fuel. The IAEA, however, has no power to do anything if it does find a nation in violation of safeguards. Its budget and staff are stretched so thin that it's doubtful it would even discover any sleight-of-hand. (The IAEA has a safeguards budget of $6.4 million and only 87 inspectors to police 315 reactors worldwide. See *Saturday Review*, January 22, 1977, p. 20.) The next few years may bring us not just the conventional arms race with its irrational, lunatic concern for greater nuclear fire-power. Sales of nuclear technology for peaceful purpose may well open up the sluice gate to nuclear disaster. Will we witness scores of Third World nations jostling each other to make it to the nuclear trough?

Western countries have already shown their willingness to do business at whatever cost. While Germany sold Brazil a nuclear reactor and uranium enrichment package that could be used to manufacture a bomb, France has sold reprocessing plants to Pakistan and South Africa and reactors to Iran and Iraq. Taiwan possesses a Canadian research reactor of the type used by India in her bomb-making.

A recent article in the U.S. public affairs magazine, *The Nation*, notes that "North America has made the possession of a research reactor a status symbol in even the most destitute of developing nations." "The United States and Canada," the article continues, "bear primary responsibility for the proliferation of nuclear technology in the Third World" (February 26, 1977, p. 238).

If a country is so determined, all the safeguard agreements in the world will do nothing to stop it from assembling an atomic explosive.

Conclusion

The nuclear power debate is a far-reaching one which touches on crucial yet unresolved questions and concerns:

1. **Our Growth-oriented, Consumer Society:** Do we need to consume ever-increasing amounts of energy? Has unchecked growth made us a happier, more peaceful and humane society? Has rampant growth alleviated poverty, poor housing and income disparities? Have we raised growth to become an end in itself?

2. **Radioactive Wastes:** Permanent safe storage seems impossible and toxic radioactive wastes continue to accumulate, low-level and high-level, liquid and solid. Can we in good conscience leave these wastes, some of which last thousands of years, to the care and control of future generations?

3. **Alternate Energy Sources:** There are energy alternatives to nuclear power. They may be safer and more democratic. Are enough resources going towards exploring them?

4. **Who Should Decide?** Canada's commitment to nuclear power has been strengthened by $20 billion in research and development by AECL, by the formation of a $1.2-billion-a-year nuclear industry, and by the endorsement of public utility firms. A nuclear route has been mapped out for us. Yet, Canada's nuclear energy policy has never been legitimized by Parliament. What voice did the Canadian people have in these decisions?

5. **Nuclear Energy and Development:** Is nuclear technology as currently encouraged and exported by the U.S. and Canada appro-

priate to development needs of the poor? Or, is it simply an extension to serve our trade purposes; an extension of our industrial patterns which serve the rich?

6. **Nuclear Proliferation:** Is it possible to separate the peaceful uses of nuclear energy from proliferation for war uses?

7. **Control of Energy Development:** Can people assert their own control over energy development or will the decisions over that commodity which is most vital to life be made by corporations, administrative boards and well-intentioned technocrats?

None of these issues can be dismissed out of hand or shrugged off as groundless anxieties. The first significant public examination of nuclear power is drawing to a close under the aegis of the Porter Royal Commission on Electric Power Planning in Ontario. A second wide-ranging three-person inquiry has been announced by Saskatchewan—the Bayda Commission. But, despite calls for a thorough national discussion on the issue by public interest groups and some M.P.'s, the federal government is unconvinced that a federal public investigation of nuclear power is necessary.

It will remain unconvinced until individuals and organizations show their interest and unless the public declares and demands its right to be informed, to be consulted and to decide on issues of basic social policy and national importance.

9 · ETHICS AND URANIUM MINING

THE URANIUM WORKING GROUP, THE B.C. CONFERENCE OF THE UNITED CHURCH OF CANADA, 1980

Preface

The Uranium Working Group, on behalf of the British Columbia Conference of the United Church of Canada, commends this report to the attention of commissioners and participants in the Royal Commission of Inquiry into Uranium Mining and Milling in British Columbia. It is additionally hoped that the analysis represented here may be a useful point for reflection and action on the part of the wider British Columbian and Canadian church.

What is placed before the reader through this document has little to do with the provision of simplistic answers or the expounding of technical arguments, an arena we enter only with the humble posture of knowledgeable amateurs. What we strive to bring before the reader is analysis of values, assumptions and world-views which characterize the testimony heard by the Commission and some thematic reflections regarding the teaching of the United Church in particular, and the broader Christian faith in general, as it bears witness to the subject being considered.

The report also seeks to critique the inquiry process and provides detailed recommendations based on our learning as participants in the Inquiry. As well, some detailed consideration is given to what we believe to be the role of ethical analysis in public decision-making processes, the subject which in many ways is as complex as it is important. The cornerstone for development of a model relating ethical analysis and public process is indicated.

What may well be most fundamental to this document is a deep belief that the way we view ourselves, the society we live in and our relationship to the world, plays a decisive role in determining our actions and our perceptions of responsibility. We believe the consequences emerging from this dynamic are of utmost importance to the life of this complex, yet fragile planet we live out our days on. In this context the Inquiry related to uranium mining becomes a paradigm through which we may begin to understand ourselves and our world....

INTRODUCTION

The Mandate of the B.C. Royal Commission Inquiry into Uranium Mining

The Royal Commission into Uranium Mining was established under the British Columbia Public Inquiries Act by Order in Council, No. 170/79, dated January 18th, 1979. That Order in Council set out the Terms of Reference of the Commission. It states that the Government deemed it expedient to cause inquiry to be made into the adequacy of existing measures providing protection as the result of uranium mining in British Columbia, and authorized this Royal Commission to inquire into the following:

1. to examine the adequacy of existing Federal and Provincial requirements for the protection of the health and safety of workers associated with exploration, mining and milling of uranium in British Columbia, and for the protection of the environment and of the public;

2. to receive public input on these matters; and

3. to make recommendations for setting and maintaining standards for worker and public safety and for the protection of the environment as a result of the exploration for the mining and milling of uranium ores.

Concerns of the United Church

The United Church has three main concerns in reference to the mandate of the B.C. Royal Commission into Uranium Mining. The first is that the Commission, interested parties and the wider public recognize the fact that values, beliefs, moral action guides and worldviews are unavoidably involved, as well as technical information, in setting public policy concerning the regulation of uranium exploration, mining and milling. Secondly, the church is concerned that there be explicit study and analysis of these value aspects. These are vital matters on which persons who are *not* technical experts on uranium matters can best make an informed and indispensable contribution. There should be significant public participation particularly by those most directly affected and by those with least influence in other levels of decision-making. Thirdly, the church advocates certain particular values and beliefs and openly seeks through the public forum to have these the prevailing ones informing and shaping judgements concerning safety standards.

Background of Church Involvement

Central to all Christian creeds is the basic commandment of Christ to love neighbour as God loves us. The conviction that humans are part of nature yet entrusted with care and stewardship of the earth in a fashion congruent with the purpose of the Creator is also in the very foundation of Christian and Jewish tradition. Of course, the church through its members is very much involved in all phases of uranium exploration, mining and milling, such members reflecting the full spectrum of views on the subject. These convictions and actual present involvement together, then, make it difficult to see how the church could responsibly not be engaged in some intentional way in an inquiry concerned with safety of workers and "the general question of public well-being and environmental protection arising out of uranium exploration and mining" (Opening Statement to the Inaugural Public Meeting of the Royal Commission into Uranium Mining, p. 3).

The church has a long history of active concern about worker safety, public well-being and protection of the environment. As a finite and fallible human institution the church's record on this is certainly not as strong or unblemished as we might wish. Nevertheless, there is a persistent affirmation of certain beliefs and values such as equal regard for the dignity of all persons, social justice, care of nature, and also a persistent effort throughout the centuries to enact these in public policy and program. Since World War II the church has grappled with the nuclear question, issues of testing, armaments and energy from the varied perspectives of its members in advanced industrialized nations and Third World countries. The United Church of Canada through adopting a B.C.-sponsored resolution as national policy in 1977—"Nuclear Option for Canadians"—provided the framework for what has become an increasingly definitive debate in recent years. The central call of the resolution was for a moratorium and a full-scale public inquiry with respect to all aspects of the nuclear fuel cycle:

... such inquiry to include everything from the mining of uranium to the storage of radioactive wastes, and deal with transportation of radioactive materials, safeguard treaties, and both the domestic and export uses of nuclear materials and technologies;... [...]

United Church groups have been active on nuclear fuel cycle issues in Ontario, Saskatchewan and Newfoundland. The United Church has participated in the ongoing World Council of Churches' series of consultations and hearings by scientists, theologians, politicians and church leaders from around the globe that began in 1975 at Sigtuna, Sweden.

The basis of the United Church's concern has been and continues to be the conviction that the "nuclear option" represents a matter demanding widespread, deliberate public participation in the decision-making process, and that Canadians be challenged to critically examine the values underlying the central issue of the debate....

ETHICAL ANALYSIS IN THE PUBLIC INQUIRY
The Role of Ethics in Public Inquiry

Our purpose in this section is to provide a synopsis of what has guided our ethical analysis with a view of enhancing the role of ethics and perhaps establishing some of the foundations for a model of ethical inquiry in questions of public policy formation....

Let it suffice to say that the discussion related to the role of ethics as the Inquiry proceeded became often confused. There is evidence ... that the Commission at one point in the discussion recognized to a considerable degree the significant role ethical analysis could play in dealing with technical information, and in relation to the issues attendant to setting standards for uranium mining and milling in B.C. However, in a later document entitled *Planning of the Ethics Phase*, released February 6, 1980, ... the Commission repeats an earlier error which reduced ethics to matters of "personally-held belief" as distinct from "evidence presented on matters of fact." In response the Uranium Working Group once again wrote to the Royal Commission of Inquiry with the goal of explaining the Church's view of the role and purpose of ethics in this public forum. It may be useful to quote from this correspondence in that it serves to summarize our position:

We recognize with the Commissioners that "ethical positions" may often be perceived to simply represent matters of "personally-held belief."

We would also want to observe, however, that "evidence presented on matters of fact" are frequently also reducible to vested interests or other more complex forms of corporate and cultural myopia. Indeed, it is here that we find the context for disciplined ethical analysis of the issues defined by the question of setting appropriate standards for uranium mining in British Columbia. It is the task of those with ethical concern and expertise to attempt, with full reference to the other dimensions of technical information, to discern the parameters of the implications of such nuclear development, to uplift the assumptions made and represented by the various parties involved, to clarify the values inherent in the options presented, and to offer this critique within the framework of a clear statement of the ethical position they represent.

We can also agree that the Commission cannot and should not be expected to adopt or make decisions about the various ethical analyses anticipated. This, in the end, is the prerogative of the political authority. Nevertheless, we do feel that the Commission is responsible to provide the decision-making bodies with, alongside their other technical findings, as complete an analysis and clarification of the nature of the political choice before them as possible.

What elements in this review can assist us in elaborating a working conceptualization for public ethical analysis?

The posture of ethics is from the outset and in the end self-critical and self-evaluative. In presuming to judge a situation or relation, the discipline of ethics invites one to reflect on the nature of one's own involvements, implications and commitments in the structure of the human interaction or behaviour under scrutiny.

The fact that ethical analysis places the self—whether individual, organization, profession or system—in relation to others, serves to dismiss the contention that ethics are matters of personally held belief. While there are certainly personal dimensions critical to ethical analysis, it must extend by its very definition to include the interaction of groups and systems.

The function of ethics is thus dynamic and not static. The character of judgement and, reciprocally, the context being judged is not determined by the simple or objective application of a set of authoritative categories against the measured features of a given environment. Rather, the character, and even the possibility, of ethical judgement is determined by the degree to which the actors engaged with each other are continually informed and altered by each other. Thus the way a public process such as an inquiry is structured to allow or even require analysis for purposes of clarifying values, assumptions, etc., is of importance not just to the Commission, the various participants and individuals—the inquiry process itself—but also to the larger society which through their government must indeed make the consequential political decisions....

Framework for Analysis

The church is not and does not claim to be an authority on the purely scientific or engineering aspects of nuclear development. To comment upon, let alone judge, the mechanical efficacy of this technique or the integrity of that chemical formula is entirely outside the bounds of its expertise. It is not the case, however, that the challenge presented by the issues of uranium mining and nuclear development are essentially or even primarily scientific or technological in nature. Rather, the decisions that we are called upon to make are fundamentally ethical, spiritual and, in the broader sense of that term, political. Nevertheless, the church's commitment to the exercise of ethical analysis in the public arena compels us to seriously and responsibly engage in the scientific and technical discussion. That is to say that the bases for judgement must be found within the scientific information and that to bring ethical faculties to bear upon this issue demands that we root our analyses firmly within the technical information before us.

The task prescribed by this approach is one of monitoring the testimony presented to the Royal Commission of Inquiry guided by a specific focal question: Does the testimony presented consist exclusively of findings and descriptions or does it represent also conclusions and judgements? In what epistemological areas do the findings or conclusions relate? Having filtered the information by means of this broad lens, a set of more specific reference points is required to organize and interpret the information according to categories that incorporate the principal areas of concern. The data identified, collected and classified by such a tool would be able to contribute to the development of an inventory or catalogue of the value assumptions, dispositions and contradictions inherent in the testimony and thus constitute the raw material for ethical analysis. This describes the analytical undertaking by the church and is, we submit, consistent with the "moral questions" recognized by the Commission in its statement of October 5, 1979.

The reference grid developed for this purpose is as follows:

1. Nature and scope of information
   (a) Professional or other vested interests
   (b) Transference of credibility: What technical authority accrues to non-technical judgements made?
   (c) What factors limit the content or range of information sought or investigated?

2. Technical certainty/uncertainty
   (a) Perception of impact of proposed activity: assumptions re nature of context
   (b) Perception of dimension of proposed activity: assumptions re extent of risk
   (c) Casualty relations: What is the perceived ability to control impact?
   (d) What problematic elements of control are being left or projected for future solution? Are these acknowledged? concealed? suppressed? unknown?
   (e) What is the attitude/concern regarding freedom of or access to information?
   (f) What variables that are currently problematic are projected as manageable in the future? How distant a future? What will be the agent effecting the change?
   (g) What limits to the research process are highlighted?—size of sampling/data base, degree of consensus in scientific community, influence of non-scientific factors, dependence on probability factors, amount of experience with phenomenon

3. Assumptions, world-view, value stances
   (a) How is the witness disposed to science/technology?
   (b) How is the witness disposed to the future? What is the basis of hope?
   (c) Assumptions regarding energy needs/demands: disposition to economy of steady growth
   (d) Assumptions concerning how human/societal needs and wants are discovered and assessed: consumer demand in marketplace? deliberate, collective priority-setting and decision-making? definition by elites?
   (e) Assumptions regarding human nature: role and purpose, ideals, how is change effected?
   (f) Assumptions regarding the relation of humanity to its environment

(g) Assumptions regarding decision-making in community/society: role of business, government, individual, interest groups, inter-group relations, scope of society

(h) Assumptions regarding risks/benefit and distribution.

(i) Assumptions regarding the nature of a hazard.

The specific set of reference points offered by this grid allows us to establish the framework for a presentation that integrates our understanding of the nature and function of ethics with the body of information and issues that it is intended to impact. Accordingly, our own participation in the ethics phase of the inquiry process in attempting to deal with the risk/benefit problematique would have to include three components:

(i) *Analysis* of the assumptions, values and world-view commitments operative in the technical testimony.

(ii) *Declaration* of the assumptions, values and world-view commitments operative in the Christian perspective.

(iii) *Critique*, bringing the Christian perspective to bear contextually upon the question of uranium mining in B.C.

Analysis of Technical Testimony

It is obvious that given the incomplete nature of the Inquiry, any application of this framework for ethical analysis to the testimony presented can only prove illustrative of the method rather than definitive of the issues. This is due not only to the fact that several essential categories were not dealt with prior to the termination of the hearings but especially because the broad range of perspective is not well represented in the testimony on record. Indeed, it is fair to say that it is predominantly the view of the nuclear industry including the mining companies, government research and regulatory agencies, and their consultants that is reflected.

This presents the commissioners with something of a dilemma in that they are confronted with, in effect, two distinct bodies of testimony of apparently largely contrasting attitudes and interests: the community hearings versus the technical hearings. Emphasis upon one data base must appear to be at the expense of the other. In the analytical task, we are confronted with a similar problem in that our selection of data will serve to isolate our biases. This in itself, however, is consistent with the self-critical nature of ethics and, furthermore, may be useful in demonstrating the fact that the issue at hand is fundamentally one of world-view and value orientation. The exercise would only be inappropriate if we were not to challenge ourselves to self-examination on the basis of the same questions. Recognizing the impossibility of a comprehensive analysis, it would not appear to be useful to work through each of the items referred to in the grid. Nevertheless, we can begin to undertake a preliminary survey of the testimony with a view to drawing attention to certain key themes.

One such theme may be described by the question of how or upon what bases groups with power and authority lay claim to public confidence. Two of the bases are obviously expertise (knowledge and experience) and ability (financial and technical resources) and the proponents of nuclear development assert that they are capable of fulfilling both these criteria and, therefore, responsibly merit public confidence. We must examine assumptions about this from a variety of perspectives.

The first standard of measurement of responsibility must be the record of the past and attitudes toward that record. An effort to disclaim the past as well as the lack of any detailed or overall record of performance is evident in several places with regard to safety measures and general technological efficacy (transcript reference 6515, 7490). There is sometimes evidence of the lack of any historical perspective whatsoever (7056). In some instances, however, failures in the past are acknowledged but seen as "not surprising" (6483). Here it is assumed that the technicians, scientists and engineers of the past (1940s to 1960s) either did not follow guidelines, were uncertain of their technology or were not concerned about safety (6549-6552). It is concluded that "it would be very difficult— or I think very incorrect—to try to reflect on the 1950s performance. Reflect on today's performance using experience from the 1950s" (6483). The basis of this suggested approach is the claim that not only has the technology available progressed but the attitudes of scientists have changed as well.

The problem in dealing with a perspective limited to the present is that it provides us with no real basis for judgement. In the absence of past benchmarks we are reduced to adopting a "better than" standard instead of one founded on an unambiguous philosophy of protection of the public and the environment. Thus, when it is expressed that all that can be expected is that we do our best and carry on (6222), even this is qualified to mean the "best practicable technology" (6288). With the present as the operative standard of judgement, our regulations assume the character of what are referred to in the curricula of some of our schools as "educational objectives" as opposed to "competency requirements."

The dismissal or disparagement of the past would appear to assume a stance that is exploitative and manipulative of the future in that the constant fluidity and current improvement of best available technology inherently suggests that previous methods were inadequate. It suggests that what is referred to elsewhere as the "traditional after the fact body counting technique" remains operative. We are dealing here with the question of the adequacy of data available for decision-making and the necessity of both using and identifying with past experience in guiding our judgement. The level of public trust assumed as well as the credibility ascribed to judgements made about the future on the basis of that trust demand examination of the disposition toward the integrity of past, present and future reflected by our scientific authorities. This connection between the question of the adequacy of information for responsible judgement and our attitudes toward our historical context is pointedly made elsewhere in the transcript.

> The lesson I think the United States experienced in uranium tells us is that thirty years ago, forty years ago, we as a society chose to ignore, to play down, to not take cognizance of existing scientific information. To place human values as secondary to other interests of importance. These were decisions that were made during the period of the desire for nuclear weapons production in the United States. Today we stand on a new horizon with regard to nuclear energy. (12979-80)
>
> Not only does the lack of research not allow us to make the predictions we need to make over the long haul, we haven't yet done the research to find out what the consequences of our past actions are. (7611)
>
> By assuming solutions in the future, we are passing on the responsibilities into the future and in our modern society presumably we are getting away from that as an acceptable way of operating. (7611)

In view of the apparent focus on the present as the operative standard, this latter point must remain an assumption to be tested.

Another way in which this limitation of perspective to the present manifests itself and betrays certain assumptions regarding the nature of the hazards involved in nuclear development is in the technical use of such concepts as "remoteness" and "conservation." To describe a site as remote is to appeal to its most relative and impermanent characteristic and to isolate it from its actual context. To use remoteness as a design criteria in building a mine or tailings dam is to assume both that this abstraction from the environment *can* be realized and that the site's remoteness *should* be a permanent reality. At several times in the testimony it is recognized that the standards and procedures surrounding uranium mining vary not solely according to the objective degree of hazard involved in handling radioactive material but also according to the demographic location of the ore body (6528, 7800). Specifically, a more "conservative" approach to safety design in waste management is adopted if the mine is in close proximity to a large population centre than if it is considered to be remote (8150). Yet, when matters of public health, worker safety and environmental protection are being discussed in relation to the development of a public resource, can any geographic area be deemed remote?

The notion that conservatism of design is an option (7904) raises serious questions about our basic approach to the issue. Do certain parts of our population and environment bear greater intrinsic value than others, for example, people in the metropolitan area more than village dwellers, industrial land more than Indian reserve land (11286)? Do we assume a distinction between construction criteria and safety factors, whereby safety precautions are "added on," or are both integral to design (7799)? Do we consider the hazards posed by uranium to both the public and the environment real and legitimate concerns or are they seen as merely psychological obstacles demanding no special or unique responsibility (8121, 11278, 12730-46)? Given that the degree of conservatism exercised in designing for long-term management is a variable, can we assume that our safety standards offer the optimum of protection? Do we assume that we know all that we need to about radioactivity and related problems (6221)? Are standards established arbitrarily or according to reliable and comprehensive information (7873, 8460, 11199, 11230)? The stance adopted by two witnesses dealing with waste management and the restoration of the environment serves to illustrate the impact of such value-laden concepts as remoteness and conservatism on attitudes to such matters.

> ... we think we understand the principles and we believe that we can successfully do this ... you know what nature is like, and you can never be quite sure of anything. That's just part and parcel of the game. (4603, 4607)

The resulting impact is impossible to predict with certainty, and one should not jump to the conclusion that the impact will be catastrophic, or even of substantial concern. (6222)

One of the constant features of the human condition is risk: we rarely enjoy the luxury of having sufficient information or confidence in ourselves to assure absolute certainty. We are called upon to exercise judgement. Yet to responsibly do so implies that we guide our behaviour by taking into account the full dimensions of the hazards involved and the extent of our knowledge about the context. Both passages quoted reflect a logic similar to that which views the past, present and future as disparate entities. Here, however, we are addressing the question of fragmentation and continuity in terms of the degree to which assumptions made about the integrity of the human and natural environments model the ways in which we deal with matters of risk. What is the effect of regarding human interaction with nature as a "game" or of assuming that the results of our intervention shouldn't be considered serious? Is it assumed that there is no burden of proof with regard to safety incumbent upon the proponents of nuclear development? Whatever the statistics may eventually indicate, any attempt to maintain that our standards and technology provide "adequate" levels of safety and "acceptable" degrees of risk (4377, 7490) must be considered within the context of the fundamental optimism and uncertainty that together characterize the predominant outlook of the technical testimony.

We have drawn attention to the fact that in the expert testimony the ability to legitimately lay claim to public trust, establish safety standards, or make decisions regarding risk often appears to be compromised by assumptions and values predicated upon a fragmentary and inadequate body of information. Indeed, it was not unusual for the remark to be heard concerning this medical finding or that environmental factor "how important that is becoming and how recent is the knowledge which deals with it" (9015). Another instance related to the perceived ability to control the impact of development that highlights the effect of this endemic separation of areas of knowledge on the structures of assumptions is the claim that engineers can design to any safety specifications set for them (4310). It is further asserted, from the point of view of the regulatory agencies, that economics plays no role in the setting of standards (11219), although it is recognized that "the selection of radiation dose limits involves subjective judgments and has economic implications..." (11289).

Both of these contentions must be interpreted in the light of the almost pivotal statement, "You don't make profits spending money on the waste end of your cycle" (7606-7). The context for analysis is given greater dimension when it is observed that all facets of the nuclear industry advocate as their functional principle not the "best possible technology" but rather the "best practicable technology" and, further, that research is directed toward the pursuit of the "least cost technology" (12922). All of this points out that it is a fallacy to simply state that there exists the technical capacity to deal with problems without defining the terms of context and raises the question of the degree to which economics is the governing factor determining not only the incentive for development but the health and safety standards operative as well (4300, 6289, 11676).

Hence, the terms relating to nuclear waste such as "disposal," "containment," "management," etc., bear more than technically descriptive meaning. They have economic connotations, that is, management suggests long-term surveillance and costs whereas disposal, which at this point means dispersion into the environment, may not involve the same expense (6584). Thus, the inconsistent and equivocal use of economics as a factor in the scientific criteria makes evident some implicit values and, again, a fragmentation of knowledge and standards. This can be illustrated by comparison of the statement that "from an engineering viewpoint, the progression of marketing is simply one of the items that must progress" (7321) with the position that health and social costs arising from development are purely matters of economics (9190). In other words, a value orientation is evident such that certain economic considerations are held to be integral to the scientific discipline itself while others, those generally found around the "waste end," are excluded from the realm of direct concern or responsibility.

A second key theme discussed during the technical hearings was that of freedom of and access to information. The central point here is contained in the fact that there is no statutory requirement under the current guidelines to ensure consultation with the public (11625). Indeed, some company witnesses regarded informal discussions with government agencies as the way to "keep all parties informed" (7494), though it sometimes appeared that confidentiality was the only real regulation exercised by the regulatory agencies (6568). Generally speaking, it would seem fair to say that the involvement of the public in considering the various aspects of proposed development was portrayed more as an obstacle and in terms of an adversarial model than as a moral obligation or legitimate right. Accordingly, one government witness could describe public hearings as a problem in that

> ... quite a bit of time is taken up in educating people into what we are talking about in regards to mining. (11633)

> ... well the public raises its objectives now. I mean they have lots of means of doing it. They do it through the press and they do it through public meetings like we had in Atlin, if it concerns them. (11635)

The posture reflected here bears a variety of assumptions regarding the value and principle of public participation in the decision-making process. For the right to know to have any authenticity, whether it be the worker's right to fully comprehend the nature of the risk to which she/he is exposed or the community's right to information about possible alteration of its environment, it must include the ability to make use of the information available. In other words, the right to know must include as a corollary the right to exercise judgement and contribute to the act of decision-making. The importance we attribute to these matters is dependent upon the assumptions held about the nature of a public resource. Is it the ambition of those with specialized expertise and ability to educate the public with a view to enhancing its capacity for critical judgement, or is the role of the public assumed to be a more passive one, that is, simply be assured that the experts have matters in hand (9036)? Does the current system by which natural resources are developed foster public awareness and control or does it implicitly encourage the withholding of information in order to enable private interests to maintain a competitive edge (7288)? Is public involvement and access to information seen as something demanded by the issues themselves and to be initiated by the scientific and regulatory process (11235)?

This focus on the role of the public raises the question of to what extent the research and regulatory facilities currently in place reflect the diversity of perspective that defines the public's concern. In effect, given the serious gaps in the adequacy of knowledge in the numerous areas noted above, the question here is: What values and commitments are affirmed in guiding and establishing priorities for research? It was frequently pointed out in the testimony that the subject of mine tailings as a waste problem is only a recently awakened interest in the nuclear research and regulatory community (7091). Furthermore, it was generally acknowledged to have become a matter of interest as a result of public concern and provocation (7573). Because of a policy decision to concentrate research efforts on the development of nuclear power generating technology such as the CANDU reactor, mining and its problems were not considered as part of the process (7541). This lack of a holistic perspective or systematic approach prompted one witness to offer the broad diagnosis that "we are limited by a lack of knowledge and a lack of methodology and a lack of research" (7525).

> I would say that there is very little basis for having confidence that research will be done on waste management prior to the crisis period if the system of decision-making on environmental research remains as it is now (7574).

In other words, it seems evident that the bodies responsible for the regulatory functions surrounding uranium mining and milling assume and are committed to the principle of increased nuclear development and make little provision for the formal expression of views "independent" of this predisposition. Correspondingly, the research community is limited in the extent to which it can freely and responsibly fulfill its mandate to discern and solve problems by the fact that it is bound to the pursuit of the objectives of a nuclear program (9179).

We have already noted that the standards and procedures that relate to this program are at least partially determined by economic factors. The justification for the commitment to the program also usually includes economic reasons: the need for energy to maintain and increase our standard of living, the need for employment (3085), and so on. Just as the relation of waste management and safety factors to profitability points to the necessity of clarifying our assumptions about the character of human responsibility to the natural environment, so here we are challenged to make explicit and choose our values with regard to our understanding of the human vocation. Does the risk and end uses of the product entailed in uranium make for "good work"? Or is this not a matter for human prerogative. Will the enterprise even produce significant numbers of jobs (4544)? Is the energy "needed" to contribute to the building of a socially and ecologically just community or to provide for the desire of increased consumption by the few? Much could be said about what assumptions relating to these matters emerged in the technical testimony heard by the Royal Commission of Inquiry. It is to be hoped that the opportunity to pursue this analysis with some intentionality will be forthcoming. It may be more useful at this point, however, to reflect on these questions from within the framework of our own perspective: the Christian tradition.

THE CHURCH'S POSITION

The above section analyzing the technical hearings reflects the first concern of the church named in the Introduction, namely, the recognition of the unavoidable interaction of technical information components and value/belief components in policy decisions concerning uranium. The following are an elaboration of the other two concerns: public participation and advocacy of particular values and moral concerns as key considerations in formulating public policy on uranium mining.

Public Participation in Decisions Regarding Uranium

The church believes that the public should have the opportunity to participate significantly in a decision that so obviously affects their well-being. The Royal Commission and its hearings provided an important vehicle for this. The assumption that such decisions should be left to the wisdom of a technological or administrative elite manifestly held by a number of witnsses at the technical hearings was disturbing. The widely held democratic principle concerning public participation has in the West been grounded in a variety of basic philosophies and religions. For Christians it is an implication of love for neighbour that respects the worth and dignity of others in a way that precludes one group or person unilaterally deciding what is best for the well-being of another group or person. It is reinforced by one aspect of the Christian understanding of human nature—the propensity of all persons and groups, even the most "enlightened" and "redeemed," to pursue their own self-interest at the expense of others frequently under the conscious or unconscious pretension of "serving others," "the good of the whole" or "the greatest good for the greatest number." No group is good enough, then, to have too much power and control over the lives and destiny of others. This is one reason, then, why democratic structures and procedures are so important.

Yet it is becoming increasingly evident that certain groups (multinationals and government bureaucracies) who control resource development which so profoundly affects the lives ultimately of us all, but certainly of the particular groups immediately affected by any particular development, have just such extensive power over others. The uranium mining issue with its question of standards for protecting persons, public and environment is but a current, especially potent illustration of this problem. There is growing frustration and anger over the widespread experience that our traditional institutions of parliament and "free market" are insufficient instruments for democratically dealing with such increasingly complex, high-technology, heavy social impact issues as uranium, nuclear energy and major-development projects. Royal Commission hearings are one of a variety of devices developed for broadening the decision-making process on such matters, increasing public participation.

A major limitation on the effectiveness of the Commission's hearings as a method for enriching the democratic process of decision-making was the very narrow mandate given to the Commission. It prevented thorough examination of some broader, underlying issues regarding nuclear power and energy policy about which the public is greatly concerned (and perceives uranium mining as but one current example) and convictions which profoundly affect judgements on matters that do fall within the narrower mandate. For example, if one believes that increased levels of energy consumption are necessary for Canada's well-being and nuclear power will soon be needed to meet that, then judgements about what degrees of radiation hazards are acceptable or "safe" will be made differently than if a contrary view were held. Any reasonable judgement about "acceptable risks" entails comparison with alternative possibilities and the risk involved with them.

There is a widespread tendency in North American society to concentrate on a specific problem or even components or aspects of problems without regard for the larger questions concerning the whole issues of purpose, desirable ends and goals, what is the good society. Sociology of knowledge would identify this as "componentiality," one aspect of the "cognitive style" that accompanies advanced technological societies. Since these larger issues do not lend themselves to easy resolution, there is additional pressure to neglect them. Yet so important are these matters in themselves that some intentionality concerning them is essential to a good society, perhaps even to civilization itself. But in addition, when more immediate problems, in this case safety standards for uranium mining, are dealt with in the absence of any explicit consideration of their connection to the larger issues, a distorted perception of that particularity results and mistaken judgements are apt to be made. The tragic stories of American involvement in Vietnam and the Watergate debacle bear witness to this point.

The termination of the Commission and its hearings has frustrated the full realization of the potential of this process for enhancing the democratic process. As we have already identified, we have found it frustrating that the "Ethical Hearings" (which promised the opportunity for careful scrutiny of what we have called the value/belief component of policy formation) have had to be foregone. This would have been about matters to which the public could best contribute. A rare opportunity for a public forum on basic value issues that would be informative to the government on a variety of public policy issues has been missed. Further, a crucial step in enabling informed public participation in this important matter— education of the public on the latest technical information (presented at the technical hearings), value/belief discussion and then their participation in light of these—was lost. We urge the government to resume some such process during the moratorium so that when the issue arises again an informed public will be ready and able to participate.

Key Considerations in Formulating Public Policy on Uranium Development

The church has not yet reached any definitive conclusions concerning the desirability of mining and milling of uranium or safety standards. We do strongly affirm, as indicated above, the right of the public affected by such decisions to participate in them and that no exploration or mining should take place until such informed participation takes place and more study is done.

Given the technical evidence presented to the Commission to date concerning the hazards of uranium, its mining and handling and transportation; the imperfect "state of the art" concerning long-term storage of tailings including the social controls needed to assure safety; plus the very ambiguous end-use of uranium in nuclear energy and destructive power of nuclear weapons, *we believe the "burden of proof" clearly rests at this time on the case for mining uranium in B.C.* rather than on the case for not doing so. Those who would mine it must show good cause as to why rather than, as has been the case, those who oppose such mining.

The following are some of the values and moral principles the church believes should form the value/belief component that so inextricably intertwines with the technical component in any policy decisions about safety regulations to protect persons, public and environment. These are some of the values and norms which we think should determine (others will if those do not) the kind of information sought, shape the direction of concern, become the criteria in terms of which judgements are made and conclusions reached. These principles are formulated here in terms of Christian theology, though their grounding in more fundamental beliefs is not elaborated here. Other bases for such values, however, exist and the values and principles command wide support on different grounds than those of Christian community.

1. *Whose safety and protection should be considered?* "Worker and public safety" should be interpreted to include not only the safety and well-being of the "near neighbour"—mine and mill workers—but also the more distant neighbour—transport workers, those impacted through the food chain and the like. In addition, the basic Christian conviction concerning the equal worth of all persons and the basic command to love neighbour as God loves us impels us to advocate consideration of future "neighbours" and their safety. Standards should be designed with the protection of future generations in mind and the necessary measures should be included in cost calculations, for example, in engineering designs for tailing storage. What safety standards are needed to protect future persons from genetic damage?

The end use of uranium, of course, has to be considered in any rational and moral decision about whether or not to mine it. But even with regard to the more restricted question of safety regulations for protection of the public some consideration of end use is necessary. Guarantee against misuse is an impossible criterion for any human project to meet, but the most usual and likely uses of uranium—nuclear power, weapons, medicine—should be considered. How is public health and safety, especially that of future neighbours, affected by these uses?

2. *What human well-being considerations should be involved in determining safety and benefits?* "Safety hazards," "benefits" and "cost" are all understood in terms of beliefs concerning human well-being. Christian thought has properly never attempted to define this with detailed precision, since obviously it will vary with individual, group,

time and place. But greater clarity is possible about the general character of well-being, minimal requirements and, negatively, what is *not* essential to it.

Central to even a modest definition of well-being are convictions about human beings, their meaning and destiny. Biblical thought recognizes the holistic nature of humans, that body, mind, spirit are interdependent and interacting, and both our "weal" and "woe" entail all three dimensions. The essentials of well-being as named in the Christian tradition are first, the necessities of physical existence—food, shelter, clothing, absence of sickness, fundamental knowledge and skills, affection and support, community and self-respect; second, a person's conscious relationship to God—a sense of meaning and purpose; third, integrity of personal identity and freedom.

Several implications for understanding "benefits" and "costs," "hazards" and "safety" flow from this sparse outline of beliefs concerning human beings and their well-being. From the first aspect of well-being, the necessities of physical existence, stem the obvious concerns for protection of bodily health. But it also pushes us to distinguish between "needs" and "wants." Affluence in terms of a high note of consumption of goods and services is clearly not essential to well-being so understood. The much discussed conflict between the physical well-being of mine workers and local communities on the one hand and the "needs" of other centres for more electrical energy on the other, turns out from this perspective not to be one of conflict between the genuine well-being of two groups but between the needs of some and the desires or wants of others. We affirm the guiding principle that "meeting the needs of all persons must take priority over satisfying the wants of any."

The significance of affection and support, community and self-respect, a sense of meaning to life and relationship with the mystery we call God listed as basic to human well-being reminds us not to limit our calculus of benefits and costs nor our standards of protection only to physical or quantifiable "goods" such as cash income, rate of return on investment, greater energy resources. The health and beauty of the environment, for example, becomes a consideration here as well as being important for its own sake. Increased employment opportunities are a "benefit" when it is "meaningful work" under healthy conditions that fosters self-respect and community, not simply when it provides a pay cheque. Nor in light of this understanding of well-being can it be automatically assumed that more energy is required by our society. Instead we are led to ask what kind of energy for what use, and at what cost to whom?

Related to these aspects of well-being is a further Christian conviction about humans that affects one's understanding of well-being. We are not primarily individuals and only secondarily members of groups, not primarily members of groups and only secondarily individuals. We are both at once. Well-being, therefore, entails both individual self-fulfillment and the common good of society as a whole in harmony with each other. Sound economic and political systems and institutions must be our concern as well as the rights of individuals. Of fundamental significance, therefore, in any calculation of benefits and costs or of hazards from which persons or the public should be protected by safety regulations are the short-term and long-term impacts upon communities and social institutions. Many of the social impacts of uranium mining would be similar to those of other resource development, but no less important for that reason. Are disrupted communities and various accompanying social pathologies hazards from which we want protection? Who pays for these costs? We need to clarify public policy as to what social impacts are acceptable and unacceptable.

But in addition to these social impacts are others peculiar to hazardous products like uranium. Of crucial concern is the potential danger that the need for person, public and environment protection from the hazards of uranium mining, milling, transportation (let alone its end uses) may require policy measures antithetical to an open society. What a political scientist observes concerning the nuclear fuel cycle in general seems likely to be true to a lesser extent for any extensive uranium mining. It

> requires continuous, though not always effective, surveillance. [It] needs people watching machines, machines watching machines, and machines and people watching people, to protect against nonroutine releases of, or exposure to, radiation,... whole cultures must be organized to guard against [uranium] hazards. The outcome is antidemocratic social control. (M. Reader, *Energy Ethics*, ed. D.T. Hessel [New York: Friendship Press, 1979], p. 99.)

We need to ask whether the stable social conditions, the value consensus and ethos of cooperation required for observance of safety regulations necessary to make uranium mining, milling and the transport of the ore viable are now present or are fostered by our current ways of developing resources. Do not the major end-uses of uranium-nuclear power, with the necessity for secrecy and severe control measures, and nuclear weapons threaten to undermine these essential social conditions?

A third aspect of human well-being noted above, personal integrity and dignity, also has implications for defining "benefits" and "safety." The principle of persons participating in decisions that affect them, discussed earlier, is involved here. An important aspect of this principle is "valid consent." If workers or others are to be subject to health hazards, what kind of regulations will assure their informed consent to be so exposed? The extensive and careful ethical discussions on "valid consent" with regard to the health sciences is pertinent to this. Suffice it to note here that one of the fundamental components of valid consent is sufficient information for a person to make a genuine, responsible decision. Precision in formulating how much information this entails is impossible. But the worker will need to know in non-technical language the likely short-term and long-term hazards and any other information he or she, not some authority, feels necessary to make a good choice. The unseen and generally less-known risks and hazards of uranium compared to dangers in other kinds of mining make this a particularly crucial factor to watch.

Finally, we affirm again the importance of persons and groups participating in defining their own well-being and concepts of benefits and costs, hazards and safety, since no group or person is free enough from the biases of their class or era to designate in detail objectively what these might mean. Corporations and governments have sufficient power to participate effectively and be heard on the uranium issue. Native Peoples, small communities, future generations are not so apt to be heard or heeded. The church, therefore, seeks to amplify their voice in the public debate.

3. *What regard is to be given to the claim of needs and protection of various groups and persons?* Intrinsic to the Christian understanding of neighbour love is the principle of equal regard for the highest well-being of all persons. This principle implies that a group's essential well-being and protection from hazards should not be neglected because of small size or little power or "remoteness" whether defined in terms of geography, class, race or size. Any proposal that would argue for lower safety standards and regulations in sites "remote" from large population centres, for example, is unacceptable.

The principle of equal regard rules out easy priority being given to the claims and protection of the present generation over those of future generations or priority of the near neighbour's needs over those of the distant neighbour. The view that focusses on present gains and benefits and sees the future mainly as a time for solving problems of waste disposal, for example, rather than as a time where such problems will inflict difficulties on others from which they are entitled to protection is from our perspective, then, mistaken.

The principle of equal regard also runs directly counter to the greatest good for the greatest number as a formula for distributing costs and benefits. What if the well-being, safety, claim to benefits of one group conflicts with those of another? We discussed earlier how this conflict should be examined to see if it is a genuine conflict between essential needs or an apparent conflict—between needs of one and wants of the other. If it is a real conflict, the moral principle of equal regard, rather than legitimating the sacrifice of the well-being of some (usually the least powerful) to that of others, pushes for the diligent pursuit of better alternatives. Are there ways of meeting the needs of both groups? This is another reason why it is impossible to make sound, rational decisions about uranium mining safety without examining its implications for energy needs, and various ways of meeting these.

If no better alternative is available or possible within the time it is needed—and much careful inquiry would be needed to establish this—the principle of equal regard would then lead us to considerations of justice. The church's beliefs about justice include concern for a fair distribution of costs, risks and benefits and opposition to any arrangement whereby one group reaps most of the latter and bears little of the former. If the costs and benefits of uranium mining cannot be equally distributed, then the distribution of benefits should favour the least advantaged.

4. Finally, a central conviction of the church has to do with responsibility for the environment. Two beliefs help to define this responsibility. The first is a vision of *Shalom*—God's promise and activity to transform persons and society toward a condition of peace with justice and harmony between persons, between people and the rest of nature, between God and all. Implicit in this belief is the awareness that social justice and environmental health are mutually dependent upon each other.

The second belief is that humans have a mandate to shape and use nature, but not arbitrarily or destructively, rather in sacred trust. This entails a recognition that we are part of that nature, bound up with it and responsible for its care in accord with God's purpose of Shalom.

Regulations and safety standards, then, should prevent or minimize negative impacts upon the natural environment. In determining such impacts, the accumulative effect of many seemingly "manageable" negative impacts need to be considered. What kinds and degrees of impact upon the environment are compatible with good stewardship and God's purpose of Shalom? One important element in the complex answer to this question is the principle that no party claiming rights to use of and income from the land has the right to alter it in a way that entails permanent destruction preventing some of its many present or potential uses. The safety standards, then, should ensure that impacts upon the environment that alter the land in such a fundamental way are prevented.

These, then, are some of the beliefs and moral convictions that the church frankly hopes will shape the direction of the Commission's recommendations and the public policy on uranium exploration, mining and milling.

FURTHER READING

Frayne, Rev. Stuart. *It's Not What It Used to Be (Nuclear Power and Energy Needs)*. The Baptist Convention of Ontario and Quebec *Christian Alternatives* series 17. Toronto: 1978.

Inter-Church Uranium Committee. *Who Makes the Rules? An Assessment of the Warman Refinery Inquiry*. Saskatoon: 1980.

Penna, James V.; Curry, Bill; and Regneir, Robert. *Human Identity and Christian Responsibility in the Uranium Issue in Saskatchewan*. Saskatoon: Inter-Church Uranium Committee, 1983.

Taskforce on the Churches and Corporate Responsibility. *Policy Formation on Aspects of Canada's Nuclear Wastes: A Brief to the Atomic Energy Control Board*. Toronto: 1982.

The United Church of Canada. *Energy and the Church* (A Report adopted by the 29th General Council, Montreal, August 8-15, 1982).

SECTION IV
NORTHERN DEVELOPMENT
AND NATIVE RIGHTS

The criticisms of the B.C. Conference of the United Church of Canada regarding both the procedures and the criteria for deciding large-scale resource development projects apply nowhere more clearly than in Canada's North. Political and business leaders seem to regard these lands as no more than a vast storehouse of mineral wealth, to be exploited as quickly as possible for their own profits. The Native Peoples who form the majority of the population in the Northwest Territories, and a sizeable minority in the Yukon, Labrador and the northern sections of all but the Atlantic provinces, are usually not even consulted about proposed developments, despite their well-established claims to ownership of the land in question.

Until recently, the churches' work with the Native Peoples of the North was characterized by paternalism and white ethnocentricity. In 1968, the Anglican Church of Canada began to question this approach and commissioned Charles E. Hendry of the School of Social Work, University of Toronto, to produce an assessment of the church's work with Native People and recommendations for the future. Published in 1969 as *Beyond Traplines*, his report set the stage for a new, more equal relationship with Native People, not just for the Anglican Church but for other Canadian churches as well.

In 1975 the Roman Catholic Bishops of Canada devoted their Labour Day message to the theme of justice for the northern Native Peoples. In this document, *Northern Development: At What Cost?* the bishops express their solidarity with the Native Peoples in their protest against exploitation by the federal government and the resource development companies, and they call for fundamental social change in Canada to develop a more just society for both the natives and southern Canadians.

This statement of the Catholic bishops was part of an intensive church response to a proposal for the largest resource development ever planned for the North—a natural gas pipeline from the Arctic Ocean through the Mackenzie Valley into Alberta. When Judge Thomas Berger was appointed by the federal government in 1974 to conduct an inquiry into the potential social, environmental and economic impact of this pipeline, both the Native organizations and various church groups took the opportunity to challenge the pipeline project and many of the assumptions which motivated those who wanted to see it built. These assumptions included the belief that the traditional Native lifestyle was no longer valid and that resource development was what the Native People needed, as well as the belief that Canada's future depends on greater supplies of gas and oil, no matter what the social and environmental costs.

The two most active religious groups challenging the pipeline proposal were the Committee for Justice and Liberty, a non-denominational Christian social justice organization based in Toronto, and Project North, the inter-church coalition formed in 1975 to support northern Natives in their struggles for self-determination and social justice. Both groups played an active role in the Berger Inquiry, both in rallying support among southern Canadians for the Natives' position and in presenting briefs to the Inquiry on behalf of the churches. One of these submissions, Project North's *A Call for a Moratorium: Some Moral and Ethical Considerations Relating to the Mackenzie Valley Pipeline* (June, 1976), is included here. Partly as a result of the arguments presented in these briefs, Judge Berger recommended that the pipeline in question not be built for at least ten years, and the National Energy Board and the federal government subsequently rejected the applications of two companies to build this pipeline. However, they later approved an alternate pipeline route through the Yukon, despite conditions there similar to those along the Mackenzie Valley.

Undaunted by Judge Berger's conclusions, an oil company and a pipeline company approached the National Energy Board in 1980 for permission to build an oil pipeline from Norman Wells on the Mackenzie River to an existing pipeline in northern Alberta. The Committee for Justice and Liberty coordinated a number of church interventions against this proposal, including that of Project North. The testimony of the Project North representatives before the

National Energy Board is included in this section. It attempts to show that the pipeline is not feasible even on economic terms, much less on social and environmental ones. In the end, however, the Board ignored all but the technical and economic aspects of the proposal and found these basically satisfactory. The federal government ment confirmed this decision, subject to a two-year delay (until 1983) to allow for the settlement of Native land claims in the area.

10 · NORTHERN DEVELOPMENT: AT WHAT COST?*

THE CANADIAN CONFERENCE OF CATHOLIC BISHOPS, 1975

Introduction

A cry for justice rings out today from Native Peoples who inhabit the Canadian North. Dramatically, on a massive scale the Native Peoples of the North find themselves and their way of life being threatened by the headlong search for new energy sources on this continent.

At the same time other voices are raising serious ethical questions about the enormous demands for energy required to maintain high standards of wealth and comfort in industrial society. A variety of public interest groups are calling for greater care of the environment and responsible stewardship of the energy resources in this country.

We, Catholic bishops of Canada, want to echo these cries for justice and demands for stewardship in the Canadian North. They tell us much about ourselves as citizens and consumers, about the industrial society of North America, about the Native Peoples of the North.

As Christians, we cannot ignore the pressing ethical issues of northern development. For the living God, the God we worship, is the Lord of Creation and Justice.

We wish to share with you, fellow citizens, some reflections and judgements on the ethical problems posed by the industrial devel-

146

opment of the Canadian North.[1] We hope that these reflections and judgements will contribute to more public debate and stimulate alternative policies regarding the future development of the North. We also ask that these expressed concerns be tested in the public arena along with other points of view.

Northern Dilemma

Since "time beyond memory," the vast land mass that covers the northern tips of our provinces and the sub-Arctic regions has been the home for many of this country's Native Peoples: Indians, Inuit and Métis.

Through time, these Native Peoples developed social, cultural, economic and religious patterns of life which were in harmony with the rhythms of the land itself.[2]

This land has been the source of livelihood for a significant portion of northern Native Peoples, along with a number of early white settlers. It has been the basis of their traditional economy: hunting, fishing and trapping.

For the Native Peoples the land is more than simply a source of food or cash. The land itself constitutes a permanent sense of security, well-being and identity. For generations, this land has defined the basis of what the Natives are as a people. In their own words, "Our land is our life."[3]

After countless generations of occupation, use and care, the Native Peoples of the North have come to claim their rights to these lands.[4] While some northern Natives are giving up their life of hunting, fishing and trapping, these lands remain essential to their future economic development. For these northern lands contain a natural storehouse of some of the most valuable resources on this continent: potential reserves of oil and natural gas, powerful river systems and rich mineral deposits.

But now the "energy crisis" in the industrial world is posing a serious challenge to the people and resources of the northern lands. The search for new supplies of oil, gas and electricity on this continent is largely focussed on the untapped energy resources of the Canadian North.

In recent years, provincial governments, crown corporations and private companies have been planning large-scale projects to harness the power potential of the northern rivers.

Dams, power plants, railroads and highways are now under construction in several provinces:

• *the James Bay hydro project in northern Quebec; the Churchill-Nelson hydro development in northern Manitoba;*

• *the Churchill Falls hydro project in Labrador; the hydroelectric plants in northwest British Columbia.*

Simultaneously, the Canadian North has been sighted as a major region for potential reserves of oil and gas. Assisted by the federal government, the giants of the oil industry—Exxon, Shell, Gulf, Mobil, Sunoco and others have led the way, through their Canadian subsidiaries, in making discoveries and initiating plans to build several major industrial projects:[5]

• *the Mackenzie Valley pipeline in the Northwest Territories to bring natural gas from Alaska and the Canadian Arctic to southern Canada and the United States;*

• *the Polar Gas pipeline designed to bring natural gas from the high Arctic to the Maritimes and the United States;*

• *the Syncrude project to develop the Athabaska and tarsands in northern Alberta*

In this way the Canadian North is fast becoming a centre stage in a continental struggle to gain control of new energy sources. The critical issue is how these northern energy resources are to be developed—by whom and for whom. We are especially concerned that the future of the North not be determined by colonial patterns of development, wherein a powerful few end up controlling both the people and the resources.

Some present examples of industrial planning give us cause for grave concern.[6] For what we see emerging in the Canadian North are forms of exploitation which we often assume happen only in Third World countries: a serious abuse of both the Native Peoples and the energy resources of the North.[7] Herein lies the northern dilemma. What has been described as the "last frontier" in the building of this nation may become our own "Third World."

Demands for Justice

Our first pastoral concern is that justice be done in the future industrial development of the Canadian North. In various parts of the northern lands the Native Peoples' protests have drawn attention to a series of injustices:

(i)   In several cases, governments and corporations have secretly planned and suddenly announced the construction of large industrial projects without prior consultation with the people who will be most directly affected.[8] As a result the future lives of these Native Peoples and their communities tend to be planned for them by southern interests.

(ii) The plans for these industrial projects are usually finalized and implemented before land claim settlements have been reached with the Native People of the region.[9] Yet, for people whose land is their life, and who wish to secure control over their future economic development, a just settlement of their land claims lies at the very heart of their struggle for justice.

(iii) The construction of these industrial projects has sometimes proceeded without an adequate assessment of their environmental and social consequences. In several instances, the building of power plants and hydro dams will cause the flooding of vast areas of land, damage to the vegetation and wildlife, and the relocation of whole communities of people whose lives have traditionally depended on hunting, fishing and trapping.[10]

(iv) The promise of jobs in the construction of these industrial projects has offered no real alternative way of life. For most of the Native Peoples, these jobs are temporary, paying relatively low wages for low-skilled labour.[11]

As a result, more and more Native Peoples are being compelled to give up their land-based economy and move into the urban centres where alcoholism and welfarism have become prevalent for many. While compensation may be offered, money can hardly replace the loss of land and what it means to the lives of the Native Peoples and their future economic development.

A sense of justice, coming from the living God, tells us there are better ways of developing the resources of the Canadian North. The Lord of Creation has given mankind the responsibility to develop the resources of nature so as to make possible a fuller human life for all peoples.[12] This coincides with the beliefs of the Native Peoples who have traditionally called for a "communal sharing" of the land which belongs to the Creator.

To develop the resources of the Canadian North is a responsibility to be shared by all who live in this country—North and South.

While Native Peoples in the North must be prepared to share in this responsibility, they rightly demand that their claims to justice be realized. In the words of one northern Native leader: "... We also want to participate in Canadian society, but we want to participate as equals. It is impossible to be equal if our economic development is subordinated to the profit-oriented priorities of the American multinationals .... the Native People are saying we must have a large degree of control over our own economic development. Without control we will end up like our brothers and sisters on the reserves in the South: continually powerless, threatened and impoverished."[13]

Across the Canadian North Native Peoples' groups have begun to articulate a common program for justice.[14] Their goal is greater control over their own economic development. The key is a just settlement of their land claims. In recent years, Native groups have been taking the land issue into the courtrooms to establish their traditional rights to these lands.

The living God calls on us to respond to these demands for justice. Christian love of neighbour and justice cannot be separated in the development of people. "For love implies an absolute demand for justice, namely a recognition of the dignity and rights of one's neighbour."[15]

Demands for Stewardship

A second pastoral concern is the demand for responsible stewardship of energy resources in the development of the Canadian North. Throughout this country, public interest groups are raising serious questions about our highly industrialized society and the current exploitation of northern energy resources.

(i) The scramble for northern energy continues without adequate measures to regulate the patterns of relentless consumption in this country. In the last 25 years alone, Canada's consumption of oil, gas and electricity has multiplied three times over.[16] This extravagant consumption of energy generates increasing demands for the rapid development of northern resources.

(ii) Northern development is also continuing without full public discussion of future energy needs. Governments and industries predict that Canada's energy needs will have to multiply four more times by the end of this century to maintain "a high quality of life."[17] But what is this "quality of life" and who determines what these future energy needs should be?

(iii) The reasons for rapidly developing northern energy resources on such a massive scale at this time have also been seriously questioned.[18] While the sale of these resources will reap large profits for the energy industry now, it may also cause the rapid depletion of non-renewable supplies of oil and gas required for the future.

(iv) In several cases, this energy is being rapidly developed now to feed the industrial centres of the United States.[19] Yet, there are many other countries, especially poor nations of the Third World, that are suffering from acute shortages of energy required for basic survival.

The United States and Canada are ranked as the highest users of energy in the world today. For these two countries, containing little more than 6.5 per cent of the world's population, consume about 43 per cent of the energy supplies of this planet.[20] All this energy goes to run the countless number of machines which have become "our energy slaves" in industries, businesses and homes. It is now estimated that given the amount of muscular power required to do the work of these machines, each North American has the equivalent of 400 "energy slaves" working for him.[21]

We North Americans have created a highly industrialized society that places exorbitant demands on limited supplies of energy. The maximization of consumption, profit, power has become the operating principle of this society. These are the driving forces behind the present continental struggle to gain control of northern energy resources.[22] These are the idols which turn many from service of man and world and, thus, from the living God.

As a culture, we have not faced up to the fact that the world God created has its limits. Many voices now warn that mankind has reached a "turning point" in history: crucial decisions must be made now to stop plundering the Earth's non-renewable resources before it is too late.[23] Yet, this industrialized society treats the resources of the Earth as if they were limitless.

In recent years, public interest groups have been calling for responsible stewardship of northern energy resources. They are calling for more effective measures to reduce levels of consumption and waste and preserve non-renewable resources. These groups contend that future resource development, which is largely controlled today by multinational corporations, must be made more accountable to the Canadian public.

The living God calls us to a life of caring, sparing, sharing the limited resources of this planet.[24] This is no longer simply a moral imperative. It has also become a practical necessity for the survival of our common humanity.[25]

Northern Alternatives

We readily acknowledge that the Catholic Church must also take a critical look at itself. We now see that, coming from another culture, the Church may have contributed to disruptive changes in Native culture while helping to bring Christianity to the North through the creative efforts of missionaries who have shared the hard lives of the people. At the same time, the Church has participated with others in the wealth and comfort of an industrial society which places enormous demands on energy resources at the expense of other people.

We look to the past in order that we may learn to act more responsibly in the present. The present industrial development of the Canadian North poses new challenges for the Church. Some of our northern dioceses have been re-evaluating their missionary work in the light of these challenges.[26] But the responsibility lies with all of us who comprise the Church in Canada.

We believe that the Spirit is challenging the whole Church to fulfill its prophetic service in society today. As the Third Synod of Bishops asserted in 1971: "Action on behalf of justice and participation in the transformation of the world fully appear to us as a constitutive dimension of the preaching of the Gospel, or, in other words, of the Church's mission for the redemption of the human race and its liberation from every oppressive situation."[27]

We contend, therefore, that there are better ways of developing the Canadian North. What is required today is a public search for alternative policies for northern development. This search is already under way through the activities of Native Peoples and public interest groups across the country.[28]

We find ourselves in solidarity with many of these initiatives. Based on the ethical principles of social justice and responsible stewardship, we believe that the following conditions must be met before any final decisions are made to proceed with specific projects for northern development:

(a) *sufficient public discussion and debate* about proposed industrial projects, based on independent studies of energy needs and social costs of the proposed development;

(b) *achievement of a just land settlement* with the Native Peoples, including hunting, fishing and trapping rights and fair royalties in return for the extraction of valuable resources from their land claims;

(c) *effective participation by the Native Peoples* in shaping the kind of regional development, beginning with effective control over their own future economic development;

(d) *adequate measures to protect the terrain,* vegetation, wildlife and waters of northern areas, based on complete and independent studies of the regional environment to be affected by proposed developments;

(e) *adequate controls to regulate the extraction of energy resources from the North,* to prevent the rapid depletion of oil, gas, and other resources which are non-renewable.

It remains to be seen whether Canada's "last frontier" will be developed according to the principles of justice and stewardship. The next two years will be a crucial testing period. In some cases, final and irreversible decisions have already been made. In other instances, there may still be a chance to alter the course of development. The Mackenzie Valley pipeline proposals presently being reviewed by the Berger Commission and the National Energy Board could provide the real test.

As Christians, as citizens, we have a responsibility to insist that the future development of the Canadian North be based on social justice and responsible stewardship. As responsible citizens are we prepared to:

(a) *study* one or more of the industrial projects in the northern parts of our provinces or the Territories?

(b) *actively support* Native Peoples' organizations and public interest groups currently striving to change the policies of northern development?

(c) *engage policy makers,* both federal and provincial, and local members of Parliament in a public dialogue about the ethical issues of northern development?

(d) *raise ethical questions* about corporations involved in northern development, especially those corporations in which Church institutions may have shares?

(e) *seek a just settlement* regarding specific Church landholdings that are subject to Native claims?

(f) *design* education programs to examine personal lifestyles and change the patterns of wasteful energy consumption in our homes, churches, schools and places of work?

(g) *collaborate* with the other Canadian churches, in every way possible, in a common Christian effort to achieve the above objectives?

In the final analysis what is required is nothing less than fundamental social change. Until we as a society begin to change our own lifestyles based on wealth and comfort, until we begin to change the profit-oriented priorities of our industrial system, we will continue placing exorbitant demands on the limited supplies of energy in the North and end up exploiting the people of the North in order to get those resources.

Conclusion

We wish to emphasize that this message is only one step in the continuing struggle for justice and stewardship in the Canadian North. For our part, we want to join with other members of the Catholic community, fellow Christians, members of the other faiths, and fellow citizens. Together, we may be able to act in solidarity with the Native Peoples of the North in a common search for more creative ways of developing the "last frontier" of this country.

Ultimately, the challenge before us is a test of our faithfulness in the living God. For we believe that the struggle for justice and responsible stewardship in the North today, like that in distant Third World countries, is the voice of the Lord among us. We are called to involve ourselves in these struggles, to become active at the very centre of human history where the great voice of God cries out for the fullness of life.

11 · A CALL FOR A MORATORIUM: SOME MORAL AND ETHICAL CONSIDERATIONS RELATING TO THE MACKENZIE VALLEY PIPELINE

PROJECT NORTH, 1976

Mr. Commissioner, the Anglican, United and Roman Catholic Churches, represented here today in Project North, would like to thank you for this opportunity of appearing before you to express some of the moral and ethical issues which we feel to be crucial to any discussion of the proposed Mackenzie Valley Natural Gas Pipeline and, indeed, to any discussion of northern development and Native concerns.

These concerns have reminded some of us of a legend of the Inuit which bears repeating.

It is called the Legend of the Raven:

> At one time, the Raven was able to talk with Man. The Raven was a great help to Man. The Raven was a great help to Man because he would fly out and search for the caribou, the seal or the walrus and would report back to Man. Man would hunt and they would share the food. They were brothers. But then, one day, greed entered the picture and the Raven wanted the food for himself. Because of this, he lost his voice and was left with nothing but a raspy croak. Today, although the Raven is seen everywhere in the North where Man lives, he no longer talks to Man and they are not brothers.

We believe this legend has a profound meaning for us today. For if we do not learn to share and live together as brothers, our survival is in serious jeopardy.

It is for this reason that *we intend today to press for consideration by this inquiry*—and through it by the people of Canada—*for a moratorium on all major northern resource development projects, including the Mackenzie Valley Pipeline*, to give Canadians an opportunity to work together to develop alternative lifestyles, based on conserver rather than consumer attitudes....

Mr. Commissioner, ... the basic purpose for the presentation of this brief to your inquiry ... is to call for a moratorium—a minimum of ten years has been suggested—on all major resource development in the North, including the Mackenzie Valley Pipeline. On March 2, 1976, the leaders of Canada's five major denominations and the Canadian Council of Churches appeared before the prime minister and members of the federal cabinet to urge upon them the necessity for such a moratorium in a document entitled *Justice Demands Action*....

We believe that the issues of the development of the Mackenzie Valley and, specifically, the proposed natural gas pipeline must be defined in a moral and ethical manner and not merely in terms of economics or political expediency.

There are those in society who would say that the Church should not be involved in political, economic or social issues. These people would argue that the Church is concerned with man's soul and lacks the expertise to deal adequately with other matters.

We reject this concept and turn to the biblical imperatives of justice and liberation for the poor, the dispossessed and the minorities of this world (Habakkuk 2:9-10; Amos 5:7-11). We suggest that the decisions of the Mackenzie Valley Pipeline must be considered along moral and ethical grounds at least as equally as political and economic grounds, because we are talking of the very soul of this nation.

So, Mr. Commissioner, we would like to ask your indulgence to reflect with us for a few moments on the role of the Church in addressing the moral and ethical issues of northern development.

In defining development, material values have been allowed to become the norm, while Gospel values are only nominally held as rather abstract propositions which do not affect public attitudes, behaviour and policies all that much. As with many of our social, educational and economic institutions, there has been a tendency for the Church to be caught up in accommodating to the established social order, an order which gives more priority to economic growth and profit-oriented values (which are called "realities") and less to social justice and human dignity (which are called "humanitarian sentiments"). In our experience we are discovering that justice and human dignity are not the automatic by-products of such economic growth.

The Gospel proclaims that God's sovereignty includes all realms of life. Nothing that is human can be outside the Church's mission. It is the love of God in Christ for man that is the basis of the Church's social and political concern. In particular, this means that we stand in solidarity with the Native Peoples of Canada who face the inseparable connection between themselves as a people, and the stewardship of the earth's resources.

Most of us live in and benefit from a socio-economic situation which is *sinful*. By social sin, we mean that we create and sustain social and economic patterns of behaviour that bind and oppress, give privilege to the powerful and maintain systems of dependency, paternalism, racism and colonialism.

The Gospel is more than mere propositions. The Good News is a cluster of living images and values for living. It brings with it a radically new vision of man. In view of this new vision of man, Christians are called to take a critical stance regarding the social reality of each time and space. The Gospel sheds critical light on the structures and procedures of our institutions, governments and corporations and calls into question many of the images and norms which prevail in the mainstream of our economic, political and social life.

Let it be clear that we are not speaking of countries far away, but we are speaking of our own Canadian society and many of its institutionalized ways of life. This state of affairs, we believe, demands not only individual repentance on the part of Christians but, even more difficult, a change of social priorities among all Canadians.

We believe the following underlying assumptions guide Canadian public policy making:

1. that our society, as it presently operates, is basically sound and, that at most, a few adjustments are required to cope with changing conditions;

2. that problems can be isolated and analyzed and that the results can be re-integrated with other factors on the basis of rational functional calculations.

Emphasis is given on continuity with present practices and rational, technical decision-making by the "experts" even though it will probably nod in the direction of citizen participation. These are assumptions that must be challenged given the existence of the serious problems of economic and cultural inequalities.

It is our belief that simple tinkering and patchwork will not suffice to bring justice to its fullest extent in our society.

We are talking about more than simple reformism and calling for more than mere individual conversion. We are calling for a conversion within our social and economic structures whereby policy-making and decision-making will begin to reflect and make practical the values of justice, dignity and fulfillment for every human being. Our corporate sins must be acknowledged and we must turn around, if we are to have a society that truly reflects the social consequences of the New Commandment. To bless the established order is to remain unconverted!

We want to share with you what was, for those of us who were in attendance at the Anglican Church's General Synod in Quebec City last June, a "moment of truth." It was the day the issue of Native rights and northern development was to be debated. It was introduced by the bishop of the Arctic, John Sperry. Using the analogy of the parable of the Good Samaritan, he asked the Synod what it should do about the robbed, beaten and broken body lying beside the road, that was Canada's Native People of today, as the white population and its governments passed by on the other side.

Sperry spoke in passionate and urgent tones:

> We must be like the Good Samaritan, who not only bound up the wounds inflicted by a cruel and heartless society that left a race of people to die, but who stood clearly beside this man and continued to support him when all others had abandoned him, and helped him morally and with action.
>
> If we today fail to place ourselves clearly on the side of Native People in Canada, and instead pass by on the other side by refusing to state clearly with words and actions where we stand, then we must return to our homes from this place and hang our heads in shame.

Mr. Commissioner, we think that to pass by on the other side means to fail to deal squarely with the issues of justice in respect to Native land claims and the cultural survival of the Native Peoples in the Northwest Territories; that it means irresponsible stewardship with respect to the exploitation of energy and mineral resources in the N.W.T.; that it means to denigrate our human and natural resources; above all, that it is to deny the Gospel of justice, dignity and human fulfillment for all God's people.

From these reflections we believe it is clear to us that we must press home the point that the federal government has a major responsibility to insist that colonial patterns of development not prevail any longer in the Canadian North, especially in the Northwest Territories where the federal government retains complete jurisdiction.

We are helped in understanding this by examining the forces that are at work in the North, the same forces that are at work in almost every "Third World" situation we know of. The world we talk about is one that is economically underdeveloped, which often has huge reserves of natural resources and has become the target for transnational companies anxious to "open up" or "develop" the North.

There have been studies undertaken which draw striking parallels between the struggle of the Native Peoples in the Amazon region of Brazil where a variety of mining, agricultural, forest and energy projects have been initiated along with the construction of highways, railroads and seaports to service these projects. Native People there have had no role in the decisions about this development; therefore we suggest a colonial pattern of resource development has emerged in that area which has had striking consequence for the Native Peoples who have inhabited the Amazon basin for centuries.

The same forces and the same patterns, we believe, are at work in the Mackenzie where Native People do not have a decision-making role in northern development....

The most important similarity is the failure to involve Native Peoples in decisions about development that affects them. Land is the essential ingredient to the lives of the indigenous peoples of the Amazon. The Native People of the Northwest Territories insist that the land is their life.

Another similarity noted by the studies is the conflict of interest in the DIAND (Department of Indian Affairs and Northern Development) that makes it similar to the Brazilian FUNAI (National Foundation for Assistance to the Indians), a government agency with a twofold objective:

(i)   to protect Native People until they are sufficiently "integrated" into national society;

(ii) to serve as an agency for the Ministry of the Interior promoting the development of the Amazon.

As you know, sir, the two hats worn by the minister of the DIAND are:

(i)   as legal guardian of Native rights in Canada, and

(ii) to ensure the development of Canada's North, in particular the Yukon and the Northwest Territories.

In many instances the same transnational corporations—e.g., Placer/Noranda; Shell Exploration/Royal Dutch Shell; Cominco/ Canadian Pacific; Brascan Resources/Brascan Ltd.; Giant Yellow-knife/Falconbridge Nickel Mines; INCO—are involved in the two areas, and the same policies of the Brazilian government in providing incentives for resource development are found in the incentives of the northern resource development programs of the DIAND.

Project North believes it is clear that the colonial patterns of resource development similar to those found in Brazil will occur in the Northwest Territories during the next decade if the plans, developed thus far in secret, of the federal government and the transnational energy corporations are allowed to proceed unchecked.

For these reasons, the churches insist that there be a moratorium on all northern development including construction of any Mackenzie Valley Pipeline.

The experience of the Amazon must in no way be allowed to occur in the Northwest Territories for while the consequences of colonial development in the Mackenzie are already tragic, their continuation would result in nothing less than disaster.

There are those within the present administration in Canada who will argue strenuously that our democratic system protects adequately the rights of Native minorities. In fact the Natives are not a minority in the Northwest Territories, as you well know, and it is clear, we believe, that their rights are not adequately safeguarded.

We cannot afford to be complacent about the protection of the democratic rights of the Native People of the North. The record is not good. The "colonial" administration of the territorial council, the lone, but hardy voice of the N.W.T.'s sole member of Parliament and the demands of a consumer-oriented southern, white majority make the guaranteeing of these rights a constant, and often losing, struggle.

For there to be equality in this struggle it is necessary for the churches and all other groups interested in the moral and ethical questions of northern development to stand officially, openly and clearly on the side of justice for and the human rights of the Native People of this country.

There must be continual demand for freedom of information, a process of accountability in decision-making by senior civil servants as well as elected representatives, and a clear statement of who decides how resource development takes place and for whose benefit.

As Canadians we have an obligation to defend the rights of minorities and to recognize that the various regions—in this case North and South—must play an interlocking role if all Canadians are to live in justice and equality.

But we suggest here, Mr. Commissioner, that the rights of Canada's Native People occupy a special status within this country and that we are talking about more than the rights of a minority: we are talking about the rights of Canada's original people.

It is also important to consider that Native People are on the cutting edge of turning the direction of our society's growth from materialism and consumerism to a more fundamentally human concept. In some ways the North is fighting the South's battles.

It is on that note, Mr. Commissioner, that we would like to turn to our basic recommendations which we hope your inquiry will consider carefully, for we believe steadfastly that time is the essential ingredient that must be considered in any application for the construction of a pipeline.

We hope to describe clearly in the remainder of this brief why we are calling for a substantial moratorium on major resource development in the N.W.T. and the feasibility of such a moratorium not only at the moral and ethical level but at what the government and oil companies like to describe as the "practical" or "realistic" or "pragmatic" level.

We believe that a moratorium on all major resource development in the N.W.T. should be declared and that no right of conveyance should be granted to any pipeline company during this period, until the rights of the Native People have been clearly defined and adjudicated.

That period would be used to achieve the following objectives through a public search for alternative policies of northern development:

(i) *Just Settlement of All Native Land Claims:* The only major settlement of land claims that has been negotiated by the federal government in recent years was that in James Bay. It was a land extinguishment settlement at complete variance with the kinds of settlement being envisaged by the Déné and Inuit. It was a settlement which the minister of DIAND has publicly indicated will be a model or "will at least contain the ingredients for other settlements." Because of the continued construction of the James Bay hydro development project during the period of negotiations and because the Native People were forced into an unrealistic deadline, from their point of view, the negotiating process was extremely difficult. The moratorium we propose would give all groups the necessary breathing space to negotiate and realize just land claims that reflect the wishes and the aspirations of the Déné and Inuit. Unrealistic deadlines could be avoided and discussions could take place in an open and suitable manner in the North, rather than being rushed through a purely white man's process in Ottawa or Yellowknife. The pressure to produce a proposal and an agreement under the threat of deadlines is foreign to Native ways of achieving settlements. The use of regional and community discussions and eventual consensus should have at least the same weight as the white man's processes.

(ii) *Native Peoples Programs for Regional Economic Development:* The slogan of the Native People, "Land Not Money", reflects the desire for self-determination and control of their own destiny. This can only be achieved, they insist, through economic development that they control and administer. We would favour policies that support Native People in regions where they do not want large cash settlements such as were negotiated in James Bay and Alaska, but rather the econòmic base that can be derived from the controlled development of their own natural resources. If a moratorium on major northern development projects such as the Mackenzie Valley Pipeline were granted, time would be available for the Native People to devise appropriate programs themselves, rather than the ad hoc method presently in vogue. These programs would take into consideration the traditional hunting, fishing and trapping of Native People as well as providing a base for local and regional government. These programs have little chance of development if the Native People are attempting to adjust to, and live within, the enormous social and economic unrest of the construction period for a pipeline. Development of their own regional economic programs would safeguard their way of life *before* resource development rather than afterwards when it is too late.

(iii) *Adequate Safeguards to Deal with Environmental Problems Like Oil Spills, Blowouts, Damage to the Terrain and the Living Creatures:* Evidence before this inquiry has made it clear that many of the environmental questions have not been adequately answered by the applicants and that because such a pipeline is the "first" in the world there is no body of experience to draw upon. The question of alternative routes that would cause less social and environmental damage in the area needs a great deal more examination.

The very real fears of the people whose lives depend so deeply on their relationship to the Beaufort Sea would be allayed if time were given to developing a safer technology for offshore drilling than is presently available to the industry. The hasty planning that has accompanied so many massive industrial and energy projects in the North exemplifies the frontier boom-or-bust mentality of colonial development. Extraction of resources rarely takes into account ecological or environmental concerns until it is too late. A moratorium, we believe, should be used to change this pattern so that adequate safeguards are planned and included in proposals before the construction phase begins.

(iv) *Adequate Programs to Regulate Domestic Consumption and Export of Energy Resources:* Canadians have no real input into a rational nationwide energy policy. The National Energy Board is not available as a forum to most Canadians. Public discussion is almost impossible because of conflicting, conditional, partial and misleading answers to energy supply-and-demand from the government and industry. A case in point is the failure to explain adequately the unbelievable discrepancy between 1971 and 1974 statements with respect to oil and gas reserves in this country. The Honourable Joe Greene, minister of energy, mines and resources in 1971, told the nation we had 923 years' supply of oil and 392 years' supply of gas and had better export these non-renewable resources before they became obsolete. In 1974, the National Energy Board reported that we would have to start importing oil by 1982 and of course the applicants before this inquiry and the same Department of Energy, Mines and Resources insist that a natural gas shortage is just around the corner.

Nothing short of a full and independent public inquiry will ever serve to give the people of the country the facts they need to make the decisions about what is and what is not in their interests. And until such a public inquiry produces some straight answers on energy supply and demand so that the public can participate meaningfully in decision-making, a moratorium on pipeline construction and offshore drilling should be in force.

Too early and precipitate approval of the Mackenzie Valley Pipeline by the National Energy Board and the federal government will serve further to confuse the issues and leave the people of Canada unable to decide whether they wish to be consumers or conservers.

The following arguments show that if the federal government takes the appropriate steps there are sufficient supplies of natural gas to ensure Canadian consumption until at least the year 2001. This would give ample time for a full public inquiry and discussion of future energy development with a moratorium on such projects as the Mackenzie Valley Pipeline until the inquiry has been completed and a responsible national energy policy established. At the same time environmental and Native concerns could be dealt with in a just manner.

1. A July, 1975, background study issued by the Science Council of Canada, *Energy Conservation* by F.H. Knelman, concludes that a serious program of waste reduction can result in a saving of 30 per cent of projected 1995 consumption of natural gas. This cutback, Knelman asserts, could add four years to supply projections.

2. Canadian Arctic Gas Pipelines admits that there is no imminent physical shortage of natural gas in Canada and says there is a 12-year supply available for delivery to all parts of Canada if the federal government takes the necessary steps to ensure that deliverability. The main problem is not availability but *deliverability* and the main reason for this is that TransCanada Pipelines cannot meet Eastern Canadian demands because the crown-owned corporation is unwilling to pay the price suppliers are asking for available Alberta natural gas.

3. Canada now exports to the United States natural gas at the rate of one trillion cubic feet a year, about 40 per cent of its annual natural gas production. Long-term contracts call for the export of

an additional 14 trillion cubic feet between 1974 and 1995. But, Mr. Commissioner, you are no doubt aware that reduction or elimination of exports is allowable under Canadian law if supply conditions warrant. If 10 trillion cubic feet of natural gas were diverted for domestic use, Canada's gas supply would be extended by seven years.

4. The Alberta government has offered to release, for Eastern Canadian consumption, the 30-year natural gas supply it maintains prior to exporting gas to other provinces. In return, the federal government must make the commitment to deliver to Alberta, at a future date, an equivalent supply of gas. Acceptance of this offer would add approximately three years to future supplies.

These four steps, Mr. Commissioner, would bring the non-northern gas supply figures to 26 years, composed as follows: present reserves, 12 years; conservation, 4 years; export cutbacks, 7 years; Alberta swap, 3 years.

Surely the churches and the Native organizations are justified in asking, "What's the rush to build the Mackenzie Valley Pipeline when there are so many unanswered questions?"

These are some of the "realities" behind our call for a moratorium and for the purpose of illustrating the fact that southern whites need not "freeze to death in the dark" while considering the moral and ethical issues of northern development.

CONCLUSION

The conclusion that we have come to in Project North is defined in terms of the following objectives:

• a reduction in the per capita use of all forms of energy consumed in Canada;

• a concerted national effort to develop alternative sources of energy;

• honouring the aboriginal rights of Natives with respect to the involvement of their lands and culture in projects designed to provide energy for southern Canadian and United States consumption;

• full satisfaction that the ecology will not be adversely affected *prior* to the commencement of any massive development project;

• the establishment of just royalty and tax provisions to reduce the unreasonable profits of multinational companies and governments;

• the expenditure of natural resource revenues for enhancing the total well-being of people instead of being solely related to economic growth;

• the gradual reduction of oil and gas exports to the United States and, instead, the export of energy, at below international prices, to underdeveloped countries.

Mr. Commissioner, we have the time and we must use it!

For the sake of ourselves, our children and all future generations of Canadians, we must learn from our Native brothers and sisters that our land and its resources are to be used for the benefit of all people and not exploited for the profits of a few.

Taking the time we have suggested requires a moratorium on the Mackenzie Valley Pipeline, a project so enormous that it will reinforce, perhaps irrevocably, the high energy consuming, materialistic, hedonistic lifestyle that is so seriously under question by so many people in so many ways.

The serious questions that are now being raised by the panic resource dash to our northern frontier may be a blessing in disguise! For we in southern Canada are being forced to address the realities of our current way of life. Are we prepared to develop new sets of values, create new social and economic structures that lead us into a less materialistically oriented society, find new forms of living and growing as people, search for alternative patterns of resource development in such a way that caring, sparing and sharing become a truly human reality? We, in southern Canada, must soon wake up to these extremely serious questions of our common survival. How we address the issues of northern development and how we respond to the cries for justice by the Native People of this country will serve to indicate the ways in which we will begin to find answers for these questions.

Since we represent positions taken by the churches, we feel we must conclude by referring our discussions back to ourselves. What is it that we can really do?

Since there are moral and ethical issues that must be raised, then we have no choice but to speak up in language that cannot be misunderstood.

We have spoken today about whether or not the project you are inquiring into makes sense from an economic point of view. We have declared ourselves on the environmental issues. We have raised the question of the development of the Native People of the North. We have indicated the serious need of all Canadians to address the basic question of personal and corporate lifestyle. Others have spoken to you over the last year and a half, and more recently, on the same subjects.

"In the final analysis," as the 1975 Roman Catholic Labour Day message reminded us,

> what is required is nothing less than fundamental social change. Until we as a society begin to change our own lifestyles based on wealth and comfort, until we begin to change the profit-oriented priorities of our industrial system, we will continue placing exorbitant demands on the limited supplies of energy in the North and end up exploiting the people of the North in order to get those resources.

Therefore, we urge upon you the deepest consideration of our position that a moratorium on northern resource development be implemented to permit the work of restoration in our society to begin, and to stop further development, exploration, drilling or the issuance of permits of any kind, until all northern Native land claims have been justly settled.

Finally, Mr. Commissioner, as an offer of real and practical help, *we pledge here today to renew our commitment to stand openly and officially and wholeheartedly with the Déné and Inuit of the Mackenzie in their struggle for justice.*

Thank you, Mr. Commissioner.

12 · BEFORE THE NATIONAL ENERGY BOARD IN THE MATTER OF THE NORMAN WELLS OIL PIPELINE APPLICATION

PROJECT NORTH, 1981

Q. Whom do you represent?

A. As members of this panel, we are here on behalf of the Administrative Committee of Project North, an ecumenical action/ research program co-sponsored by seven national churches in Canada. Project North was originally organized in 1975 to support northern Native Peoples in their struggle for justice in the face of large-scale plans for the industrial development of the North. Initially, Project North was formed by the Anglican Church of Canada, the Canadian Conference of Catholic Bishops, and the United Church of Canada. In recent years, the sponsorship has been enlarged to include the Lutheran Church in Canada, the Mennonite Central Committee, the Evangelical Lutheran Church in Canada, and the Canadian Religious Conference....

Q. What are the general objectives and programs of Project North?

A. First, the basic purposes are rooted in the biblical tradition of socio-economic justice and responsible stewardship of resources. By social and economic justice, we refer to a central theme in the Scriptures in which Yahweh is understood as the God who defends the poor, the downtrodden, the weak and the oppressed (e.g., Deuteronomy 15:4-11; 24:14-15; Exodus 22:22-25; Leviticus 19:13). To know God, therefore, entails seeking justice for the poor and the oppressed (e.g., Matthew 25:31-46; Mark 10:42-45; Luke 4:18-20; James 2:1-13; Amos, Jeremiah, Hosea, Micah, etc.). By responsible stewardship of resources, we refer to those themes in the Scriptures wherein men and women are charged by God with the responsibility of being the custodians and caretakers of Creation (e.g., Colossians 1:15-20; Isaiah 24:1-12; Jeremiah 34:8-17). The resources of the earth are to be developed, caringly and sparingly, to serve the Native People for a more fully human life (e.g., Leviticus 25:1-7, 23-28; Luke 4:16-22; Amos 5:11).

Secondly, the program of Project North is organized around two interrelated objectives:

1. to support the creative activities of Native People engaged in struggles for justice and self-determination in the North, particularly in the recognition and implementation of their claims and their aboriginal rights;

2. to challenge and mobilize church constituencies in southern parts of Canada to become involved in creative action on the ethical issues of northern development....

Q. What is your basic position with respect to the proposed Norman Wells oil pipeline?

A. It is our position that little or nothing has changed since the historic decision was made regarding the proposed Mackenzie Valley natural gas pipeline in 1977. At that time, you will recall, both the Berger Commission and the National Energy Board recommended that a natural gas pipeline should not be built along the Mackenzie Valley in the near future. After three years of travelling to all the Native communities, listening to the views of the people, and evaluating an enormous number of social, economic and environmental impact studies, the Berger Commission concluded that a ten-year moratorium should be put on pipeline construction in the Mackenzie Valley and that no pipeline should be built until the Native claims have been settled and implemented. And the NEB, after hearing testimony from hundreds of witnesses and evaluating volumes of documentation, also concluded "that a pipeline should not be built along the Mackenzie Valley at this time," noting among other reasons that "the Déné might lose more than they would gain by a pipeline development in the immediate future" (*NEB Report*, vol. 1, p. 164, vol. 3, p. 207). (*Please note*: By *NEB Report*, we are referring here to the National Energy Board Report, *Reasons for Decision: Northern Pipelines*, 1977, vols. 1, 2 and 3. By *Berger Report*, we are referring to *Northern Frontier/Northern Homeland: The Report of the Mackenzie Valley Inquiry, 1977*, vols. 1 and 2.)

It is our contention that the concluding judgements of the NEB and the Berger Commission, which were based upon substantial social, economic and environmental impact studies, are applicable to the proposed Norman Wells oil pipeline. Our contention there rests upon the following premises:

1. that the proposed oil pipeline project must be viewed as part of plans for an energy corridor along the Mackenzie Valley;

2. that the federal government has made little or no progress toward the settlement and implementation of Native claims;

3. that the proposed pipeline offers no real economic benefit to the Native People of the North;

4. that no serious social impact studies have been conducted with respect to this pipeline;

5. that there are alternative forms of energy investment which would be more beneficial and productive than the proposed pipeline.

Q. What are Project North's concerns about the nature of this proposed pipeline in relation to an energy corridor?

A. The applicants imply that the Norman Wells oil pipeline bears no resemblance or relation to the larger natural gas pipeline which the NEB rejected in 1977. To be certain, the oil pipeline would be smaller (12 inches versus 38 inches) and shorter (560 miles instead of 2,400 miles). We must remember, however, that the studies and judgements of the Berger Commission and the NEB in 1977 were not simply based on the construction of a single pipeline. The primary concern was not a single pipeline alone, but rather what the Berger Commission called "the corridor concept," whereby the construction of one pipeline would open up a transportation and energy corridor throughout the Mackenzie Valley.

The federal government's pipeline guidelines of 1970 and 1972 outline this concept of an energy corridor. Together, they constitute what the Berger Commission called "the cornerstone of Canadian policy with regard to the construction of northern pipelines" (*Berger Report*, vol. 1, p. 9). The operating assumption was that an oil pipeline would be constructed first, followed by a gas pipeline in the Mackenzie Valley or vice-versa. In addition to pipelines, the guidelines envisaged the opening up of a whole transportation corridor containing roads, a railroad, hydro-electric transmission lines, and telecommunication facilities. The cumulative impact of a pipeline followed by an energy corridor would be enormous with respect to the social, economic and environmental future of the North.

Thus, the proposed Norman Wells oil pipeline, regardless of its size, will likely serve as a triggering mechanism for the construction of a major energy and transportation corridor through the Mackenzie Valley. The construction of this oil pipeline will very likely be followed by the construction of a gas pipeline and related transportation facilities. This is why the pipeline guidelines called for an examination of the social, economic and environmental consequences of an energy corridor rather than any single pipeline. As the Berger Commission noted, any attempt to disaggregate the policy and to assess the impacts in a piecemeal fashion, should be resisted (*Berger Report*, vol. 1, p. 10).

Q. What are Project North's concerns about the settlement and implementation of Native claims in relation to the proposed pipeline?

A. The Berger Commission report in 1977 declared that the settlement and implementation of Native claims was an essential precondition to the construction of any pipeline in the Mackenzie Valley (*Berger Report*, vol. 1, p. xxv). Contrary to statements by the applicants of the Norman Wells pipeline, the Déné people have not been negotiating land claims settlements with the federal government since the Berger Inquiry (cf. *Applicant's Socio-Economic Impact Assessment*, p. 132). (*Please Note: Applicant's Socio-Economic Impact Assessment* refers to the study of Esso Resources [Can. Ltd.,] and Interprovincial Pipeline [N.W. Ltd.] entitled, *Norman Wells Oil Field Expansion and Pipeline Project Regional Socio-Economic Impact Assessment, 1980.*)

Indeed, the federal government cut off all negotiations with the Déné Nation following the Cabinet decision not to proceed with the Mackenzie Valley pipeline. In addition, all funds required for research and preparation regarding land-claims negotiations were suspended. Indeed, the federal government's actions since 1977 have largely contributed to the lack of significant progress in the settlement of the Déné claims and implementation of the Berger Commission's basic recommendations.

Yet, the applicants are obviously proceeding on the assumption that they can go ahead with pipeline construction before the Déné claims are settled and implemented. This was precisely the option which the Berger Commission steadfastly rejected. Moreover, the applicants wrongly contend that Treaties 8 and 11 "... provided the federal government with full control over resources ..." (*Socio-Economic Impact Assessment*, p. 21). Witness [Fr. René] Fumoleau has conducted extensive documentary research on Treaties 8 and 11, demonstrating that they were primarily understood as "peace" and "friendship" treaties with no reference to the transfer of "full control of resources" to the federal government. There is also evidence to show that many of the signatures on these treaties were fraudulent. All this led Mr. Justice Morrow to grant the Déné a caveat to the land in the Mackenzie Valley in 1973.

In the documentation available to us, there is certainly little indication that the applicants have given only passing references to the Déné claims position. After careful study, the Berger Commission concluded that there were no legal or constitutional objections to the Déné entrenching their rights to self-determination through their own political institutions in the North (*Berger Report*, vol. 1, pp. 172-74, 193-95). Yet, it appears that the applicants have decided to proceed without serious reference to these claims. References are made instead to the model of land-claims settlement being negotiated in the western Arctic under the pressures of Dome Petroleum's drilling program in the Beaufort Sea. Yet, nothing is said about the enormous pressures exerted by Dome Petroleum on COPE and the Inuit communities nor the Déné's repeated rejection of this model of land-claims settlement.

Q. What are Project North's basic concerns about the economic impact of the proposed pipeline?

A. In 1977, the NEB reached the following conclusion after studying the economic impact of the then proposed natural gas pipeline:

> The Déné might participate in some of the unskilled and semi-skilled jobs during construction, but on balance the construction would have negative impacts since it would frustrate their attempts to develop their own institutions based on a renewable resource-based economy and the operations phase would have little to offer the Déné. (*NEB Report*, vol. 1, p. 144)

The report further states, "the white segments of society would, in the Board's view, gain from pipeline developments, particularly local business" (*NEB Report*, vol. 1, p. 144).

There is no evidence to suggest that the NEB should conclude any differently with respect to the proposed oil pipeline. The project will simply continue the "boom and bust" pattern of development with little or no benefits going to the Déné population. The applicants themselves admit that while employment opportunities will increase, "...this trend will not marginally affect the high rate of unemployment ... and most new positions will probably be filled by in-migrants" (*Socio-Economic Impact Statement*, p. 25). Beyond this, the applicants have given little serious attention to such factors as the inflationary impacts generated by pipeline projects like these in local areas.

Moreover, the proposed oil pipeline is likely to further frustrate the possibilities of developing what the Berger Commission called a mixed economy based on a balanced development of both non-renewable and renewable resources designed to really benefit the people of the North (cf. *Berger Report*, vol. 1, pp. 120 ff.).

Yet, the problems of economic impact run deeper than this. Even if the Déné were offered thousands of jobs through the construction of this pipeline, it would not begin to compensate for the losses and damages incurred. A job in the wage economy is certainly no substitute for the loss of land and the valuable resources it contains. To cast the Native People in the role of wage earners is to deny them their proper role as land owners. When all is said and done, the fact remains that the Déné are denied the right to decide whether and under what conditions such a pipeline should be constructed on their land. At the same time, they are denied the right to appropriate adequate rents in return for the extraction of valuable non-renewable sources of oil from their land. As long as this model of northern development continues, the Déné and other Native Peoples in the North will remain trapped in a state of economic dependency.

Q. What are Project North's concerns about the social impact of the proposed pipeline?

A. In 1977, the NEB made the following judgements with respect to the natural gas pipeline proposal: "The Board can only point to the fact that pipeline construction impacts are more likely to be a negative rather than a positive influence on the social fabric of the North..." (*NEB Report*, vol. 3, p. 198). At the same time, the NEB concluded that "on balance, pipeline projects probably have a negative social impact" (*NEB Report*, vol. 1, p. 143). Once again, we believe that the NEB's judgements on social impact apply to the proposed oil pipeline as well as the natural gas projects.

There is an overwhelming tendency on the part of pipeline applicants generally to underestimate and understate the social impact and social costs of pipeline projects in the North. The Norman Wells application is no exception. No attempt has been made to do a serious independent study of the multiple factors involved: costs of welfare, crime and violence, health services, the influx of migrant workers, the pressures on Native women, the resulting social inequalities and the problems of identity and self-respect. At best, passing references are made to the problems of alcohol in the applicant's socio-economic impact statement. There is no attempt to refer to the historical experience of what happened to the Native communities when the oil refinery was constructed at Fort Norman or when the Mackenzie Valley highway was extended to Fort Simpson (e.g., *Berger Report*, vol. 1, p. 148 f.). And, recent comparative case studies on the social impact of pipelines on Native communities are completely ignored. (See, for example, *The Alaska Pipeline: The Social and Economic Impact on Native People*.)

Indeed, the social impact assessments furnished so far by the applicant are simply inadequate. They are largely based on the assumption that social impacts can be measured quantitatively in terms of population statistics and their relation to housing, health care services, and education facilities. There has been no serious attempt to study the potential social impact in terms of the intricate realities of the Déné culture and the lives of the people to be affected. Moreover, there has been no attempt to assess the cumulative social impact of this pipeline as part of an energy corridor. The social impact of this kind of development, the Berger Commission concluded, would be "devastating—and quite beyond our capacity to ameliorate in any significant way" (*Berger Report*, vol. 1, p. 143).

Q. What are Project North's concerns about the proposed pipeline as an energy investment?

A. In 1977, the NEB firmly stated its position "that a vigorous conservation program should be a prime goal of a Canadian energy policy and that conservation appears to offer the lowest cost option for balancing the energy budget in the near term ..." (*NEB Report*, vol. 1, p. 67). The proposed oil pipeline, however, is not designed to promote conservation but the rapid depletion of the Norman Wells oil field. If this pipeline is built and recovery proceeds at a rate of 25,000 barrels a day as planned, the field would be exhausted in 27 years. If, on the other hand, the oil at Norman Wells were to be recovered at its present rate of 3,000 barrels a day, it would last another 250 years.

For Canada, the expenditure of some $735 million ($360 million for the pipeline, $375 million for enhanced recovery at Norman Wells) to produce an additional 22,000 barrels a day of oil, appears to be a bad energy investment in the long run. The fact is that more oil could be saved at less expense through adequate conservation programs. It has been estimated, for example, that if 500,000 Canadian homeowners, or roughly 15 per cent of Canadian homes, heated by oil furnaces, were lent $1,300 each to invest in improving furnace efficiency and weatherproofing their homes, then some 23,000 barrels of oil a day could be saved at a cost of $650 million (based on a formula developed by Professor W. Ross, Environmental Science Department, University of Calgary).

We believe it is important for the NEB to give serious attention to such alternative energy investments while studying proposed pipeline projects. In addition to saving non-renewable oil supplies required for the future, a vigorous conservation program will create more jobs. For example, a conservation program like the one noted above would generate two or three more times as many permanent jobs than the number of temporary jobs involved in the construction phases of the proposed Norman Wells pipeline.

Q. Do you have any conclusions or recommendations to offer the National Energy Board?

A. The NEB may well find itself faced with a test of credibility when it comes to make its decision on the proposed Norman Wells pipeline. Three years ago, after many months of intensive study and evaluation, the NEB decided against the construction of a natural gas pipeline down the Mackenzie Valley. It has been our contention that little has changed in the past three years. If anything, the basic reasons for rejecting pipeline construction in the Mackenzie Valley are even more pronounced than they were in 1977. We, therefore, urge the NEB to reaffirm its judgement that a pipeline should not be constructed in the Mackenzie Valley at this time. Indeed, we urge the NEB to call for a moratorium on all northern pipeline construction in the North until Native claims have been justly settled and implemented.

The applicants will, undoubtedly, charge that Canada is about to face an oil crisis, exacerbated by the present war between Iraq and Iran, and that this pipeline must be built in the national interest. In recent years, whenever a decision is to be made on whether to proceed with a northern pipeline, the petroleum industry makes a dramatic appeal to the impending energy crisis and the national interest. Yet, the present pipeline proposal raises deeper moral questions. To what extent are we prepared, as a nation, to sacrifice the Déné people and their culture for the sake of increasing our oil supply by less than 1 per cent? To what extent does this state of affairs reveal a moral crisis in our society that begs to be resolved in the national interest?

Indeed, we have reached a critical turning point in our own history. To a large extent, Canada's future energy policies are inextricably linked with the future development of the Canadian North. We are now at the crossroads where some fundamental choices must be made. As a country, we could continue along the present energy path, which is largely dominated by a foreign-owned petroleum industry and which places high priority on the rapid development of non-renewable supplies of oil and gas to meet short-term energy needs. The end result may very well be genocide for the Native Peoples of the North and the exhaustion of energy supplies required for the future. Or, as a country, we could decide now to vigorously chart an alternative energy path, a decentralized energy system based on forms of public or community control, which places priority on the development of renewable energy sources (e.g., solar, wind, water, farm and forest products), effective conservation measures, and a much more balanced development of non-renewable energy resources. The result of this alternative course could well mean the entrenchment of Native rights to self-government in the North and the responsible stewardship of resources to save long-term energy needs of future generations.

We believe that this choice between two energy paths is the central issue of national interest facing this country today. In our view, the only sane choice is to develop a truly alternative energy path for the sake of future generations. To achieve this end, a moratorium on major resource development in the North is necessary, not as a delaying tactic, but to take the time necessary to develop a viable alternative energy policy for Canada and achieve a just settlement and implementation of Native rights in the North. We submit, Mr. Chairman, that time is of the essence. Decisive action is required now, before it is too late.

FURTHER READING

Committee for Justice and Liberty. "Fighting for a Way of Life: The Norman Wells Pipeline Hearings." *Catalyst for Public Justice*, December, 1980, pp. 8-20.

Committee for Justice and Liberty. *Newsletter* (December, 1976), *In the Public Interest: CJL before the National Energy Board.*

Hendry, Charles E. *Beyond Traplines.* Toronto: Miracle Press, 1969.

McCullum, Hugh, and McCullum, Karmel. *This Land Is Not for Sale.* Toronto: Anglican Book Centre, 1975.

McCullum, Hugh; McCullum, Karmel; and Olthuis, John. *Moratorium: Justice, Energy, the North, and the Native People.* Toronto: Anglican Book Centre, 1977.

Project North. *Northern Native Rights Campaign.* Toronto: 1979.

The United Church of Canada, Department of Church in Society. *Issue 12, Land for the Future: Native Land Claims* (1976).

The United Church of Canada, Department of Church in Society. *Issue 16, The Berger Report: A New Departure* (1977).

SECTION V
CANADA, QUEBEC AND THE CONSTITUTION

All of the economic issues dealt with thus far have had an important political dimension. This section will focus on a—perhaps *the*—Canadian political issue, the place of Quebec within Canada. Along with the division of powers between the provincial and federal governments, this issue dominated the extended debate over the patriation of the British North America Act, Canada's constitution, from Great Britain. When Parliament finally passed the Constitution Act in December, 1981, it did so without the agreement of the Quebec government. The alienation of the French-speaking people of Quebec from English Canada has only been intensified by the outcome of the constitutional debate.

The Roman Catholic Church in Quebec was the focus of Quebecois nationalism for over 200 years, until the "Quiet Revolution" of the 1960s. For much of this period, however, the Church maintained its powers and privileges by collaborating with the English-speaking elite which controlled the economy of the province. When, as a result of the Quiet Revolution and especially after the election of the populist Parti Québécois government in 1976, economic and political power shifted to French Canadian nationalists, the leaders of the Church were uncertain where their allegiance should be. The Parti Québécois had promised, as part of its election platform, a referendum on independence for Quebec, and when the date of the referendum was announced for the spring of 1980, the Catholic bishops of the province decided to state their position on the matter. In two documents, *The People of Quebec and Its Political Future* (August, 1979) and *Building a Better Tomorrow* (January, 1980), the bishops disengage themselves from the English and French federalist forces by affirming the right of the Quebec people to self-determination.

179

They themselves do not choose either for or against independence, but they state that neither option is incompatible with the Christian faith.

In the end, Quebecers did vote against independence, and the political debate turned to the constitution. The Quebec Catholic bishops attempted to convince the other Canadian bishops that they should make a joint statement on the Constitution which would insist that any new agreement must have the approval of Quebec. The English-speaking bishops would not agree to this provision, and there was no statement on this issue from the Canadian Conference of Catholic Bishops.

Although it is predominantly Anglophone, the United Church of Canada did not share this reluctance to affirm Quebec's right to self-determination. In their *Brief to the Joint Committee of Parliament on the Constitution of Canada*, they defend the rights of all minority groups in the constitutional process, especially Native Peoples and French-speaking Canadians. According to this document, there is no justification for a new constitution and charter of rights and freedoms which is unacceptable to or ignores the needs of minority groups in Canada.

13 · THE PEOPLE OF QUEBEC AND ITS POLITICAL FUTURE

THE ROMAN CATHOLIC BISHOPS OF QUEBEC, 1979

To address the political choices offered to Quebecers today constitutes, especially from the viewpoint of Christian faith, a difficult and sensitive undertaking. However a twofold reason prompts us to do so. As servants of the Catholic community in Quebec, we must support our brothers and sisters as they seek commitments inspired by the Gospel. As servants of the Word of God, we must, in relevant language, submit its contents in all things and to all persons of goodwill. We wish to adopt an attitude of dialogue open to one and all. We are faced with complex realities and we expect a great deal from those comments to which our statement shall perhaps give rise. We make no claim to absolute truth, nor is our message the final word in this matter.

Staying Close to Events

As bishops of Quebec, ours is a tradition of staying close to life in Quebec society. This presence, which has always been sustained by a clergy in turn close to the people, has assumed a variety of forms which today are sometimes the object of contradictory assessment. Such critical assessment does not always take into account the needs and ways of thinking of the past. Nevertheless, our faithful presence has never faltered. This is our heritage and we are not prepared to break with it now.

At a time when so many changes are simply taking place, are sought after or predicted, we would hope to serve, by shedding the light of the Gospel in the midst of problems confronting the conscience of our society. We shall seek to impose neither political option presented to us, as well as to all our fellow citizens. Above all, it must be made clear that we firmly intend to remain servants of the people of God regardless of the option that ultimately shall prevail. However, now that major political changes are upon us, we cannot yield to a false sense of discretion by keeping silent, or to an overly cautious hesitation by waiting too long.

Some would readily remind us that one "should render unto Caesar that which is Caesar's," and that the Kingdom of Christ is "not of this world." It is precisely because of the distinction between God and Caesar, between this world and the Kingdom, that all in turn should be reminded that there is nothing absolute in any political or constitutional option. Christians must cope with all the complexities and contingencies of all options put before them. Different and even divergent choices may be inspired and enlightened by the same faith. We believe it timely to set forth a number of considerations in order that each and every one of us be able to grasp the implications of the Gospel in the various proposals laid before us, and to test the Christian foundation underlying our decision.

In varying degrees, and over and above the sometimes divergent viewpoints on how to go about doing so, Quebecers wish to establish better relations with the rest of Canada. Those of us who wish to be inspired and to abide by the Gospel are most deeply concerned about bettering relations, not only between individuals, but between communities as well. Christians must certainly have services to render and responsibilities to assume among people striving for improved relations.

The People of Quebec

Christians are not only members of God's people. Their lives are enrooted in the great many peoples of the world. Each and every Christian belongs to a socially identifiable community, or "people," within which he or she must assume a share of responsibility. Applying the concept of people is never an easy task, and in Quebec, the many distinctions which have to be made are especially sensitive and difficult. It would seem that the present situation calls for some clarification.

> It is beyond dispute that the French-speaking community of Quebec has a right to exist, to develop normally in all spheres of life, to have social and political institutions suited to its own culture and needs, and to enjoy that autonomy without which its existence, prosperity, economic

and cultural growth could not be guaranteed. (Collective letter of the Bishops of Canada for the Centennial of Confederation, 1967).

French-speaking Quebecers, beyond doubt, constitute a distinct community of people, by virtue of their language, their common personality, traditions and spirit, their feeling of solidarity and their desire to thrive. Their history and their culture stand apart among Canadians, not only from those of Anglophones, but also from those of other French-speaking groups such as the Acadians. Quebec Francophones have reason to be proud of the people they form. However, they alone do not make up the whole reality of Quebec.

In the Province of Quebec, account must be taken of the presence of a large Anglophone community, and of several communities of Native People and other ethnic groups. Indians and Inuit have been living on Quebec soil from time immemorial. Many Anglophones have deep and long-standing roots in Quebec. Immigrants who have adopted English as their language are also deeply attached to Quebec.

Although these different minority groups often feel, as do many Francophones, that they belong, first and foremost, to the "broader Canadian mosaic," they are also a part of the Quebec community, and enjoy equal rights within it. Both by tradition and conviction, the Francophone majority has always respected them. It is together with these groups that the Francophone people of Quebec today ponder their future and search for answers.

Therefore, the future of Quebec shall not be decided by the .Francophone majority alone, but by all its citizens, that is, by all those who live within its boundaries, develop its economy, form a significant community, enrich its common culture, share the same legal and political institutions inherited from a common history; it is in this sense then, and providing for all the necessary nuances, that one may refer to the "people of Quebec."

Seeking and Searching

By virtue of the British North America Act, the Province of Quebec has been a member of Canadian Confederation since 1867. Within this framework, the people of Quebec retain the right to determine their own destiny and to re-examine or question, if they so desire, the ties that bind them to their partners. Referring to political life in Quebec, the Canadian bishops recalled, in 1972, that principle reiterated by the Synod held in Rome the previous year: "Peoples should not be hindered from attaining development in accordance with their own culture" and "through mutual cooperation, all peoples should be able to become the principal architects of their own economic and social development" (Ottawa, CCC, 1972). In this sense, it is only natural that the people of Quebec attempt to determine on their own what they wish to become in the future, and how they wish to live within the community of peoples, particularly among their present partners in Confederation.

"Self-determination" is defined precisely as the right of a people to decide its own political future and on how to proceed in doing so. By virtue of self-determination, Quebecers can decide either to accept the present or some other federal structure, to declare sovereignty, or again to enter into association or confederation with others. Self-determination is not a constitutional status in itself, but rather consists in the freedom to decide, without constraint, on the status deemed desirable.

The Gospel calls us to live in freedom and brotherhood with our fellowmen. This twofold invitation applies to peoples as well as to persons. In exercising its right to self-determination, Quebec may choose to remain within a federal type of structure which would give concrete recognition to its specific character. Or it may also exercise this same right to self-determination by declaring sovereignty. In either case, it must always remember that modern nations live in a situation of interdependence, and that thus it would have to maintain some form of relations with its neighbours.

In either situation, Gospel imperatives of responsible freedom and human brotherhood can be met to their full extent. Until that freedom of choice is exercised by the people, there should be no attempt to exert any misleading influence by intimating, for instance, that sovereignty always implies a rejection of others, or that adhering to some form of federalism is equivalent to total submission or capitulation. Relations between peoples may take on various forms, none of which is dictated by faith. Every person must seek out those forms of relations which he deems the most appropriate, and adhere to them in the spirit of the Gospel.

The Quest for Better Relations

In the eyes of Christians, the unity of all human beings in God constitutes, for the peoples of the world, the highest possible aspiration. The grace of God which was bestowed on us in Jesus Christ, permeates the world with the Spirit of Pentecost, gathering together, in a single prayer of praise, all human beings of all nations under the heavens. "And there are no more distinctions beween Jew and Greek, slave and free, male and female, but, all of you are one in Christ Jesus" (Galatians 3:28). This Gospel revelation never ceases to be demanding.

Although self-determination may constitute, for the people of Quebec, the exercise of a legitimate right, and although either sovereignty or a federal system may be adhered to in accordance with the Gospel, the cooperation which is necessary among peoples always carries with it its own obligations.

Many international organizations are striving today to develop this kind of cooperation. While remaining true to themselves, all peoples are called upon to overcome the barriers which divide them and to foster the most suitable form of mutual relations. The accession of many peoples to sovereignty and the emergence of many new countries have been hallmarks of our century. And, without there being any contradiction in this, it has also been the century of worldwide bodies and continent-based organizations. Countries joining organizations do so freely, and if they sometimes renounce part of their sovereignty, they do so of their own accord and for the common good.

The situation is not quite the same in the case of the union of two or more communities of people living in the same country, under a common government invested with real powers. As a rule, such a union is the result of a choice freely made. But it may also happen that a union of this kind is dictated by factors foreign to the will of at least one of the partners. As a consequence of war and conquest, or political or economic conditions of a particular era, through former colonial presence or the initiative of leaders holding no mandate, peoples have at times been placed under one political authority, and through no choice of their own, have lost a large share of their sovereignty.

Whether united through free choice or by history, peoples forming a political unit must always be willing to define or redefine, to negotiate or renegotiate, the terms of their co-existence. Otherwise it would have to be admitted that, by uniting, they had lost their dignity as peoples.

Quebecers may rightfully demand that, in their relations with other Canadians, they be treated as partners endowed with full rights as a people. As Quebecers ponder the changes which they might wish to see made in their present union with the rest of

Canada, two extreme attitudes threaten to damage, each in its own way, the good relations that are so desirable.

The first attitude flows from a misguided search for the unity proposed in the Gospel. It condemns as a sin or crime the questioning of Quebec's belonging to the present federal system. In this view, the concept of Canadian unity is bound up with the idea of Confederation, it becomes intimately related to the concept of the unity of peoples, and does not allow for the possibility of any substantially different form of relationship between Quebec and the rest of Canada. Through a sequence of subtle and sometimes not so subtle (even if well intentioned) statements, some Christians have come to consider the proposals put forward by the proponents of sovereignty as opposed to the unity willed by Christ. Such proposals may be considered debatable for political or economic reasons which remain to be evaluated by the people of Quebec. But if such judgement is passed in thinking that the proposals are in themselves contrary to morality or to the Gospel, then this illustrates an unfortunate confusion, and is bound to result in profound ambiguity.

The second attitude reflects narrow-minded "sovereignism." It tends to consider as cowardly any involvement with the historical experience of Canada as a whole, especially since 1867. It sees nothing positive in what has come out of this experience through those years, and concerning the future of Quebec, it considers as subordinate and superfluous any reference to the rest of Canada. Quebecers have sound reasons to show dissatisfaction with present political institutions and with the behaviour of their partners. They have done more than their share to keep Canada together. But they would be seriously wrong if they were to elevate refusal, rejection and revenge as proper attitudes towards the rest of Canada as a virtue. In so doing, they would indeed offend the ideal of the Gospel and unity among peoples.

On both sides, it behooves everyone to respect all others, be they opponents, and constantly to seek that atmosphere conducive to the clarification if not to the reconciliation of positions. Refusal to discuss, and the *a priori* rejection of democratically expressed opinions would jeopardize, from the outset, the earnestly desired quest for better relations.

It is obvious, however, that in spite of everyone's good intentions, both current demands for change, and those changes which will eventually come about, will inevitably cause a certain amount of unrest and give rise to conflict. The Gospel challenges us to become instruments of that fullness which flows from the attainment of our deepest human aspirations. "Happy are the peacemakers: they shall be called sons of God" (Matthew 5:9). Every Christian is called upon to cooperate in setting up and maintaining conditions conducive to establishing peace. And therefore, in the present debate, many Christians show concern in the name of that peace which the Gospel proclaims.

Yet the peace that Jesus brings to the world will not fully come about until the coming of the Kingdom of God. It would be a display of unreal attitudes and wishful thinking to imagine, in this world, a society without conflict.

Christians will do more than resign themselves to conflicts. They will do their best to turn them into positive and fruitful experiences, striving, even as they experience them, to show respect for others. While divided on questions of a temporal nature and even in their theological views, and yet united in one faith and in one Lord, Christians can and must bear witness to the possibility of experiencing conflicts in a spirit of mutual respect and in adherence to common values. More than others are they called upon to demonstrate that the dignity of individuals and the search for a consensus on essentials can be maintained in spite of divergent opinions and interests.

If we adopt a healthy attitude towards them, current conflicts within Canadian Confederation and regarding the aspirations of Quebecers can contribute to create a more just society. History has shown again and again that when they are sustained with proper attitudes, conflicts can foster the evolution of society and help establish better relations among individuals as well as among peoples.

Conclusion

With an objective to serve the people of Quebec in their search for new ways of self-fulfillment and co-existence with others, we have attempted to define the broad lines of a Christian outlook and interpretation. In order that this search be conducted in the responsible exercise of freedom and according to the requirements of unity and peace, we offer our services within the limits of our abilities.

We shall gladly listen to those who may care to react to our considerations, and we shall closely follow coming events. We wish to repeat, however, that none of the political options put forth at the present time in Quebec concerning its constitutional future is binding in the name of the Gospel, and that we shall pursue our work of proclaiming the Gospel, whatever may be the ultimate option democratically chosen.

14 • BRIEF TO THE JOINT COMMITTEE ON THE CONSTITUTION OF CANADA

THE UNITED CHURCH OF CANADA, 1980

INTRODUCTION

The United Church of Canada shares both the exhilaration and concern of these present days of constitutional debate. Exhilaration, because the debate marks an important step in establishing a new ethos and identity for Canada. Concern, because the debate, as it attempts to move us to a new and firmer unity, has had the unfortunate effect of straining relations and sharpening differences.

We in the United Church are sharing in the wide sense that there is nothing inevitable about the arrival of a new dawn of Canadian unity with justice for all. For too long we have been uncritically optimistic. Recent events make us reflect in a new way that nothing as momentous as turning the corner of our history can be achieved without mental and spiritual struggle by all the social, ethnic, religious, economic and political communities that comprise Canada. For this reason the Executive of the General Council of the United Church has called for an extension of the hearings by the Joint Committee, and that hearings on the government of Canada proposal be made widely accessible.

As representatives of the United Church, privileged to appear before the Joint Committee, we do not have a mandate from our membership to speak on the wisdom of patriating the Constitution as proposed by the government of Canada. We do have the mandate to raise with the Committee certain concerns pertinent to the constitutional question which reflect the ongoing positions of the United Church's General Council and other policy bodies within the United Church. This is particularly so with respect to Native Peoples' rights.

As a church we have a commitment to stand in solidarity with the Native Peoples until their rights are ensured in full.

For us there is a call to speak for human rights and the sharing of wealth that arise out of a Bible-shaped faith. The United Church has repeatedly affirmed mission goals related to personal and distributive justice. It would be inconsistent to remain silent when national attention is focussed on these areas through the constitutional debate.

AREAS OF PARTICULAR CONCERN WITH RESPECT TO PATRIATING THE CONSTITUTION TO CANADA

Native Peoples and the Constitution

Among all the groups in Canada that are concerned about guaranteeing essential rights and freedoms in the proposed Constitution, the aboriginal peoples stand out as a special case. We draw their situation to the attention of this committee with the utmost urgency.

The proposal to patriate the Constitution in the very near future has created a state of emergency for the aboriginal people of this country. In some cases, they stand in danger of having the diminished rights they now experience virtually cast in stone, with little room left for manoeuvring. As great an obstacle as their rights represent to the development plans of some provinces, the aboriginal peoples are unlikely to find many supporters of their rights during the post-patriation period. Theirs is therefore a case that must be dealt with before patriation.

The British Crown recognized the aboriginal nations, guaranteeing all rights and sovereignties in the Royal Proclamation of 1763. Yet these peoples have endured numerous efforts by settlers to extinguish their aboriginal rights and to enforce their assimilation into the new society established in this land.

As we all know, many aboriginal nations never did sign treaties. Today, they are still struggling to hang on to the aboriginal rights guaranteed to them by the British Crown. For a variety of reasons, various governments have found it more convenient to negotiate with aboriginal nations as if the only issue in dispute were hunting rights on pieces of property. The discussions of the past decades have focussed on "land claims" negotiations: but such a phrase obscures the real issue.

By functioning as if this were a simple negotiation over the use of a piece of land, we perpetuate the myth that the aboriginal peoples of Canada are simply another ethnic minority, who require special status to protect them. Few recognize that the "land claims" nego- tiations are actually between the representatives of nations—the aboriginal nations and the government of Canada.

Our involvement as a church with Native groups in their strug- gles for justice in the North has convinced us that the pressure on them to simply abandon their aboriginal nationhood is enormous. Foreign and domestic oil companies offer tempting proposals for development of northern resources, with the jobs and the royalties most Canadians want. But the oil is only accessible to those compa- nies if it belongs to the government of Canada. Until the aboriginal nations and the government of Canada reach satisfactory agree- ments on the question of aboriginal rights, every decision to go ahead and develop oil found on traditional Native land simply creates another precedent for believing that we are dealing with a trou- blesome group of people who want to hold up development of land that is really ours by virtue of our greater need, or our numbers.

We have been appalled at the willingness of companies, govern- ments, and indeed of many Canadians to simply put aside the ques- tion of negotiations between aboriginal nations in the rush for the resources of the North. At this point, the rights of the aboriginal nations within Canada are supposed to be guaranteed by the Crown. If aboriginal rights can be brushed aside under present conditions, what assurance can be possibly drawn from the brief reference in Section 24 of the Canada Act? In fact, Section 24 is so weak that it calls into question our claim that we will bargain in good faith with the representatives of aboriginal nations once the Constitution has been patriated. Our fear is that once the Canada Act becomes law, the status quo rights of Native Peoples—i.e., the reduced rights, with no recognition of aboriginal nationhood—will be virtually guaranteed.

Our experiences with partner churches throughout the world have taught us to be extremely wary of weak and vague "guarantees of the rights of Native People." In country after country, the aborig- inal peoples have been forced off their land, assimilated into the poorest segments of the local population, and sometimes killed, whenever the resources under their land became attractive to industrialists. One of the most tragic cases has recently been widely reported in our papers: the slaughter of the native population of the Quiche province of Guatemala, where the discovery of oil on their land brought them into direct conflict with the government and military of that country.

The attacks on aboriginal peoples of the world have become so widespread that they are the subject of the hearings of the Russell Tribunal in Rotterdam at this very time. A global pattern of oppression has been developing, one in which we do not want to see Canada participate.

It is unthinkable that the aboriginal peoples of Canada would be treated as others have been in Guatemala or in Chile, or in other parts of the world, but neither did aboriginal peoples elsewhere expect the treatment they have received. In a world where nations have been known to go to war over resources, particularly oil and gas, we believe that the Canada Act must reflect the obligations we have undertaken as a former British colony, as well as the reality of the pressures that will probably be placed on us as the world grows increasingly energy-hungry. As a civilized nation, let us respect the agreements made by the British Crown and let us guarantee that we will negotiate with the aboriginal nations in good faith. Let us do nothing to jeopardize that process.

We therefore strongly recommend that Section 24 (or another section) clearly set forth in detail guarantees with respect to the aboriginal and treaty rights of Native Peoples as understood by them, and that representatives of aboriginal nations be full members of all future constitutional talks.

Quebec and the Constitution

The United Church of Canada is overwhelmingly an Anglophone middle-class church. Nevertheless, it has recognized that considering itself a national church requires that it learn about, appreciate and seek to support the aspirations of cultural and social minorities that make up the fabric of Canada. The two peoples that the church has concerned itself with most have been the Native Peoples and Francophones. We have already discussed the Native Peoples in terms of the constitutional debate, so let us turn to the Francophones.

Though the United Church has been involved in parish work with the Francophones for many years, it is the church's involvement in political concerns that is relevant to the present discussion. The United Church has always seen its role as one of identifying some of the underlying value questions rather than endorsing one or other political option. In fact, at the 1972 General Council in Saskatoon, the church stated "that no political structure or movement to change such structure ought ever to be regarded as sacred or as more than an instrument to serve human ends" and further, "that a crucial factor in the shaping of future political structures must be the deliverance of French Canadians from any sense of subjection and that such deliverance requires an openness to a reconsideration of the present structure of Confederation" (1972 General Council).

As the General Council met in Calgary in 1977, it was very aware that the Parti Québécois, having won the November 1976 election, was preparing for a referendum sometime in the future. The church reiterated its support for the democratic right of peoples to self-determination and in that context recognized that

> this new context offers an opportunity to grow in our comprehension of what constitutes a human right. We expect protection for the rights of individuals, the right to a fully human life, the right to a personal cultural identity, the right to participate in social, economic, and political decisions, the right to express opinions differing from those of the majority. But we also call attention, as did the General Council in 1972, to collective rights, to the rights of communities and peoples. In this we include the right to take what measures are necessary for collective survival and fulfillment. (1977 General Council)

At the same time within Quebec, the Francophones represent the majority and have within their boundaries various minorities who similarly have rights that need to be respected. "We call for safeguards of both individual and collective rights in a situation full of conflicting interests." The 1977 statement recognized that "no solutions are ideal. New political solutions bring with them new political problems" (1977 General Council).

The constitutional discussion was seen as being broader than just a debate between Quebec and Canada.

> It is vital in the entire debate that other groups of people in this multicultural country not be ignored ... the many issues concerning the rights of the native peoples, minorities and immigrants come crowding in for attention, and must be discussed and dealt with. A reworking of the Canadian Constitution would provide an exceptional opportunity to take these other groups into consideration, and to respond to the native peoples' demands for justice, in particular. (1977 General Council)

The church acknowledged that conflict was inevitable but saw that as an opportunity for growth and participation and not as a tragedy or reason for avoidance. "We know that there must be a solution worked out in the context of a political process of which conflict is an essential element. Christians believe God acts in history, therefore Christians are urged to view the present political struggle in the light of God's living Presence in history and to participate in it on the basis of this faith" (1977 General Council).

In August of this year, 1980, several months after the Quebec Referendum, General Council was meeting in Halifax and again turned its attention to the Canada-Quebec debate. The church again reiterated the vital importance of the involvement of many participants in the discussions on the future of Canada.

> The heart of the matter within the process of designing the future is the recognition of the right to self-determination of peoples in Canada without prejudging the eventual structural and constitutional result. This involves the acceptance of minorities as responsible participants in building the future .... Unilateral action in designing solutions to problems, without adequate participation, would only demonstrate the attitude against which minorities have protested. (1980 General Council)

RIGHTS OF MINORITIES

Let us turn briefly to several other minority groups the rights of whom the United Church has been concerned with and whose voices seem not to have been heard so far in this discussion. As the Canadian government in 1972 was preparing Bill C-25, the Canadian Human Rights Act, the Department of Church in Society of the United Church urged that several further categories be included on the basis of which discrimination would be prohibited in employment, accommodation, and access to services. Those categories were "physical handicap," "mental and emotional handicap" and "sexual orientation." We were pleased that "physical handicap" was included in the Act but disappointed that it related only to employment.

We are aware that the Advisory Committee of the Canadian Organization on the International Year of Disabled Persons 1981 is encouraging the government to amend Article 15, Clause 1, to include "physical and mental disability." We support their efforts. Physically and mentally handicapped persons have experienced discrimination for years but with next year designated as the International Year of Disabled Persons, the timing is particularly critical for such protection to be extended.

The inclusion of "sexual orientation" is admittedly a more controversial though no less important area. Though there continues to be differences of understanding about homosexuality in Canadian society and in the church, there nevertheless is a growing consensus of the need to have "sexual orientation" as one of the categories on the basis of which discrimination is to be prohibited. Mr. Gordon Fairweather, the Canadian commissioner of human rights, has long advocated that the government amend the Act to make such an inclusion. We support him and others who argue that the proposed Charter of Rights and Freedoms include "sexual orientation" as one of the grounds on which discrimination is to be prohibited.

Three of the most deprived groups within our society, with respect to protection under human rights legislation, are refugees, immigrants and the inmates of both penal and mental institutions.

If Canada is to be a just country, and to be seen as such in the eyes of the world, then justice must extend to all, and not exclusively to those who are holders of full and intact Canadian citizenship.

(i)   The provision of cities of refuge was written into the law of ancient Israel (Numbers 35:14). We would like to see it written into Canadian human rights legislation (entrenched or otherwise) that political refugees whose bona fides are established by the United Nations high commissioner for refugees may find asylum in Canada as a right. In the proposed Charter of Rights and Freedoms a section to this effect could strengthen the universal cause of human rights and serve as a model for other countries.

(ii) A measure of the justice of every country is its hospitality and fairness to newcomers. Will the Charter of Rights and Freedoms be specific with regard to the rights of immigrants before they achieve full citizenship; e.g., will it be stated that immigrants are to have all the human rights accorded full citizens? Will the rights of illegal immigrants be also stated?

(iii) Offenders of the law and the mentally disturbed are still persons. Is it enough to write into law that "everyone has the right not to be subjected to any cruel and unusual treatment or punishment" (Section 12)? Does not this section need some strengthening by mentioning the right to normal levels of health care, exercise and sanitation; the right to communicate with family; and the right of access to legal counsel and to members of Parliament or provincial legislatures?

THE RIGHT TO A BASIC STANDARD OF LIVING AND SOCIAL SECURITY

It encourages us to learn that the proposal to guarantee equalization is not a matter of contention between the government of Canada and the provincial governments, or between provincial governments. The practice of equalization is one of the distinctive features of Canadian polity and is a development that has been healthy for Canadian unity and a sense of national identity.

The need for equalization through taxation and sharing measures is obvious in a federal country where the natural and human resources to meet the needs of people are distributed unevenly. While it is important to provide a balance between regions through equalization grants, the fundamental concern is to ensure that all individuals and families across the country are brought up to a basic physical standard of living and are assured of basic services related to health, education and old age.

For over a decade the United Church of Canada has supported the concept of the guaranteed annual income and other related income security measures. In addition we have supported medicare, social housing, and employment opportunity programs.

If there is to be a constitution which guarantees human rights and equalization, it is our opinion that the section on equalization must have a footing in the Charter of Rights and Freedoms with a section on the rights of individuals and families to a basic standard of living and social security. (See Article 25 Universal Charter of Human Rights.)

A charter of human rights should properly include the right to work, the right to a minimum standard of housing, the right to a minimum standard of nutrition and the right to a minimum income. Other rights are hollow without these rights, and in turn the denial of basic living standards and services becomes the source of extremism and disunity.

THE RIGHTS OF WORKERS TO JOIN OR FORM UNIONS AND TO JOIN IN COLLECTIVE ECONOMIC ACTION

The right of workers to join or form unions is basic. The denial or suppression of workers' rights to (a) become part of a collective bargaining unit or (b) withhold labour during a legal strike, is indispensable in a free society.

These rights should be ensured in a framework of law that will protect both the workers within a particular enterprise and the larger public. We do not minimize the complexities that surround the guarantee of these rights. Every right is a standard to be upheld in the context of competing rights. We contend, nevertheless, that workers in every sector of the economy have the right to enter into collective bargaining associations for their mutual protection and benefit. States which suppress the rights associated with collective bargaining inevitably go on to suppress other human rights. The whole fabric of human rights is weakened unless these rights are ensured. (See Article 23 (4), Universal Declaration of Human Rights.)

SUMMARY

1. The Executive of the General Council of the United Church of Canada believes that the creation of a Canadian Constitution that will reflect the aspirations of both majorities and minorities can be best achieved through an unhurried process of participation by many groups.

2. Section 24 (or another section) of the proposed Constitution should set forth, in detail, guarantees with respect to the aboriginal and treaty rights of Native Peoples. Representatives of aboriginal nations should be full members of all future constitutional talks.

3. A Charter of Rights and Freedoms should include sections on the rights of refugees, immigrants, and inmates of penal and mental institutions. The rights of the physically and mentally disabled should be stated. Discrimination on the basis of sexual orientation should be prohibited.

4. The basic purpose of equalization should be identified in the Charter of Rights and Freedoms under a section on the right to minimum standards of housing, nutrition, income and services.

5. A Charter of Rights and Freedoms cannot serve its intended purpose without including a section on the rights of workers to join unions and take collective economic action.

FURTHER READING

Le référendum: un enjeu collectif. Montreal: Fides, 1979.

The Roman Catholic Bishops of Quebec. *Building a Better Tomorrow.* Montreal: 1980.

The United Church of Canada, Department of Church in Society. *Issue 11, Quebec: A Province 'Pas comme les autres'* (1976).

The United Church of Canada, Department of Church in Society. *Issue 22, Canada/Quebec: Where the Roadmap Ends* (1979).

SECTION VI
POPULATION, IMMIGRATION
AND REFUGEES

As was the case with several of the issues dealt with above, it was a government initiative which prompted a renewed religious response to immigration policies and practices. In February, 1975, the federal minister of manpower and immigration tabled in Parliament a four-volume *Green Paper on Immigration* which recommended, among other things, that the flow of immigrants to Canada be related more closely to the employment needs of this country. Many religious organizations submitted briefs to the Special Joint Committee of Parliament (Senate and House of Commons) which was established to study this Green Paper and make recommendations to the government. The first document in this section is the Brief of the Canadian Catholic Conference of Bishops to this Committee (1975). The bishops criticize the Green Paper for its assumptions as much as for its conclusions, and they call for a better understanding of migration and a less selfish Canadian stance towards potential immigrants.

The principal church agency in the immigration debate was the Inter-Church Project on Population, formed in 1973 to promote public discussion on population issues. ICPOP conducted an extensive public educational program around the Green Paper, which was funded by the Ministry of Manpower and Education. In their report to the Ministry, they reiterate and extend the Catholic bishops' criticisms of the Green Paper and make a number of proposals for changes in Canadian immigration policy.

In response to such criticisms, the federal government did make certain modifications to the Green Paper proposals before introducing legislation to revise the Immigration Act. While welcoming some of these changes, ICPOP and the Inter-Church Committee on

Human Rights in Latin America both felt that the legislation was still defective, especially regarding refugees. Based on their experience with Chilean refugees, ICCHRLA contended that political refugees should not have to satisfy normal immigration criteria. Since the new Immigration Act came into effect in March, 1978, the churches have continued to press for better treatment of refugees. The Refugee Concerns Project of the Canadian Council of Churches presented a brief to the minister of employment and immigration in May, 1980, which contained specific proposals for more just treatment of refugees. This is one issue where the churches' recommendations and actions have exercised some influence on government policy, as was evident during the exodus of the "Boat People" from Vietnam and Kampuchea in 1979-80. Church sponsorship of refugees at this time shamed the government into greatly increasing its quota of refugees for those years.

15 · BRIEF TO THE SPECIAL JOINT COMMITTEE OF THE SENATE AND OF THE HOUSE OF COMMONS ON IMMIGRATION POLICY*

THE CANADIAN CONFERENCE OF CATHOLIC BISHOPS, 1975

INTRODUCTION

This brief is submitted as a contribution to the public opinion upon which you are to report to Parliament. As we understand your mandate, you are exploring what kind of society we want for the future. Mr. Andras has pointed out that this far-reaching question underlies the government's more specific inquiry into Canadian views about immigration and population policies. While there will be other stages in this public discussion, your report will have a central role in shaping subsequent discussion. For this reason we want to add our contribution to the other viewpoints that you are hearing and weighing.

Our brief will reflect the way we understand God's Word and the social teachings of the Church. From this starting point, we hold that migration is a right, not merely a privilege. As Pope John XXIII said in his letter, *Pacem in Terris*, every human being must have the right to freedom of movement and of residence at home, and, for just reasons, the right to emigrate to other countries and take up residence there. For, the fact that one is a citizen of a

---

* Copyright © CCC, 1975.

particular state does not detract in any way from membership in the human family, nor from citizenship in the world community and common ties with all persons.[1] Thus we see today that we are all called more and more to become a people without frontiers. Migrants, therefore, whether they move within Canada or come from beyond our shores, have a right to be received not as strangers but as sisters and brothers, with respect for their nationality and their own culture, and with no discrimination, whether based on race or social or economic condition.[2]

In particular, our brief will further develop the basic principles outlined in the recent "Pastoral Statement on Immigration and Population Policies" by our Episcopal Commission for Social Affairs. As expressed there, one of our major concerns is that immigration policies for the future be approached as an aspect of overall planning for the redistribution of power and wealth, opportunities and amenities. For the essence of migration is that people move in search of better life chances. People are prompted to migrate to Canada and within this country largely because they experience socio-economic disparities. Thus, the redistribution of wealth, not the control or exclusion of people, is the long-range goal towards which we should aim in building the kind of future society we want.

In this spirit, then, we shall offer our views as pastors and citizens. Much of our information about the current debate has come through our participation in the Inter-Church Project on Population. We also draw on what we have learned from the news media, the minutes of your committee, and other related sources.

REVIEW OF DEBATE

Potentially, the current discussion about immigration and population policies could become a great upsurge of creative thinking about the future. It seems from what they say that this is what people really want. People worry that the times are somehow out of joint. They express increasing concern that if creative new steps are not taken, the lot of future generations will be bleak indeed. But if there is this deep longing for fresh thinking, is it being satisfied in the current discussion? To date it does not seem so, and several explanations for this can be suggested.

During your cross-country hearings, members of your committee frequently emphasized that the government's Green Paper is only a discussion starter, not a policy statement. Yet the Green Paper has become the predominant factor in defining the situation for this debate and so limiting it. People have tended to agree or disagree with the Green Paper, but hardly ever to go beyond it. Like the Green Paper itself, this debate rarely has looked beyond Canada's present or recent immigration laws and regulations, or those of some comparable nation. Those who have been identified and given special place as experts on immigration policies have discussed details of familiar concepts more frequently than they have explored new ones.[3] There has been a marked lack of critical analysis of popular assumptions and conventional opinions, and a distinct scarcity of proposals for alternative perspectives. Past and present experience seems thus to stifle any imagination that might give rise to new approaches.

This tendency, which in a general way characterizes both the briefs you heard and the questions your committee posed to witnesses, has been reinforced by the news media, which seem to have been less than industrious about seeking out views other than those immediately generated by the Green Paper.[4]

For all its importance for the future, this then is a debate that so far has remained largely boxed into its initial framework. It is one of your responsibilities to try to take it beyond such limits. In particular, we hope you will see your task as more than just proposing details of a new Immigration Act that seems suited for today's conditions in Canada. These conditions themselves must be rigorously examined for the sake of the future that is to be built. As a contribution to this, our brief will have more to say about today's conditions than about details of a new Immigration Act.

Such a new Act, in turn, must *not* be written and administered as an instrument of Canadian self-interest and protectionism. Rather, let us make it an expression of our increasing openness and generosity, especially towards those immigrants and refugees who are the most deprived and in need of our solidarity and assistance. To this end, we affirm many of the suggestions you have received in other briefs, from churches and other groups, especially to separate immigration and manpower issues, to develop a clear and open policy on refugees, and to assure that there be no discrimination of any kind in practice as in principle.

RECOMMENDATIONS

Our recommendations have to do with the operating assumptions of your final report to Parliament. We are especially concerned that your report reach beyond the limited framework of the Green Paper to seek out fresh approaches to the issues of migration and the building of a future society.

Towards the writing of your final report, we have three sets of recommendations to offer:

1. dispel some popular myths about migration,

2. clarify the basic causes of migration,

3. contribute to goals for building a New Society.

Migration: Popular Myths

The current debate about immigration in Canada has given popularity to a number of myths. These myths foster the idea that migration—the movement of people—is a major cause of all our social problems. The immigrant, therefore, tends to be made the "scapegoat" of our social ills. In part, these myths were fostered by the operating assumptions of the Green Paper. At the same time, the news media have played a large role in popularizing them. Your Committee, in your report to Parliament, has a major responsibility to dispel and reject the following myths about migration:

(i) that migration of peoples can be singled out as a significant cause of such problems as urban crowding, housing shortages, traffic congestion, pollution, etc. The primary causes of these problems are to be found in industrial strategies, land-holding systems, the money market, planned obsolescence, the promotion of consumption, etc. They will never be solved by efforts to control movements of people.

(ii) that increasing immigration is turning Canada into a racist society. This is a myth in the sense that the roots of racism are far deeper than present patterns of immigration. The exclusion of strangers will not eliminate selfishness and hatred, nor put an end to covert racial discrimination that is an expression of these.

(iii) that immigration explains rising unemployment in Canada. Cyclical patterns of unemployment have to do with industrial planning in this country and our failure to establish and maintain a stable and equitable economy.

(iv) that future immigration will cause a rapid depletion of Canada's valuable resources. The major causes of resource depletion lie elsewhere: in our industrial policies, in corporate production and marketing practices, and in our affluent consumption habits.

Migration: Basic Causes

The current immigration debate has either confused or neglected the real causes of migration. There has been a pronounced tendency to look only at the impact of migration on other social factors. As a result of such one-direction analysis, much attention is directed to the "effects" of migration but almost none to its causes. Neither the Green Paper nor the media have done much to identify and clarify the primary causes of migration. The question of what motivates people to move is of central importance to the study of immigration policies. We believe that the Committee has a major responsibility to set forth the primary causes of immigration.

We, therefore, recommend that your report to Parliament start from study of migration within Canada in order to understand the primary causes of immigration into this country. Thus, it will be seen:

(i) that people move primarily because they see their situation as one of need, deprivation and poverty. That is, people migrate because they sense they can do better somewhere else. People move in search of greater access to the necessities and opportunities of life.

(ii) that migration within Canada primarily reflects regional disparities and rural underdevelopment. People move from the hinterland and rural areas of Canada to the metropolitan centres where wealth and opportunities have been overly concentrated by political and economic decision-makers.

(iii) that immigration to Canada is largely caused by persistence of poverty, underdevelopment and oppression elsewhere in the world. Refugees flee oppression and danger. Immigrants come to escape conditions of poverty and exploitation in search of their fair share of opportunities and wealth.

(iv) that domestic and global industrial strategies both plan and exploit the socio-economic imbalances and inequalities that induce people to migrate. One example has been the promotion of immigration from depressed areas in order to make low-cost labour available in other areas.

(v) that it is not particularly fruitful to take the view that immigration is primarily the result of overpopulation—surplus people—elsewhere in the world. Such a view is at odds with the position taken at the 1974 World Population Conference by many Third World delegations. They held that their social ills, which motivate migration, should be seen as stemming from the rich-poor gap and their deprivation and underdevelopment. This view is reinforced if the causes of migration within Canada are taken as a basis for understanding immigration into this country.

Migration: New Approaches

The current immigration debate has given expression to various responses concerning the question of what kind of society we want to become. The debate has shown people to be frustrated over a host of societal problems. Underlying most of these problems is the sense of deprivation, poverty and powerlessness arising out of the inequitable distribution of resources within Canada and throughout the world.

Immigration law reform will not really touch these problems. What is required is the creation of a new social order in Canada and the world, based on a redistribution of wealth and power for the sake of justice and peace. This implies among other things that, "wherever possible, the work to be done should be taken to the workers, not vice versa."[5] Your Committee has a major responsibility to address these concerns.

We therefore recommend that your report to Parliament emphasize the following objectives regarding the future of Canadian society:

(i) that humanitarian values be given primacy over economic ones as a basis for future societal goals oriented toward the full development of peoples at home and in the world;

(ii) that immigration policies for the future be approached as an aspect of overall planning for the redistribution of wealth and power in Canada and the world at large;

(iii) that present patterns of urbanization—whereby two-thirds of Canada's population are concentrated in three or four metropolitan centres—be seen as neither inevitable nor irreversible;

(iv) that creative industrial strategies can and must be designed for the purpose of overcoming regional disparities and rural underdevelopment in Canada;

(v) that this country's governments, corporations and all citizens undertake a greater responsibility for creating a New International Economic Order.

CONCLUSION

We believe it possible to conclude that you can rightly reach beyond a narrow definition of the mandate you have from Parliament. Despite the fact that many witnesses discussed immigration only in a narrow and technical way, you heard ample testimony to conclude that what's wrong in this country is not an excess of immigrants. Conversely, you have heard considerable opinion that the management or restriction of immigration will have little to do with the difficulties we do have. Specifically, immigration curbs and controls will not solve unemployment, metropolitan congestion, housing shortages, loss of arable land, or damage to the environment. These conditions are signs of sinful greed and selfishness, of thoughtlessness, carelessness and mismanagement.

We urge you, instead of designing a legal stockade to keep Canada as it is, to aim at contributing to a global policy intended to help move all peoples to full realization of their capacities and worth as persons.

In this spirit, the content and application of a new Immigration Act for Canada should be based on generosity and openness, especially towards the most deprived and oppressed families and individuals who come to us as immigrants or refugees. This implies that you add your influential voices to a call for personal and collective change of heart, and fundamental changes in structures and systems, so that human relations can be normalized in justice and fraternity.

As economist Barbara Ward has written: "To live simply, to love greatly, to give without stinting, to see a brother in all mankind— this is no longer a remote theory of ethical behavior. It is the inescapable recipe of planetary survival."[6] To put such a challenge to the Parliament and people of this country is the only fitting conclusion to your summer's work.

16 · REPORT ON THE IMMIGRATION DEBATE

INTER-CHURCH PROJECT ON POPULATION, 1975

INTRODUCTION

This is a progress report on an inter-church venture into public discussion of Canadian immigration policy. In the House of Commons—on September 17, 1973, when he announced plans for an immigration policy review, and again on February 3, 1975, when he tabled a Green Paper—the Honourable Robert Andras, minister of manpower and immigration, emphasized the value of public discussion about immigration policy. He invited Canadians to take part. One of the ways in which representatives of Canadian churches accepted that invitation was as this report will describe.

This is a progress report, as distinct from a final one, because there will be continuing and even increasing inter-church involvement in this debate about the future of Canada's and the world's peoples. This report will indicate some lines of future inter-church activities....

Approach

In ICPOP since 1973 we have developed an approach to the question of Canadian population policy that we have carried forward into our involvement in the immigration policy debate. We pursue these three questions: Who is shaping Canadian policy? What are the visions, values and goals of the policy-makers? What alternatives have we to propose, from our understanding of our society and of our commitment to Christ?

We have found that too few people are deciding policy, and that their views, values and goals are too limited. As an alternative, we are trying to increase participation and to promote broader social justice perspectives, values and goals....

When he tabled the Green Paper, Mr. Andras also announced plans to involve provincial governments and to have hearings in each province. ICPOP therefore decided to emphasize provincial groupings and recruited an inter-church coordinator for each province. Our work on population issues was known to Manpower and Immigration officials who invited us to submit a public discussion project for federal funding. Our project was designed at a Winnipeg meeting of ICPOP's national staff and provincial coordinators in March of this year.

Our Vision

When we accepted the government's invitation, we realized we had assumed a difficult and challenging task. The spirit in which we did so, and our deep concern about immigration matters, are expressed in the title under which we proposed to group our various contributions to the immigration policy debate: It would be a *Rainbow Paper*. Why did we choose this title? Why do we turn to the biblical symbol from the story of Genesis 9? It is mainly for two reasons.

First of all, green is only one of the seven colours that constitute the full spectrum of the rainbow. We in ICPOP feel that the Green Paper has overtones that are too green—green being the colour of our dollar bill. Canada should not make immigration primarily a matter of dollars and cents: immigrants are welcome when the economy needs them, but unwelcome at the sign of a recession. It is our conviction that immigration is not just a matter of manpower. Our policy towards strangers coming to this land is a concern of all Canadians and thus of the whole government with all its departments.

This leads to the second reason that ICPOP proposes a Rainbow Paper on this matter. Responsibility in immigration policy is not only one of the government to this nation, nor of one nation to other nations; in the final analysis, it is our human responsibility to God. Hence in our report we speak about God, His people and His world.

When the rainbow appeared for the first time, God spoke words of promise. The earth would not be destroyed any more. The earth would serve man so that "seedtime and harvest ... shall not cease" (Genesis 8:22). In the rainbow, God offered man His *shalom*, His care for man's well-being and safety. Noah represents the new beginning of mankind; he is God's man for all the world. God accepts man as he is and invites him to make use of God's free gifts in a worthy manner. God uses the rainbow to remind Himself of this (Genesis 9:16), and not Noah or man. Now if God does this, should we, recipients of God's goodness, not strive to reflect His goodness to as many people as possible? What can be more truly human than the imitation of God's goodness? Hence in immigration matters not only the government but the entire people should be creatively and generously involved.

It is a long time since the rainbow appeared for the first time. God has maintained His rainbow policy throughout the ages. Furthermore, the Bible gives us a projection of the future. In the end, the rainbow of God's love will again be seen around His throne. The city of the future, the new Jerusalem, is an open city with gates on every side to receive a multitude without number from every nation (Revelation 21:12,14). This is the vision that has inspired and shaped our efforts to stir Canadians to support an immigration policy that is consistent with God's own rainbow policy....

THE CANADIAN DEBATE

... Looking back to its starting point, it is clear that the current immigration debate is especially bedevilled by a confusion of *policy* and *law*. This confusion is often expressed as a tension between long-run and short-run viewpoints, but it goes as far as basic social power questions about who decides just what is up for decision, and who controls the debate....

Confusion about what the government is driving at has plagued the public debate, frustrated citizens and thereby placed in jeopardy the process launched so expansively by Mr. Andras. While there may be no agreement about just how to define a policy, many Canadians clearly are concerned about "longer-term demographic economic, cultural and social objectives." Invited to study and discuss underlying policy, they found themselves being urged to hurry on to deal with detailed revisions of the law. The pressure in this regard, as expressed by the government's deadlines for the public debate, has produced negative reactions: skepticism on all sides, dissatisfaction and frustration and, too often, anger.

For our part, ICPOP entered the immigration debate with a point of view. Our perspective calls for social change in the direction of justice and fraternity. It calls for social goals and therefore new policies as a basis for new laws. To test our views, and as a contribution to the immigration debate, we are trying to rally people around our social justice perpective. Our future strategy is to continue to propose and to discuss a social justice perspective, a viewpoint that we hope to deepen and clarify in other rounds of public debate on immigration and population issues. As Mr. Andras said, "... at issue is nothing less than the future of Canada's population..." (Hansard, p. 2819).

The Green Paper

The Green Paper, though meant to be "a helpful basis for public discussion" (A.E. Gotlieb letter to Mr. Andras, December 1, 1974, reproduced in the Green Paper, vol. 1), proved to be a limiting factor. Much of the debate was about the Green Paper itself, not about policy options going beyond what it said.

We also found that the Green Paper is not a neutral discussion paper. It contains a rather narrow line of argument from a fairly clear set of assumptions. Its argumentation is suggestive of the "zero population growth" school of thought. Its underlying assumptions set the economy over people, look more to control and management of people than to human rights, define "quality of life" in economic terms, treat economic interests as the touchstone for policy decisions, define the national interest in static terms, and generally focus attention more on problems of maintaining the status quo than on possibilities for fruitful social change. Over all, its technical tone projects a view that immigration is an affair for experts rather than a topic for ordinary people talking about their own lives and those of possible new neighbours.

Moreover, we found that the Green Paper and some of the news media tended to popularize a number of myths about migrants: that migration of peoples can be singled out as a significant cause of such social problems as urban crowding, housing shortages, loss of arable land and environmental deterioration; that increasing migration is what causes racial distrust and hatred; that immigration explains rising unemployment; that future immigration poses a serious threat to natural resources. In fact, these would be Canadian problems even without immigration.

The news media ... did not generally probe deeply into policy issues. The headlines tended to shout about racism and to feature the small but disruptive demonstrations. At the provincial hearings, serious reflections about the state of affairs in Canada and about its future went largely unreported and therefore unshared.

Findings about the Real Issues

The Green Paper launched the idea that immigration has become a problem that Canadians should confront and solve through new policies and new legislation. It is our finding that other problems have been given priority by the people who have spoken in the immigration debate. We will list these as hinterland problems and metropolitan problems, although there is some overlap. (Montreal, Toronto and Vancouver are the centres of metropolitan areas in question. The Atlantic and Prairie provinces, and the rural areas of all provinces, make up Canada's hinterlands.)

Hinterland Problems

In general, inequality with the metropolitan areas is seen to be the fate of outlying areas. There are fewer kinds of jobs and few job opportunities over all. Prices on finished products tend to be higher. Housing is more difficult to find, mortgages and building programs being city-centred. Small businesses get little support and get taken over. The price of land is being forced upward—by offers to purchase (a "land grab"); by corporations (as a part of vertical integration); by wealthy Americans and Canadians seeking retirement havens; by speculators generally. There is also an inflation of fuel, machinery and other farm costs, so that young Canadians cannot easily settle on the land. Educational opportunities and social facilities are fewer, and indigenous cultural activities tend to be disparaged and so discouraged. The exodus of young people and the absence of young immigrants of various racial backgrounds tend toward an older, less cosmopolitan, more conservative hinterland population. Rural Quebec, in turn, has all these problems plus those of a linguistic nature, which amplify all the others. And hinterland Native People face total loss of land and lifestyle in the face of takeover by the energy industry.

Metropolitan Problems

While industrialization and urbanization creates metropolitan population concentration, this is a mixed blessing. Capital and people are centralized. There are more jobs and social amenities. But most of Canada's officially poor and unemployed are in these same metropolitan areas. Crime and violence are high and increasing. Personal isolation and loneliness are endemic. Many who are born in or move to the large cities say they would prefer to live elsewhere *if they could*. The costs of housing, food, clothing and cultural activities are not in fact reduced by the larger market. The large city, said by the Green Paper to be growing inevitably because of its attractiveness, is the same big city that is said by the Green Paper to be so beset with problems that no more immigrants should be allowed to go there.

The minutes of the Special Joint Committee show that all these, *and not immigration itself* were listed as the hinterland and metropolitan problems that many Canadians think should have priority of attention. This was also the finding of all provincial ICPOP groups. There is concern on the part of many Canadians in all parts of the country about city-centred industrialization as the dominant model for development. There is a resulting gearing of political, social and cultural factors to suit the urban model. The education system everywhere, even for Native children, is geared to urban corporate needs and values. Quebec's linguistic difficulties stem from the dominance of English as the language of the economy. The metropolitan mentality tends to the idea that bigness is best, a mind-set perhaps most evident in the notion that success equals maximization of material gain. Capital and, therefore, power being urban-centred, there is a resulting notion that this concentration is inevitable and irreversible. The sense of powerlessness that follows from this is to be observed in all areas of Canada. A lot of the frustration and anger shown at the summer hearings can be related to this.

Findings about Causes of Migration

ICPOP discussion animators found it helpful to examine internal Canadian migration as a way to understand why people want to move into Canada. People know why they leave hinterland areas of Canada. It is first of all because the metropolitan areas are favoured, economically and politically, and opportunities are in fact centred there—though many city dwellers do not share in them.

Alongside that general motivation for moving, other motives such as family reunification and sense of adventure also are to be found. Inversely, many in the large cities know that what brought them there was not an overwhelming love of large cities but the fact that they cannot make their living elsewhere under present economic arrangements in Canada.

From this, it is our finding that people tend to understand immigration in a new light when it is related to why people move within Canada. Regional disparity within Canada and its consequences are seen to have parallels in the divisions between rich and poor countries. Also, consideration of the scope of internal migration helps to put immigration into perspective. Data on migrant status from the 1971 census show that immigrants made up only 4 per cent of the total population while internal migrants comprised 19 per cent. (Cf. Warren E. Kalbeck, "Demographic Concerns and the Control of Immigration," *Canadian Public Policy*, Summer, 1975, p. 303.)

We found that people come to see—not universally but increasingly—that the policies underlying the metropolitan concentration of capital within Canada are part of policies directed to concentrating capital in industrializing countries such as Canada. It can be seen, for example, that Canada is presently industrializing and urbanizing because of policy decisions made by identifiable people since the 1870s. Entrepreneurs and politicians since that time have decided that Canada's future prosperity lies in industrialization and urbanization, not in rural and hinterland development on a resource base.

The subsequent settlement and particular development of the Prairies, and the consistent underdevelopment of the Maritimes, have resulted from the same decisions: the arrangement of Canada's hinterlands has been mainly on the basis of the decision to industrialize and so urbanize the Montreal, Toronto, Hamilton area.

The continuous concentration of population, the refusal to disperse capital, do not happen because of inevitable economic laws. Things are so because that is the policy—the line of action adopted and pursued by some people. This, we find, *is* the basic Canadian population policy. It is also the basic immigration policy. People have been brought in or excluded mainly in terms of the manpower needs of urban industrialization, deliberately planned.

As for laws, we find that they clearly flow from and express policy. Thus the dominance of a policy of centralized industrialization as a basis for Canadian development is reflected in all legislation. The reasons currently suggested by the Green Paper for possible change in the Immigration Act show that no basic socio-economic policy change is anticipated. The urbanized industrial economy remains the touchstone; metropolitan viewpoints dominate.

Yet, it is our finding that the population problems we have in Canada—metropolitan overdevelopment and hinterland underdevelopment—can be solved precisely because they have come about because of direct human decisions and planning, private and public. That is, there is a possibility of personalizing what is going on, and making it understandable, as a first step to making it manageable.

PROPOSALS

Regarding Citizen Participation in Policy Reviews

1. *Provide sufficient time and information.* Citizen participation in policy discussions is "underdeveloped." The immigration debate so far shows the problems of poor timing and of insufficient discussion material. Now these problems seem to be about to be duplicated regarding the National Demographic Policy Secretariat's proposed program of public information and participation. Although announced last February 3, no citizen awareness of this project has yet been developed.

2. *Reveal who does influence policy.* Citizens have the impression that they have no influence, and that a business elite always prevails. Perhaps daring, certainly novel, but necessary to allay citizen skepticism, would be revelation by government of just who does influence each step of policy decisions. The policy issues for the future are too awesome to be left subject to conventional bureaucratic secrecy.

Regarding Population and Immigration Policy

1. Population and immigration policy for the future should be part of planning, from *now* on, for a new economic and social order in Canada and for the world as a whole. The economic policy pursued in Canada since the 1870s is clearly inadequate. It is the basis of the system that creates poverty, as the Senate report, *Poverty in Canada*, said.

2. In working for a new socio-economic order, Canadian governments at all levels should make the needs of the poorest people in

the country and in the world the yardstick for measuring more specific policies and plans.

3. We propose an immigration policy that starts from the concept of migration (movement) as a basic right, which can be qualified in the light of the rights of others but is never seen as just a social contract privilege.

4. We propose an immigration policy that seeks to distribute immigrants in Canada not by legal restraints but by decentralization of real opportunities for both Canadian citizens and newcomers.

5. We propose a Canadian immigration policy of particular openness to the poor, unskilled and most-threatened immigrants and refugees. Their settlement training and personal fulfillment as fellow citizens should be a specific Canadian goal.

Proposals on a New Immigration Act

1. Reflecting policy proposals sketched above, a new Immigration Act should start from the concept of migration as a human right, not just a privilege.

2. The law and regulations under the law should favour and facilitate entry into Canada of Third World immigrants who are poorest, least skilled and most in need of new life chances.

3. To facilitate this, immigration offices abroad should be drastically redistributed, particularly by an increase in the number of offices in Asia, South America and Africa.

4. A new Act should guarantee all refugees immediate temporary asylum and subsequent immigrant opportunities, without any delay or discrimination.

5. A new Act should guarantee North America's Native Peoples uninhibited border privileges according to their tribal or other aboriginal customs.

6. A new Act should specifically state that racial considerations may not be taken into account in any discretionary judgements by immigration officials.

7. A new Act should establish a separate Ministry of Immigration, without industrial manpower responsibilities, and related to all other departments.

8. The concept of family should be defined broadly so as not to discriminate against peoples of other cultures, especially of Third World countries.

9. The category of prohibited immigrants should be greatly reduced, especially with regard to curable and controllable illnesses whose victims could have opportunities for cure and rehabilitation in Canada.

10. Intensive training of Canadian immigration officers should be guaranteed, with special emphasis on skills and sensitivities related to matters left to their discretion. Information and counselling in countries of origin should be stressed.

11. Appeal procedures should take special account of the possibilities of discretionary errors and, more generally, should emphasize prompt recourse and guaranteed rights comparable to those of citizenship.

12. The practice of importing non-immigrant "guest" workers should be curtailed. Anyone employed in Canada should have a choice to become a citizen. Sanctions should be applied to prevent employers recruiting "guest" workers.

13. Especially in view of their susceptibility to exploitation as cheap labor, so-called illegal immigrants presently in Canada should be accorded new and liberal opportunities for immigrant status.

14. To prevent insofar as possible the build-up of illegal cases, tourist or visitor controls should be improved.

15. Students from overseas attending accredited Canadian educational institutes should be accorded a special immigrant status for a limited term.

16. Services to immigrants, such as language training, should be made a priority of government, industry and all citizens. Special aid and encouragement should be directed to non-government providers of such immigrant services.

17. The practice of changing immigration policy and law by Order-in-Council changes in regulations should be curtailed.

CONCLUSIONS

We undertook to stimulate discussion of population and immigration policies. We have done that especially by proposing to look at immigration as a matter of social justice, not as an industrial strategy. While we have tried to express our viewpoint in terms of new policies and laws, our main concern is to contribute to the building of a new socio-economic order.

We realize that the principles we affirm call for a great deal of both "education" and "conversion" on the part of all of us in Canada. We pledge ourselves to work at educating and converting ourselves and others. Of our government we ask that it join, and not delay, such efforts.

17 · REFUGEE CONCERNS: A BRIEF TO THE HONOURABLE LLOYD AXWORTHY, MINISTER OF EMPLOYMENT AND IMMIGRATION

THE REFUGEE CONCERNS PROJECT COMMITTEE, CANADIAN COUNCIL OF CHURCHES, 1980

INTRODUCTION

This document has been prepared by the members of the Refugee Concerns Project of the Canadian Council of Churches. Our objective is to promote equitable and compassionate reception and treatment for refugees seeking refuge in Canada. We believe that our experiences give us much to contribute to the development of appropriate Canadian refugee policies and programs.

We speak as witnesses to the Gospel and as participants in the struggle for social justice for all, especially the refugees of the world. We have participated in a turbulent history as people both seeking and providing refuge. This turmoil continues and even grows worse.

For many years, concerned groups in Canada acted on behalf of both the refugees and the receivers of refugees. Submissions, briefs and verbal presentations have been made regarding Canadian immigration and population concerns: foreign policy; human rights in Latin America; refugee sponsorship, criteria, admission and determination procedures; information for refugee claimants; and Canadian policy towards refugees from Latin America.

We believe that these interventions have helped to bring about a more equitable and humane refugee policy in Canada. Refugee status has been specifically recognized in the Immigration Act; special humanitarian programs for Europe, South-East Asia and Latin America have been developed; some steps have been taken to improve the processes for the determination of refugee status in Canada; and thousands of Canadians have participated in the sponsorship of Indochinese refugees. The following brief presents concerns still in need of our attention and combined efforts.

SEPARATION OF REFUGEES AND IMMIGRANTS

The differences between a refugee and an immigrant, although acknowledged in the Immigration Act, are not reflected or carried forward in the procedures that regulate their admission to Canada. A humanitarian response to the situation, needs and human rights of refugees requires more than just a few privileges we may accord them. Since refugees are not immigrants either by definition or by the situations which force them to flee their country, we believe that there are compelling reasons for the complete separation of refugee and immigration policies and programs.

As during the immigration debate of the 1970s, Canadian church representatives continue to insist that *refugees should be separated from immigrants, and given special status and treatment.* We believe our position has been confirmed by recent Canadian experience with refugee quotas, admissions, sponsorships and assistance, and determination of refugee status procedures.

REFUGEE QUOTAS

At present, the refugee quota is linked in several ways with the immigration level set each year under provisions of Section 7 of the Act. This means that humanitarian considerations for refugees and other such persons get caught up in the arithmetic of the economic considerations that dominate decisions about immigration levels. The refugee movement has been controlled as a percentage of the annual immigration level. The rights and needs of refugees do not figure in the calculations reported to Parliament regarding immigration levels for 1979 or 1980. Moreover, the *Report to Parliament on Immigration Levels: 1980* said the federal government is exploring options to "provide more scope ... for the admission of immigrants who are selected against economic criteria." We are concerned that that may mean providing less scope for the admission of refugees who live in fear of persecution, torture and death. We acknowledge that for the admission of refugees, some planning is required. *However, in determining the scope of a refugee plan, the primary consideration should be the willingness to act quickly and adequately in sudden crisis situations which produce refugees. Another key consideration should be response to world resettlement needs in respectable and sufficient numbers reflecting Canada's vast natural and human resources.*

SELECTION CRITERIA

The Immigration Act acknowledges that the Canadian government is a contracting party to the United Nations Convention relating to the Status of Refugees, and mentions the intention to follow our humanitarian traditions. However, the Act and Regulations fail to identify selection criteria for refugees which recognize the unique needs of the refugee. Like any immigrants, they are selected on the basis of likelihood to resettle successfully (and government officials define "success").

In briefs and presentations to the Standing Committee on Labour, Manpower and Immigration during 1977, the churches made a thorough critique of the selection process for refugees. The churches questioned the priority given by Canada to the criterion of successful establishment and identified criteria more appropriate to refugee needs: priority should be given to applicants who are in danger of persecution, incarceration, torture or death. These considerations should be given more weight than factors such as the occupational demand in the applicant's profession or the ability to speak either English or French. The churches thus submitted that, while recognizing the long-run importance for immigrants of successful establishment in Canada, for refugees other criteria should have priority. After considerable debate, the Standing Committee on Labour, Manpower and Immigration accepted the proposals and the suggested amendment was made. It was a major disappointment to learn that the new Immigration Act and Regulations did not incorporate these refugee selection criteria.

We return to these points. *We believe that the selection of refugees should be based on criteria that give priority to resettling people in fear of persecution, torture and death.*

ECONOMIC REFUGEES

In addition to direct persecution, many people are forced to flee because of economic oppression. For example, in countries that are struggling for economic survival or have social, political or human rights struggles, people who disagree with their government's policies may find themelves unable to survive. What may appear to be an economic motive often involves a political element that precipitates the need to flee. *Canada needs to be sensitive to these situations, and should attempt to develop specific criteria for these refugees. The criteria should apply to people from all areas where political and economic oppression interface.* Response to these refugees should follow an adequate response to directly endangered people. *The Canadian government's first concern must be for refugees in fear of persecution, torture and death.*

SPONSORSHIP, RESETTLEMENT AND JOINT ASSISTANCE—A SHARED RESPONSIBILITY

Sponsorship

Sponsorship provides an opportunity for many Canadians to respond in some tangible way to the overwhelming needs of the world's refugees. This program has brought into play a number of dynamics that we believe should be acknowledged and enhanced in a continuing partnership program for resettlement of refugees.

The government and the sponsoring groups have complementary and interdependent tasks. At the onset, the initiative of the government was essential for the development of the sponsorship program. This principle is clearly recognized by the voluntary sponsoring groups; *we urge the government to clearly acknowledge its role in the partnership.* We welcome the announcement on April 2 which re-established some government responsibility. This decision begins to restore the credibility of the government as a true partner with the voluntary sector, and can, together with a satisfactory consultative process, ensure continuing support of sponsoring and assisting groups, and their involvement in ongoing and repeated responsibilities.

Resettlement Programs

The intake of Indochinese refugees within the last year has challenged the resources and services of private individuals and voluntary and government agencies. The speed and efficiency with which we have responded to resettlement needs marks a proud moment in our refugee history. These experiences have provided all involved individuals, groups and agencies with expertise in helping refugees become quickly orientated to Canadian life. Work on behalf of the refugees has also led to the identification of gaps in settlement services which should now be collectively addressed.

We are concerned about such matters as:

• the establishment of uniformly available services within all sponsoring communities;

• the availability of the same language and training services and emergency health provisions for all refugees;

• effective responses to resettlement concerns such as urban migration, racism and refugee-sponsor breakdowns;

• the need to augment settlement policies and programs, recognizing the special physical and mental conditions of many refugees.

We recognize that beyond the provision of specific services, there must be broad community support and assistance for all refugees. We pledge ourselves to working with other groups to this end.

Joint Assistance

We welcome the intention of the government to aid some of the most needy refugees through a program of joint assistance. This program was incorporated into master agreements signed last year. The subsequent long delay in implementing the program has been a cause of great concern. Consultations between the government and the churches have yet to produce mutual agreement on matters of selection criteria, participating groups, and shared expenses. We are, however, most anxious to proceed and *urge the government to give immediate high priority to the joint assistance program.*

We welcome the information that the program will be available for assistance to refugees from all areas of the world. In addition to the well-known needy cases in South-East Asia there are a smaller number of difficult and forgotten cases in Argentina and other areas of Latin America. We will seek to assist as many of these refugees as possible.

INDOCHINA AREA CONCERNS

The Indochinese refugee program has reconfirmed a number of church positions regarding sponsorship and response to those refugees most in need of our support. In general, we welcome your April 2 announcement that the federal government will sponsor an additional 10,000 Indochinese refugees this year and also enable private sponsorships to continue. In the present state of affairs, your quota of 10,000 appears to us to be a minimum figure. *Hence the importance of allowing private sponsorships to continue, over and above the government quota.* We assure you of our continuing determination to encourage private sponsorships for refugees not only from South-East Asia, but from all areas of resettlement need.

However, we will not be satisfied by sizeable quotas alone. *This country should give priority to aiding the most needy.* Therefore, the government's selection criteria and procedures are of crucial concern to us. Because refugees are defined as immigrants, there is a grave risk that priority will in fact be given to refugees deemed to be "most likely to resettle successfully," rather than those in most need. In this way, during 1979 the more difficult Indochinese cases were scarcely touched; and they are now to be included only in the slow-moving "joint assistance" program. This is not good enough. Likewise, we are concerned about the low numbers of Kampucheans and Laotians admitted last year, although they make up the majority in the Thai camps. Our concern in this regard extends to the displaced Kampucheans in Thailand as well as in Vietnam. Even if not formally considered as "refugees" according to some political definitions, they should not be entirely excluded from Canadian generosity. *We ask you to facilitate private sponsorships to enable family reunifications for them.*

LATIN AMERICA AREA CONCERNS

The pattern of gross violation of human rights and the institutionalized use of torture, arbitrary detention and disappearance exists in many Latin American countries. Although the national composition of refugees fleeing these situations in Latin America fluctuates, the need for response and assistance remains constant. Official persecution for political and religious reasons continues, for hundreds in Chile and Paraguay, and for thousands in countries such as Guatemala, El Salvador, Argentina and Uruguay.

The current number of refugees from Latin America accepted through Canada's annual refugee plan does not constitute an adequate response to the refugee resettlement needs of that area. *We urge the government to accept a minimum of 3,000 Latin American refugees during 1980.*
This recommendation recognizes that the acceptance of a significantly larger number of Latin American refugees necessitates an increase of Canadian resources in Latin America, and an improvement of the procedures which now impede the process of refugee selection and resettlement. Past representation by the churches on behalf of the refugees seeking resettlement from Brazil have found little response. The constant UNHCR caseload of 200-300 refugees consists of 50 per cent Argentinians and 40 per cent Uruguayans. The number and the percentage of Uruguayans continue to rise while those from other countries remain stable. Each month about 40 new cases are added to the list of those seeking a third country.
The length of the Canadian process and the inflexibility regarding changes in this process resulted in the Canadian government accepting fewer than 10 of these refugees in 1978 and 1979. The result has been demoralizing to the point where neither the refugee-aiding agencies nor the refugees in Brazil look to Canada as a country willing to accept them.
Recognizing the persecution and suffering undergone by those refugees seeking temporary asylum in Brazil, and the present lack of trust in Canada's willingness and ability to respond, *we recommend that the Canadian government take strong initiative to develop faster and more flexible procedures for receiving refugees in Brazil.*
For people who need to leave their country quickly to escape torture, detention and possible death, the visitor's visa requirement imposed on Chile and El Salvador creates serious problems. The escape route to Canada is now virtually closed. *We urge that El Salvador and Chile be restored to the list of countries exempted from visa requirements. We further recommend that the Canadian government not impose visa requirements on any country with serious human rights problems,* such as Argentina, Guatemala, Paraguay and Uruguay.

POLITICAL PRISONERS

Although political prisoners have been released from several Latin American countries this year, political detentions have continued in Chile and Paraguay. In 1979, over 1,200 people were detained in Chile—the majority for relatively short terms. A marked deterioration in the political situation in Colombia, Guatemala and El Salvador has resulted in mass detentions, kidnappings and killings. Argentina and Uruguay continue to have the largest number of political prisoners in Latin America. Both countries deny the majority of the prisoners their constitutional rights to exchange imprisonment for exile.

We heartily endorse the initiatives which were taken by the government of Canada to develop political prisoners programs in Chile and Argentina. The Chilean program has been more or less completed, but of 100 visas offered for Argentinian political prisoners only seven persons have actually arrived in Canada, due to the slowness of the Argentinian authorities in releasing the prisoners. Argentinian human rights organizations and the committees of relatives of the political prisoners emphasize the importance of the program in providing moral and material support and protecting the lives of many political prisoners.

We recommend that the Canadian government publicly state its strong concern regarding the Argentinian government's failure to release those prisoners with promises of Canadian visas, and make direct representation to the Argentinian authorities regarding its lack of cooperation.

We recommend that the Canadian government make a firm commitment to increase its quota for Argentinian political prisoners held under executive power as soon as the 100 visas now offered have been issued.

We recommend that the Canadian government cancel the requirement of interviewing prisoners before offering them visas as this step seems to serve no effective nor productive purpose in the Argentinian situation.

We recommend that the Canadian authorities investigate the possibilities of responding to a small number of Uruguayan political prisoners, particularly those whose release would be facilitated through the offer of a visa to a third country, or who, upon release, must find a third country quickly in order to prevent a further detention.

CLAIMING REFUGEE STATUS IN CANADA

Church groups, humanitarian organizations, lawyers and doctors are directly involved with people who are claiming refugee status in Canada. The experiences of these individuals and organizations have produced the conviction that legislative and administrative changes are essential for an improvement of existing determination procedures.

In March, 1979, the churches participated with a delegation of concerned legal, medical, labour and humanitarian organizations to present a brief to Mr. Cullen entitled *Recommended Changes in Canada's Refugee Status Determination Procedure.* We are encouraged by the fact that several of the recommended changes have been implemented. However, the major concern remains: a refugee claimant still has no right to an oral hearing. Such a person has the right only to apply in writing to the Immigration Appeal Board for a hearing. We firmly believe that credibility cannot be properly assessed without the benefit of an oral hearing. In order to ensure this right for a refugee claimant, and to ensure that refugee appeal cases are heard by a board that possesses the necessary expertise and special skills, *we strongly urge that the Refugee Status Advisory Committee either make a determination that a claimant is a refugee, or refer the case, if turned down, for an automatic oral hearing to a competent refugee review board, unless the case is obviously frivolous.*

As already noted, the churches believe that refugees have needs and rights which must be addressed outside of the considerations which influence immigration decisions. The principle of complete separation of immigration and refugee policies and programs which was recognized in the Refugee Status Advisory Committee should be carried through. *We support the establishment of a separate Refugee Review Board whose sole function shall be to hear and determine claims for refugee status referred to it by the Refugee Status Advisory Committee....*

FURTHER READING

Canadian Conference of Catholic Bishops. *Strangers in Our Midst.* Ottawa: 1979.

Frayne, Rev. Stuart A. *Immigration and Social Justice.* The Baptist Convention of Ontario and Quebec *Christian Alternatives*, 2 (1975).

Inter-Church Committee for Refugees. *Who Is My Neighbour? The Challenge of the Continuing Refugee Crisis.* Toronto: 1981.

Inter-Church Committee for Refugees. *Refugee Concerns Submission to the Sub-Committee of the Standing Committee on External Affairs and National Defence on Canada's Relations with Latin America and the Caribbean.* Toronto: 1982.

The United Church of Canada, Department of Church in Society. *Issue 3, Chilean Refugees: Canada's Reluctant Response* (1974).

The United Church of Canada, Department of Church in Society. *Issue* 7, *Work We Will Not Do...* (1975).

The United Church of Canada, Department of Church in Society. *Issue* 9, *The Politics of People: The Green Paper on Immigration* (1975).

SECTION VII
CANADA AND THE THIRD
WORLD

The attention paid to immigrants and refugees by the Canadian
churches is but one aspect of a far-reaching concern with global
issues. Several of the inter-church agencies deal specifically with
Canada's involvement in the Third World: the Inter-Church
Committee for World Development Education, GATT-Fly, the Taskforce on the Churches and Corporate Responsibility, the Inter-
Church Coalition on Africa, and the Inter-Church Committee on
Human Rights in Latin America. These groups attempt to analyze
and evaluate Canada's ambiguous role on the international scene
as both an exploiting country in relation to the Third World and
as exploited by the U.S.A. and multinational corporations. They
call for more justice in our dealings with Third World nations and
for greater firmness and self-reliance in relation to those who dominate us.

Most of the documentation produced by these agencies is not
explicitly ethical. They assume a moral concern for social justice,
but they seldom stop to analyze how and why Canada's political
and economic activities contravene the principles of religious ethics.
They are generally satisfied with the presentation of the appropriate factual information, in the hope that right-thinking individuals will draw the proper moral conclusions. The three selections
in this section do, however, analyze Canada's relations with the
Third World from the perspective of religious ethics. The first is
a statement by the leaders of Canada's five largest Christian churches
entitled, *Development Demands Justice* (1973). It covers a variety of
trade and aid issues as well as the need for changes in the Canadian
economic system to facilitate more just relations with other countries.

The second item is from the *Submission to the Canadian Ambassador to the 36th Session of the United Nations Commission on Human Rights* by the Inter-Church Committee on Human Rights in Latin America (1981). Ever since the 1973 military coup in Chile, Latin America has been a major focal point of the Canadian churches' involvement in international affairs, and ICCHRLA has been the principal church agency for this area of concern. In their *Newsletter* and other publications as well as their submissions to government bodies, they have demonstrated that their sources of information in Latin America, especially regarding human rights violations, are far superior to those of the Canadian government.

The other principal area of concern for the churches' international social justice activities is Southern Africa. Since its beginning, the Taskforce on the Churches and Corporate Responsibility has devoted much of its time and energy to the issues of Canadian trade and investment with the white-minority regimes in that area. In addition to its lobbying with governmental officials, TCCR has attempted to dissuade Canadian corporations and banks from financial dealings in these countries (see selection 6 above). In their brief to the secretary of state for external affairs and the minister of industry, trade and commerce (1981), they update earlier briefs to government on relations with South Africa and argue for a termination of certain specific policies and practices of the Canadian government which serve to buttress the apartheid system.

18 • DEVELOPMENT DEMANDS JUSTICE

CANADIAN CHURCH LEADERS, 1973

INTRODUCTION

As church leaders in Canada, we have come together for the purpose of making an urgent appeal to the Canadian people about the problems of world development.

We do not come with any special technical competence or solutions regarding the complex problems involved. We come instead with ethical questions about the values and goals underlying our present models for development. Our common concern for humanity throughout the world demands that justice be realized in the development of people and nations. This common ecumenical concern was clearly articulated recently by the general secretary of the World Council of Churches:

> We cannot speak of the church's mission to proclaim the gospel of Jesus Christ without seeing that the gospel has political implications. We cannot speak about renewal of persons and groups without facing the issues of power and authority, or of service without coming to grips with the struggle for justice.

We challenge the widespread assumption that the problems of development are solely or even mainly technical matters. On the contrary, the problems of development are primarily ethical questions pertaining to choices of social goals and human values. In our prevailing models for development, value choices have been made about "what constitutes the good life" and "what constitutes a good community." We invite our fellow Christians and other citizens to join us in a public discussion of the value choices underlying our models for development in Canada and the Western world.

We also challenge the assumption that leaders in government and business institutions alone have the prerogative to interpret the values and decide the goals of our development programs. All Canadian citizens should have the opportunity to participate in determining what our development goals as a nation should be. Therefore, we urge our fellow Christians and other citizens to join us in participating more actively in shaping new Canadian goals for world development.

The Development Gap: A Critical Problem of Injustice

The poor of the world, including the poor in Canada, are justly outraged by the widening gap that persists between those who "have" and those who "have not."

In Canada, the gap between the rich and the poor has not changed despite major expansions in our Gross National Product. If anything, the gap has widened. The top one-fifth of the Canadian population take home twice their share of the national income while the bottom one-fifth continue receiving only a third of their share.

In the world, it is the same story. Major increases in the aggregate wealth of the world have not narrowed the gap between the rich and the poor countries of this planet. One quarter of the world's population, including affluent Canadians, continue to control and consume three-quarters of this planet's finite resources and services.

This development gap between the rich and the poor can no longer be taken for granted "as the way things are." There is nothing "inevitable" about the realities of being "rich" and "poor" in the world today. Nor can the gap be explained away by references to divine law or the depths of nature. The gap is the product of our own making as men of history. We have the responsibility of choosing the kind of social order we want to develop as a human family.

The development gap is first and foremost an ethical problem. Our planet contains all the resources and services necessary to maintain a decent living for the present world population. Yet there are gross inequities in the distribution of these resources and services among the people of the world. The development gap is no less than a critical problem of injustice for mankind.

The causes of the development gap are many and complex. On the surface, it is clear that the gap itself is created and maintained by our prevailing models for development. In turn, these models for development are based on the economic system of the industrialized countries. (In our discussion of the industrialized countries here we are referring more specifically to the Western industrialized countries, including Canada.) Herein lies the major cause of the development gap between the rich and the poor. It is our economic system which is primarily responsible for the inequitable distribution of society's resources and services. The Special Senate Committee on Poverty in Canada reached the same conclusion when it declared in 1971:

> The economic system in which most Canadians prosper is the same economic system which creates poverty.... What society gives with the one hand it often takes away with the other.

Our established models for development, therefore, are firmly grounded in the economic system of the industrialized countries. Here, "development" is conceived mainly, if not exclusively, in economic terms. The primary goal is to maximize economic growth. The underlying assumption is that ever-expanding production and consumption is the road to the "good life." Moreover, it is commonly held that all people will eventually benefit from increases in the Gross National Product. According to this "trickle-down" theory of distribution, an increase in aggregate wealth will automatically result in benefits for everyone. In short, equity is believed to be a natural by-product of growth.

This model for development was imported as the paradigm for development in the Third World countries of Africa, Asia and Latin America. Following the disintegration of the colonial empires, most of the newly independent countries found themselves with a crippled economy dependent on either a single agricultural product (e.g., coffee) or a single raw material (e.g., tin). Following the industrialized model for development, the new countries explored various means for expanding their economic growth. Efforts were made to gain a reasonable share of the world market for their individual products and to encourage foreign investment and aid in their countries in order to acquire the capital requisite for economic development.

However, the desired goals for economic development were never achieved. The Third World countries soon learned that the rules of the "development game" were mainly formulated by the governments and corporations of the industrialized countries, including Canada. The rules were formulated for the main purpose of maximizing the economic growth of the industrialized countries. As a consequence, the amassed profits from foreign investment automatically became concentrated in the hands of the investors in the industrialized countries who owned the capital and the technological resources. At the same time, the profit margin of the poor countries in the Third World has been far too small to compete for the capital and technology required for their own indigenous economic development.

Of course, there have been exceptions to these rules in the "development game." But the general application of the rule is all too pervasive and true.

In playing the development game, the industrialized countries have employed a variety of institutional mechanisms for creating, maintaining and extending the gap between the rich and the poor. Among the major mechanisms have been the dominant patterns of (1) international trade, (2) corporate investment and (3) foreign aid.

1. **International Trade**: The first mechanisms are the dominant patterns of international trade. The industrialized countries, including Canada, dominate the trade patterns between nations through the exercise of their own economic and political power. Since the Second World War, there has been a steady deterioration in the terms of trade between the industrialized countries and their suppliers of agricultural and raw materials in the Third World.

On the one hand, the industrialized countries have repeatedly refused to pay adequate prices for basic agricultural commodities (e.g., coffee, rice, cocoa, tea, sugar) and raw materials (e.g., tin, copper, petroleum). On the other hand, the industrialized countries have increasingly charged the poor countries escalating prices for their finished products. For example, in 1954, Colombia could exchange 10 bags of coffee for one jeep. By 1967, the same jeep cost 39 bags of coffee. In other words, production in Colombia would have to increase four times in order to purchase the same amount of finished products from the industrialized countries.

2. **Corporate Investment**: A second institutional mechanism is the dominant pattern of corporate investment. Foreign-owned corporations from industrialized countries, including Canada, have invested a large amount of capital and technology in the countries of Africa, Asia and Latin America. Many of these corporations have received generous tax concessions as incentives for using their capi-

tal and technology to develop the kind of indigenous industry that would meet the development needs of the Third World country. However, most of these corporations have been mainly concerned with maximizing their own profits rather than the economic development of the Third World.

As a result of the patterns of corporate investment, many of the Third World countries have increasingly found themselves trapped in a state of economic dependence. They discovered that their control over their own raw materials and their own processes of industrialization was decreasing. Far more capital was leaving the country in the form of profits and tax concessions than was coming in through investments (an estimated three dollars for every dollar invested). Moreover, many of the entrepreneurial skills and resources in the country were going to the foreign companies rather than the development of indigenous industry. In effect, the needs of the foreign company were being met by the investment of capital and technology rather than the more basic needs of the country itself.

3. **Foreign Aid**: A third institutional mechanism is the dominant pattern of foreign aid. The dominant pattern has been "tied aid." The industrialized countries, including Canada, usually grant aid on a unilateral basis with the result that they can determine exactly what the aid will be used for and what the conditions of its use will be. The receiving country is usually required to use the aid grant for purchasing the products of the donor country. For example, approximately two-thirds of Canadian government aid is required to be spent on Canadian products and services.

For many Third World countries, foreign aid amounts to a net loss. Often, more money leaves the nation to pay off "aid loans" than the amount of money coming into the country in the form of aid programs. All this has contributed to the progressive debt incurred by the Third World countries. In 1968, the total debt incurred by poor countries of the Third World amounted to $47.5 billion. By 1972, the debt had risen to $60 billion.

These then are some of the major mechanisms employed by the industrialized countries in the development game. Their one net effect has been to maximize the economic growth of the industrialized countries and, at the same time, continue the economic underdevelopment of the poor countries in the Third World. Taken together, these mechanisms function to create, maintain and extend the development gap between the rich and the poor throughout the world.

The injustice of the development gap and its causes compel us to re-examine the goals and values that underlie our prevailing models for development. We Canadians have chosen economic growth as the primary goal of our model for development. But "equity" has certainly not been the by-product of "growth"—at home or in the world. Is it clear that economic growth is to be valued above everything else? Especially when the cost of maximizing economic growth is increasing inequality, or increasing dominance and dependence, between the peoples of the world?

ALTERNATIVE MODELS FOR DEVELOPMENT: A CRITICAL CHOICE FOR CANADIANS

Among the peoples of the Third World, there is a growing resistance to the prevailing industrialized models for development. There is a desire to reaffirm the values of their traditional societies and their capacities for self-determination.

Increasingly, these countries are resisting the pressures for modern industrialization where the human cost is too high. Many people in the Third World are rejecting the goal of maximizing economic growth, especially where the cost is increasing domination and dependence. The late Lester B. Pearson anticipated this emerging resistance over 15 years ago when he said:

> Perhaps only in North America every man feels entitled to a motor car, but in Asia hundreds of millions now do expect to eat and be free. They will no longer accept colonialism, destitution and distress as pre-ordained. That may be the most significant of all the revolutionary changes in the social fabric of our times.

In recent years, a variety of Third World countries have begun a serious search for alternative models for development. Several Third World models have been proposed which, in essence, call for a moderate yet adequate level of living for all citizens. In contrast to the Western industrial models, the primary goal is not maximizing economic growth with supposed "trickle down" benefits to the poor. The goal is to attain a balanced growth with an equitable distribution of income across the board.

Tanzania's president, Julius Nyerere, spoke for many Third World peoples when he articulated the vision of Tanzania founded on a traditional society. By a traditional society, Nyerere referred to the notion of "an extended family in which all contribute to the prosperity of the whole." He envisioned a society in which every one is a worker, and where each member regards everybody as his brother. In 1970, President Nyerere outlined the implications of this vision of society for development itself:

> The purpose of development is man. It is the creation of conditions, both material and spiritual, which enables man the individual and man the species to become his best....
>
> ... (We are committed) to the belief that there are more important things in life than the amassing of riches, and that if the pursuit of wealth clashes with things like human dignity and social equality, then the latter will be given priority.... This may seem to be a very academic point, but in reality it is very fundamental.

While following these guidelines for development, Tanzania has rejected foreign aid with strings attached and foreign investment that inhibits self-determination. Third World countries like Tanzania are no longer willing to sacrifice their humanity in order to become "modern industrialized nations." The growing resistance against the Western models for development is reinforced by the belief that the Third World countries can achieve adequate living conditions for all its citizens without economic dependence on the industrialized countries. Along these lines, Makbul ul Haq, advisor to the World Bank, advocated in 1972:

> The developing countries have no choice but to turn inwards, much the same way as Communist China did 25 years ago, and to adopt a different style of life, seeking a consumption pattern more consistent with their own poverty—pots and pans and bicycles and simple consumption habits without being seduced by the life styles of the rich. This requires a redefinition of economic and social objectives which is of truly staggering proportions, a liquidation of the privileged groups and vested interests which may well be impossible in many societies, a redistribution of political and economic power which may only be achieved through revolution rather than through an evolutionary change.

These Third World alternatives pose a major challenge for all of us in Canada and the Western world. They offer us a vision of a new world order—not a world based on ever-expanding growth, production and consumption, but a world based on equity, on "caring, sharing and sparing."

In effect, the voices of the Third World are telling us that "Development Demands Justice." And justice, in turn, demands a major redistribution of economic resources and decision-making power in the world today.

This is no longer simply a moral imperative. The finite resources of this planet are rapidly being exploited to the point of exhaustion by current levels of consumption and production. Violence and civil unrest continue to mount among the oppressed peoples of the world who are demanding their fair share of the earth's resources. What was once considered a moral imperative for justice is rapidly being recognized as a practical necessity for the survival of our common humanity on this planet. Economist Barbara Ward recently articulated these realities:

> To live simply, to love greatly, to give without stinting, to see a brother in all mankind—this is no longer a remote theory of social behavior. It is the inescapable recipe for planetary survival.

Today, we Canadians are faced with a critical choice between alternative courses for the future. We can decide to continue our present course of maximizing economic growth, earnings and consumption. Or we can decide to join the poor in the struggle for a just distribution of economic resources and political power in the world.

Throughout the history of Canada, we have heard a chorus of demands for justice in the development of this country. We have a diverse and rich tradition of protest against the injustices of increasing economic growth and expansion—by the Native Peoples, by the Quebecois, by the farmers in the West and the coal miners in the East. Much of this tradition is still alive and active at this very moment. In recent years, some people have moved from a critique of the industrialized model for development to a creative search for alternative models. This trend was given official recognition recently when the prime minister himself asked the Canadian people in May, 1971:

> Why ... do Western governments continue to worship at the temple of the Gross National Product?—Shouldn't we be replacing our reliance on the GNP with a much more revealing figure—a new statistic which might be called "Net Human Benefit"?

The goal of "Net Human Benefit," however, requires specification in terms of our relations to the Third World. It must be considered in terms of what will be required to advance the purpose of narrowing the development gap between the rich and the poor. We must ask ourselves what kind of alternative policies for development are required to narrow the development gap in the world. For example:

1. Are we prepared to start paying fair prices for basic agricultural products such as coffee, cocoa, rice and sugar? Are we prepared to give trade preferences to the commodities of Third World countries, thereby giving them a more equitable share of our market?

2. Are we prepared to place less emphasis on maximizing profits in our foreign investments and more emphasis on developing viable economic institutions that meet the particular needs of the developing countries and preserve their right of self-determination?

3. Are we prepared not only to increase the quantity of foreign aid but also to improve its quality by not "tying" it to the purchase of Canadian goods and by channelling more aid through the United Nations and grass-roots agencies?

We must recognize, however, that such alternative policies for development will require major changes in the economic structures of our society and the social order of our lives. We must ask ourselves whether or not we are prepared to accept the social and personal implications of these changes. For example:

1. What kind of structural changes are required in our economic system in order to bring about a more equitable distribution of economic resources?

2. What would happen to the economy if affluent Canadians adopted a more modest way of living? What would happen to the manufacturers, the workers, the advertisers, the media people? What kind of political trade-offs would be required?

3. How many relatively affluent Canadians are prepared to level off or even cut down on their living standards? How many would be prepared to accept the personal and family consequences of a national policy for limited growth, restrained consumption and generous sharing?

Such questions compel us as Canadians to re-examine our personal values and our social goals as a nation. This kind of critical re-examination of goals and values is worthwhile at any time. But today, the development gap between the rich and the poor is advancing rapidly. A re-examination of our national goals and values for development is absolutely essential at this particular moment in the history of mankind.

19 · SUBMISSION TO THE CANADIAN AMBASSADOR TO THE 36TH SESSION OF THE UNITED NATIONS COMMISSION ON HUMAN RIGHTS

INTER-CHURCH COMMITTEE ON HUMAN RIGHTS IN LATIN AMERICA, 1980

The Inter-Church Committee on Human Rights in Latin America (ICCHRLA) is pleased to accept the invitation to have representatives meet with you and the other members of the Canadian delegation to the United Nations Commission on Human Rights in its 36th Session. In the past, we have found this type of meeting very useful as a forum for sharing mutual concerns and for highlighting major human rights issues as we have experienced them.

The Inter-Church Committee on Human Rights in Latin America is an ecumenical body supported by the Anglican, Lutheran, Presbyterian (observer), Roman Catholic, and United Churches, and by religious orders of the Roman Catholic Church such as Scarboro Foreign Mission Society, Canadian Religious Conference of Ontario, Upper Canada Province of the Jesuit Fathers. The Canadian Conference of Catholic Bishops and the Canadian Council of Churches also provide official support. There is an effective collaboration with the Comité Chrétien pour les Droits Humains en Amérique Latine in Montreal.

We see our work in the human rights arena as a Christian response to the Gospel to foster and preserve the sacredness of all life. It is aimed at struggling against all that dehumanizes and destroys, and

241

at promoting conditions in which respect for human life can flourish. The ICCHRLA's efforts focus on the human dilemma as it unfolds in one part of the world. We receive evidence of brutal and flagrant repression against the people in the majority of Latin American countries through direct fact-finding missions by the members/staff of the ICCHRLA several times each year.

At other times we organize and sponsor such investigative missions in which we invite persons beyond our direct membership to travel to a particular area. The most recent example was the November, 1979, mission to investigate the new indigenous law in Chile. These multiple first-hand contacts result in ongoing, in-depth communication with our staff and denominational representatives via carefully dispatched correspondence and documents, as well as urgent telephone calls in emergencies. The broad ecumenical network and direct relationships with human rights and popular organizations in a large number of countries give rise to a constant flow of international reports, pleas from relatives of disappeared persons, telegrams alerting us to the use of savage torture and serious acts of repression against peasants and workers who seek to overcome economic/social exploitation. Our response therefore is an expression of the Canadian churches' long-standing relation with the people and the churches in Latin America struggling for social justice.

The ICCHRLA began as an Ad-Hoc Committee on Chile in response to grave human rights violations following the 1973 military coup. It gradually became clear that the erosion of human rights in Latin America was not limited to Chile but extended into Argentina, Uruguay and Brazil, where continued torture and imprisonment prompted an increasing number of appeals for help. By 1977 ICCHRLA was formed to deal with human rights violations throughout Latin America. Our focus is currently on the countries in the Southern Cone and Central America.

The Rationale for Our Concern

The ICCHRLA sees its work as an element in the global struggle for a "just, participatory and sustainable society," envisioned by the World Council of Churches. We operate within a Christian theological perspective in our concern for human rights. It comes from fidelity to the tradition of Christian accountability to God for the welfare of all, made clear in the life, death and resurrection of Jesus Christ, and from the strong prophetic element of the Old and New

Testaments, revealing God as the champion of the poor and oppressed, showing the Kingdom of God to be profoundly based in right relationships and social justice. This has been elaborated by major teachings of the Latin American bishops at Medellin, Colombia, in 1968 and at Puebla, Mexico, in 1978, as well as by evangelical and Protestant churches and the social teachings of the World Council of Churches derived from biblical sources.

We believe the struggle is one not only for political rights but for social, economic and cultural rights as well. We cannot overlook the organized and systematic quality of much of the repression. Nor can we fail to see that the major targets of repression are often the leaders of community organizations, the labour movement, peasant groups, student bodies and religious workers who are struggling for social justice and stand in direct conflict with military rulers and small elites who benefit from the status quo.

We were pleased to receive an advance copy of the Commission's agenda and applaud the broad definition it takes in human rights matters. As in previous years, we would like to take the opportunity of our meeting with you to present documentation available to our Committee, and to make recommendations for the development of an appropriate Canadian response to the issues raised on the Commission's agenda.

Last year, Canadian officials spoke out more frequently and with greater clarity on human rights problems, both at home and in international forums like the UN. At last year's Commission, Canada took a leadership role in the discussion of the very serious international problem of disappeared persons.

These efforts reflect the concern of Canadians. There has been a rapid increase in domestic attention on human rights which is seen in the growth of church, labour and community human rights actions and in the development of organizations like Amnesty International across Canada. While our Committee is aware that the impact of diplomatic statements can be limited, we encourage clear and more-frequent initiatives by our government and diplomats on human rights. We believe international pressure can bring results. During 1979, we saw powerful elements in El Salvador, in a context of intense domestic social conflict, replace the hard-line Romero government with more moderate faces to counter the report of the OAS investigatory team and to sidestep the expected international censure at the October OAS meeting in La Paz.

We are concerned, however, that Canadian efforts in the human rights arena have failed to adequately consider the causes of repression, and the reasons why violations are so widespread in the "Western world." We encourage you, and the Commission, to consider these matters in depth when you meet. We are pleased to see that agenda item 8 provides for a discussion of social, economic and cultural rights and suggest this might provide a suitable time for a looking at some of the most important questions at hand.

Our Committee is convinced that to affect the causal basis of human rights violations, it is necessary to address the structural problems inherent in the international economic order. The existing economic and political structures between nations and within nations have given rise to a distorted world system of development that promotes gross disparities, both between developed and underdeveloped countries, and between small national elites and the majority of populations. While we cannot ask the Commission to develop policy for a new international economic order, we urge you to consider the links between the existing economic order in which Canada participates, and the violation of human rights.

We realize Canadian representatives at the Commission must be grounded in Canadian policy and fear that, as in other international forums, effective Canadian action (at the Commission) at the multilateral level will be hampered by bilateral considerations. During 1979, Canadian church representatives met with members of Parliament, the minister of the Department of External Affairs and the minister of the Department of Immigration. We presented briefs and documents on matters we consider to be crucial for effective action on the violation of human rights.

We lament that Canadian statements on the global stage have not been matched by effective economic measures. Church people have asked business and government leaders repeatedly why Canada is doing business in countries where there are gross violations of human rights and why Canadian dollars and Canadian expertise are being used in any way that reinforces repressive regimes. But no mandatory action regarding Canadian corporate investment in South Africa, Chile or Argentina and no official action against bank loans to regimes like that of the now deposed Somoza dictatorship have been taken.

Canada has failed as well to link human rights questions with a strategy for disarmament or a campaign to stop arms sales to repressive governments. Our Committee is concerned that Canadian international policy regarding human rights will amount to little more than a colourful balloon if it is not matched and connected with Canadian economic and defence policies. Canada's concern for human rights should be demonstrated in positive support for countries that overthrow repressive governments. To date, the Nicaraguan people's immense process of reconstruction has not received substantial bilateral aid from Canada. If Canada is to appear serious in its concern about human rights matters, Canadian statements must be supported by positive action.

Canadian Policy and Latin America

As churches we are committed to the world struggle for a just, participatory and sustainable society and we look forward to working with government in developing initiatives that give body and force to our concern for human rights.

One of our principal concerns is an adequate Canadian response to refugees and political prisoners in Latin America. Canada's past initiatives to resettle over 7,000 Latin American refugees in Canada and to develop programs for political prisoners have been important. But we were dismayed by the December 20 change in immigration regulations which affect Chilean nationals' entrance to Canada. New visa requirements will make it almost impossible for an individual fleeing from persecution in Chile to make a refugee claim in Canada. To us, this seems to fly in the face of genuine human rights concerns, given both our first-hand knowledge of continual violations in Chile and the November, 1979, report of the UN Special Rapporteur that indicated a deteriorating human rights situation.

Given ICCHRLA's expertise in the area of Latin America, we would like to outline certain other considerations and certain steps that might be involved in the development of a more sensitive Canadian policy towards Latin America.

Canada's impact on Latin America is growing. Canadian investment projects in Brazil, Guatemala, the Dominican Republic, Chile and Panama are significant in size and impact in the global context. Canadian banks are important sources of capital for a variety of purposes in Latin America.

The Canadian government, through its commercial network and through assistance and encouragement to such business lobbies as the Canadian Association for Latin America, has encouraged increasing contact and alliance between Canadian business and their Latin American counterparts.

Canadian aid agencies and crown corporations like the Export Development Corporation are increasing the amount of money flowing to Latin America. All this adds up to give Canada increasing economic leverage on human rights affairs in the continent.

In addition to action through United Nations Human Rights Commissions and General Assembly Forums, we suggest the Canadian government could, and should, undertake significant policy development and review measures at home.

The first step would be an assessment of ways in which Canadian aid, the operation of Canadian banks and corporations assist and sustain repressive regimes. The Department of External Affairs and colleague ministries may be able to undertake important data-gathering operations in this field for the Canadian public. A case in point has been the relationship of Canadian private business to South Africa. The churches have addressed the question on codes of conduct and disclosure of large international bank loans, and await government action which would be mandatory and thorough in the collection and publication of data. The urgency of further initiatives is raised by agenda item 7, but applies to cases other than South Africa as well. If a dictatorship like that of Somoza in Nicaragua was sustained by Canadian private bank loans, by military aid from third powers and assistance from multilateral sources, is not the fight for self-determination, social justice and human rights of the people of such a country jeopardized? Is this not a matter for public concern and review? It would be most useful if in addition to initiatives by government departments in the collection of relevant information regarding investment and other ties, public hearings on a periodic basis, undertaken by a parliamentary committee, could be held. A broad non-governmental input to such hearings would be essential.

A second step could involve establishment of a mandatory code of international corporate conduct by the Canadian government which would apply equally to government departments and agencies and to private corporations and banks, and which would prohibit aid investment or credit to any country which persistently violates human rights or uses torture. This would naturally make mandatory improved methods of information gathering on the actions of Canadian corporations and make imperative the amendment of the Bank Act to enforce disclosure of large private loans to foreign regimes.

A third step might involve the extension of Canadian environmental, health and safety standards to the international operations of Canadian-based corporations as a minimum set of guidelines. Should a moratorium be put on the extension of Canadian nuclear facilities at home, pending a full inquiry of questions of risk and safety, then a moratorium on sales abroad should be mandatory. We urge the Canadian government to take initiatives to bring the question of ecological threat and damage from nuclear development and other foreign investment into the discussion of item 8 on the Commission agenda.

If Canada is to create a more positive relationship with the Latin American people, and work with them for the achievement of their human rights and the satisfaction of their basic needs, a clear-headed view of possible differences with American policy will also be required. We are of the opinion that independent Canadian initiative might on occasion offer a creative alternative to a situation in which U.S. policy is clearly in conflict with the aspirations of a Latin American people, although that Canadian initiative might run the risk of periodic increases in tension between Canada and the United States. Under item 10 at the Commission, we urge the Canadian government to initiate discussion of the question of the U.S. participation in foreign military and security training, and assistance in the origination and development of torture and other cruel treatment....

GENERAL CONCERNS

As we move forward into 1980, the ICCHRLA has engaged in some reflection about developments in Latin America over the past year. We have examined the ways events in one country have influenced, and have intertwined with, those in others, and have deciphered certain trends for the continent as a whole. In the area of human rights, we see four recurring problems that we would like to highlight as our general concerns.

The Disappeared

Thousands of people are now listed as "disappeared" in Latin America....this problem is particularly serious in the Southern Cone countries, Argentina, Chile and Uruguay, and in Guatemala.

We have noted a marked increase in human rights violations that involve the collaboration of police and military forces from various Southern Cone countries. In the report on Uruguay, we detail cases of coordinated action including that of the two Uruguayan children who disappeared in Argentina and later were found in Chile.

We believe disappearances should be viewed as a form of political repression in the same vein as political detention and political murder. Repressive Latin American regimes are currently under some international pressure to clean up their human rights images abroad and we fear that some governments and police forces may try and reduce prison populations and eliminate those who have experienced brutal torture by augmenting their lists of disappeared.

Disappearances are a brutal and continual psychological torture for many Latin Americans who have lost relatives and loved ones and who know nothing of their whereabouts or their safety.

We urge Canada to take a strong position on the issue of the disappeared in discussion of agenda item 10b at the Commission's hearings.

We recommend:

(a) that Canada bring forward to the UNHCR the resolution adopted by the Sub-Commission on Prevention of Discrimination and Protection of Minorities concerning the disappeared;

(b) that Canada initiate or support a motion of condemnation of disappearances as a grave violation of human rights by supporting the adoption of this resolution;

(c) that Canada ask the Commission to undertake a special investigation into the fate of disappeared persons in Latin America.

Violation of Economic Rights

In many countries of Latin America, the majority of the population has to struggle to secure basic necessities such as food, housing and clothing, much less minimal care or education. The enjoyment of economic and social rights is denied by massive unemployment and the combination of low wages and high prices, as the UN Special Rapporteur stated in his 1979 report on Chile.

In many Latin American countries there has been an increase in repressive legislation like that of the new labour laws in Chile and Argentina that abolish any effective means that workers have to defend their interests and improve their economic situation. These laws have the effect of institutionalizing poverty and legalizing economic repression.

We recommend:

(a) that in the Commission's discussion of item 8 on the question of the realization of economic, social and cultural rights Canada take a strong stand to denounce measures of economic repression as a serious violation of human rights.

Violation of Indigenous Rights

In Latin America, as industrialization and large-scale resource development have penetrated previously isolated regions, indigenous people have been routed from their traditional lands and forced to adapt to an unfamiliar environment, or die. In Brazil, Chile, Guatemala, Ecuador and Paraguay, the existence of whole tribes of indigenous people is currently threatened as government leaders and government agencies strip them of their rights.

Chile's new Indian Law is just one example of legislation that dictates forced integration with no regard for Indian tradition or the special cultural concerns of indigenous people. The Mapuches were not consulted in the development of the law, although their existence will be altered by it. The law has been denounced internationally by Indian leaders as a serious threat to indigenous survival.

As Canadians, who must also struggle to ensure that our own indigenous people achieve a fuller expression of their human rights, we believe Canada should take a leadership role on questions of indigenous rights during discussion of item 20a and item 23.

We recommend:

(a) that Canada condemn Chile's Indian Law as a gross violation of indigenous rights;

(b) that Canada support the proposal for a United Nations Year of Indigenous People to focus on the plight of indigenous rights around the world.

Religious Persecution

The ICCHRLA wishes to alert the Canadian ambassador and the Commission to the dramatic increase in religious persecution throughout Latin America.

Traditionally religious persecution is understood as the activity of a secularized state which prohibits, prevents or punishes religious teaching and practice (e.g., USSR), or as a result of a conflict between dominant and minority religious forces (e.g., Ireland or Iran), but neither understanding is relevant in the case of Latin America. The persecution of the churches in Latin America is part of the general and systematic repression against all those who struggle for social justice.

The Christian churches in Latin America increasingly are taking up the concerns of the workers, peasants and oppressed people who face hunger and unemployment, torture and imprisonment, and lack of freedom and political rights. Rather than give priority to their own institutional needs or to the needs of their privileged constituency, some churches and church personnel are heeding a religious call to stand on the side of the poor and to defend human rights and liberty. This has often brought the churches into direct opposition with repressive governments and small elites who benefit from the status quo.

Over the past decade, some 850 members of the Latin American clergy—bishops, priests, and sisters—as well as countless Christian leaders, activists and lay people, have died violently at the hands of the state and right-wing death squads. The year 1979 has produced particularly dramatic examples of religious persecution in El Salvador and Guatemala. The victims are invariably accused of political crimes or labelled subversive. In fact, these Christians suffer and die as a result of their seeking to respond to the total demands of their faith, which includes concern for the material bases and historical conditions of life.

We recommend:

(a) that in the discussion of agenda item 18 on religious persecution that Canada raise and condemn the grave incidence of religious persecution in Latin America....

20 · CANADIAN POLICY TOWARDS SOUTHERN AFRICA

TASKFORCE ON THE CHURCHES AND CORPORATE RESPONSIBILITY, 1981

INTRODUCTION

In spite of differences in histories and interpretations of the Christian tradition, the various branches of the Church of Jesus Christ represented on the Taskforce on the Churches and Corporate Responsibility have found a renewed unity in our common heritage of God's working among men and women throughout the world for just relationships that will make and keep human life human and as full for each person as God intends. In Jesus Christ the heritage of God's concern for justice and the well-being of all peoples came to fulfillment as God himself took flesh and dwelt among us. No more eloquent testimony to the value and dignity of human life could be conceived than the incarnation. No clearer indication of the focus of God's concern could be found than his work among and for the poor, oppressed and marginalized as he walked this earth. As Christ's body, the Church, we strive to keep alive that passionate concern for just relationships among all people.

The Taskforce on the Churches and Corporate Responsibility is one expression of the renewed unity we have found in this common heritage. It places a special emphasis on the means whereby our corporations, financial institutions and government agencies that support them, affect the quality of life for those who feel the impact of their operations.

Since the establishment of the Taskforce in 1975, Southern Africa has remained an area of primary concern for the member churches because of the conditions affecting the black populations of that area. Member churches maintain their historical ties, based on a

251

mission partnership, with their Southern Africa sister churches. They accept a continuing obligation to resist the sin of one group against another, particularly where Canadian institutions are involved.

The Taskforce has been active in coordinating efforts on behalf of its members to keep this concern before the management and shareholders of the economic institutions in which they own shares. In addition, conversations with government departments and agencies concerned with the economic links between Canada and Southern Africa have played an important part in our efforts. In all this work, we are attempting to be faithful to a God who has demonstrated a passionate and concrete concern for the value and dignity of human life in all its dimensions throughout this world.

The member churches of the Taskforce believe that Canada has a significant role to play in the events that shape the future of Southern Africa. As a member of the Commonwealth, she has in the past assumed a mediating and constructive role, which has earned her the respect and trust of Africa's emerging nations. Given the uncertain and, to us, alarming foreign policy directions the new administration of the United States appears to be adopting in regard to South Africa, it seems important that Canada join in greater measure those middle powers which have a consistent policy position in opposition to the *apartheid* state.

In its public statements, the Canadian government has expressed its opposition to South Africa's apartheid system in uncompromising terms. It has not been deceived by South Africa's attempts to put a more acceptable face on its racial policies through measures which have been heralded by less astute observers as "important changes." As recently as September, 1980, the secretary of state for external affairs, speaking to the General Assembly of the United Nations, asked:

> Where is there greater evidence of resistance to change than in the perpetuated insult which South Africa represents to any human being who cares about human dignity?

The Canadian government has also stated on numerous occasions that it favours peaceful solutions to the problems of racism in Southern Africa. This position is shared by the member churches of the Taskforce. Moreover, like the Canadian government, they have recognized the legitimacy of the long struggle for liberation in Southern Africa. It follows that in this situation, anyone who prefers a peaceful solution must demonstrate the sincerity of this commitment to the abolition of apartheid by doing all that one can to make possible such a peaceful solution. Those within South Africa and in the international community who are concerned about ending apartheid recognize that if peaceful change is still to have a chance, it is essential that Western nations apply economic pressure upon the apartheid government. Indeed, the Canadian government associated itself with this view when, in 1977, it announced a series of policy changes in regard to South Africa which were designed to curtail Canadian government economic links with that country.

However, the churches submit that the 1977 policy announcements have not been followed through by subsequent measures that had been intimated in 1977. Even the first set of measures has been insufficiently implemented or neglected. What appeared then as a resolute beginning towards a more forthright Canadian policy in regard to Southern Africa appears now to have been the most the Canadian government was willing to offer. We are left with the disturbing inconsistencies, long identified in Canada's relations to South Africa, between strong rhetoric on the part of the Canadian government and rather weak and half-hearted policies and actions. It is hypocritical to proclaim that one is against violence and prefers peaceful change while neglecting to act in a manner most likely to result in peaceful change. This neglect is tantamount to aiding a regime which by definition violates all standards of human rights.

It is our contention that the 1977 measures which have been implemented were those that relate mainly to the activities of the Department of External Affairs and were largely of symbolic rather than practical value. On the other hand, measures whose implementation would require the cooperation of the Department of Finance and of the Ministry of Industry, Trade and Commerce have received little or no attention since they were announced. This is why we address ourselves today to both the secretary of state for external affairs and the minister of industry, trade and commerce.

GOVERNMENT POLICIES RELATING TO SOUTH AFRICA

The last extended discussions about Canada's policy towards Southern Africa between representatives of the Canadian churches and a secretary of state for external affairs of the Liberal government took place in November, 1977 (cf. a brief presented to the Honourable Donald C. Jamieson, secretary of state for external affairs, by the Taskforce on the Churches and Corporate Responsibility, November 15, 1977.) On December 19, 1977, the Honourable Donald Jamieson announced that "Canada is phasing out all its government-sponsored commercial support activities in South Africa." We shall address a number of issues arising directly from that policy statement which we believe ought to be reviewed and offer policy recommendations in regard to them.

Corporate Connections

1. **Export Development Corporation (EDC)**: The government announced the "withdrawal of all EDC Government Account support from any transactions relating to South Africa." The government account represents only a small fraction of the EDC's account; it has not been activated to support transactions relating to South Africa during the decade previous to 1977. However, the EDC's considerable *corporate* account was exempted from this measure. As recently as September, 1980, and again in January, 1981, the EDC used this corporate account to provide support facilities for commercial transactions with South Africa. Neither the nature of the export nor the amount involved was disclosed.

To announce the withdrawal of all government-sponsored support activities and yet to continue EDC financial support for private-sector activities with South Africa is inconsistent with the government policy as stated. This is particularly disheartening given the fact that the EDC, as a crown corporation, includes, on its Board of Directors, senior civil servants from the Ministry of Finance, the Ministry of Industry, Trade and Commerce, and the Department of External Affairs.

We ask that the EDC be instructed to withdraw its corporate account support from any transactions relating to South Africa. (*Recommendation 1.*)

2. **Canada Development Corporation (CDC)**: Texas Gulf, a company which is 30.7 per cent owned by the CDC, holds mineral rights in the western Transvaal. It has clearly not been instructed to divest its South African holdings, since it is presently engaged in a major research program designed to enable it to enter effectively into South African platinum and chromite extraction and marketing.

In addition, Connaught Laboratories, Ltd., which is 100 per cent owned by the CDC, owns 75 per cent of Dumex. Dumex continues to operate research laboratories in South Africa and manufactures drugs, nutritional products, and baby foods.

In 1971, the then secretary of state for external affairs, the Honourable Mitchell Sharp, instructed another crown corporation, Polymer, to divest itself of its $4-million South African investment. This was done because the Liberal government at the time felt that a crown corporation ought not to profit from gains made under the apartheid system. The continuing operations in South Africa of Texas Gulf and Connaught Laboratories, owned fully or partially by the CDC, represent a retreat from the policy position of the Liberal government in 1971, notwithstanding the 1977 policy announcements, which suggested progressive policy changes.

We note in passing that the CDC Annual Report for 1980 makes no mention of an adherence to the Canadian Code of Conduct for its South African operations.

In the interest of consistency, it would seem appropriate for the CDC to use its considerable influence to have Texas Gulf discontinue its South African operations and certainly to have the wholly owned Connaught Laboratories dispose of its investment in Dumex in South Africa.

At the very least, the CDC should insist that Texas Gulf not expand its corporate investment in South Africa and, if it remains at all, the CDC should file its Code of Conduct Report as other corporations are expected to. (*Recommendation 2.*)

3. **Ford Motor Company of Canada, Ltd**: Ford, South Africa is a subsidiary of the Ford Motor Company of Canada, Ltd. Although its South African subsidiary is run almost entirely by the Middle East and Africa Division of Ford, U.S., the Canadian-incorporated parent company and the Canadian government are nonetheless responsible to hold Ford, South Africa to account for its activities.

Motor vehicle manufacturers, including Ford, have been designated "Key Point Industries" by the South African government. Under the 1970 South African Procurement Act, they are obliged to supply the military and police with required vehicles in emergency situations or face a take-over by the South African government. Since October, 1980, the South African Defence Force has been requiring foreign companies to store weapons on the premises and to organize all-white militia reserve units to protect their plants in case of serious unrest. The penalty for refusing to do so is $25,000 or five years imprisonment for executives. Companies were asked to keep these measures secret. Ford, South Africa is intimately involved in the maintenance of apartheid. It already has a contract to supply South Africa's defence forces and the police with vehicles.

We discuss Canada's position in regard to the mandatory arms embargo below. At this point we wish to state that it is for us an intolerable circumvention of the arms embargo to have a Canadian subsidiary supply the South African police and military with vehicles. It seems equally unacceptable that a Canadian subsidiary could be asked to assist in the protection of supplies for the South African military in the event that apartheid needs to defend itself against black discontent. South African blacks may justifiably inquire whether Canadians are serious about their aversion to apartheid.

We ask the Canadian government publicly to inform the Ford Motor Company of Canada and all other Canadian companies operating in South Africa:

(a)   that it considers contracts with the South African police and military a contravention of the mandatory arms embargo;

(b)   that it will disallow as normal operating expenses for purposes of Canadian tax deductions taxes paid to the South African government on military and police contracts and costs incurred through the organization of white militia units and the storage of weapons.

We further ask that the Canadian government request Ford, Canada that it instruct its South African subsidiary to cancel all existing police and military contracts and not to enter into new contracts; and that the Canadian displeasure about the military and police contracts be communicated to the Ford Motor Company in the United States and to the South African government. (*Recommendation 3*.)

4. **Massey-Ferguson**: On May 21, 1979, and June 8, 1980, *Business Week* reported the sale of technology by Perkins, a British subsidiary of Massey-Ferguson, to the South African military. Atlantis Diesel Engine Co. (ADE), a newly established company owned by the South African government, embarked on a program to produce diesel engines designed by Perkins and Daimler-Benz. Diesel engines produced by the new engine plant will be used for heavy trucks for the South African Defence Force, among others. According to *Business Week*, this program will serve the South African government's drive to ensure its strategic self-sufficiency. The announcement of this agreement followed a series of discussions in May, 1979, of the defence staff relating to the integration of political, military and economic planning in South Africa.

It is noteworthy that diesel makers in the United States were prohibited from bidding for the ADE contract because American law forbids U.S. firms from selling technology for use by the South African military or police forces. While the Canadian government has been partially underwriting Massey-Ferguson's financial reorganization at home, it has, at the same time, urged the company to continue vigorously its international operations because of their greater profitability. One of these international operations involves the sale of technology benefiting South Africa's "total strategy."

We urge the Canadian government to take the support by Massey-Ferguson for the South African military seriously. We object to a situation whereby a Canadian company, finding itself in financial difficulties, relies on Canadian taxpayers to partially underwrite its debt while it sells strategic technology to the South African Defence Force. That it is able to do so, without being legally constrained by Canadian government regulations, is a major flaw in Canada's enforcement of the mandatory arms embargo.

We ask the Canadian government to inform Massey-Ferguson that it considers the company's sale of technology to the South African military as a breach of the mandatory arms embargo, and to insist that it cancel its contract with Atlantis Diesel Engine Company of South Africa. (*Recommendation 4.*)

5. **Krugerrand Sales in Canada**: During 1979, sales promotions in Canada of the South African gold coin known as Krugerrand increased markedly. In 1967, South Africa introduced this coin as a means of selling the largest possible portion of South Africa's gold at premium rather than market price. Today, 25 per cent of South African gold production goes into international Krugerrand sales. Such sales in private transactions help to buoy up the price of all South African gold sold on international bullion markets. Thus, the increase in Krugerrand sales has a substantial effect on the gold market and on the economic well-being of the apartheid regime by earning the South African government large amounts of foreign exchange. Advertisements for the Krugerrand portray South Africa as a stable and reliable state, while the sale of the coin provides South Africa with the resources to maintain racial oppression....

We ask the Canadian government to institute measures to prevent the Krugerrand from being sold in Canada. (*Recommendation 5.*)

Code of Conduct for Canadian Companies Operating in South Africa

In April, 1978, the Government of Canada published a "Code of Conduct Concerning the Employment Practices of Canadian Companies operating in South Africa." When this code was published, the government expressed the hope that Canadian companies operating in South Africa would promote employment practices based on the principle of equal treatment for all employees and for practices "which are consistent with basic human rights and the general economic welfare of all people in South Africa." That hope is hollow when the direct and indirect collaboration between some Canadian companies and the South African military and police undermine this code and render it inconsequential. The Canadian churches pointed out before and after the publication of the Canadian code that even within its own very limited parameters, the Canadian code is timid and lacks precision. It does not even require the accountability found in other codes, notably the British code which requires itemized annual reporting to a body appointed by the government to receive and scrutinize such reports.

The Canadian code merely states that companies *should* make annual public reports. The code does not answer the question of who receives such reports, assesses them and publishes them. Companies do not have to present itemized comparative statistics and even if they were reported and found wanting, there would be no consequence for a given company because the code is entirely voluntary....

We ask the Canadian government to reassess the usefulness of its present Code of Conduct with the view of amending it to include:

(a)   the abolition of the migrant labour system;

(b)   the abolition of influx controls;

(c)   securing the right of workers to live with their families;

(d)   equality in education;

(e)   equal access to housing and health care services;

(f)   making adherence to the code legally binding and establishing penalties for non- or inadequate adherence;

(g) requiring companies to file an annual report which would include comparative data on an itemized basis as well as all contracts with South Africa's military or police;

(h) establishment of a public review committee to include representatives of the Canadian Labour Congress, the churches and other concerned organizations. (*Recommendation 6.*)

SECURITY COUNCIL MANDATORY ARMS EMBARGO AGAINST SOUTH AFRICA (RESOLUTION 418)

Canada's Policy and Its Implementation

During Canada's term on the Security Council, 1977/78, Resolution 418 was enacted. Canada supported this resolution. It did not, however, deem it necessary to enact legislation in response to the mandatory resolution, nor did it issue official regulations under the Canada United Nations Act. The Canadian government insists that the machinery by which it adhered to the voluntary arms embargo under Security Council Resolution 181 of 1963 makes it unnecessary to enact specific legislation.

The arms embargo against South Africa is administered by the Department of Industry, Trade and Commerce through the Export Control List. This list contains two categories: the first is a published list of all military store items proscribed for sale to countries of the Warsaw Pact and to countries engaged in armed hostilities. This proscription does not extend to sales to the United States with whom Canada has a defence-sharing agreement or to countries belonging to the Western defence system.

A. **Munitions of War**: In 1963, South Africa, so we are told, was added to the number of countries excluded from Canadian exports of arms and military equipment. Our main concern about this aspect of Canada's South African arms embargo relates to its scrupulous enforcement concerning items on this list.

We cite as an example of our concern the case of Space Research Corporation (SRC) which straddled the Canadian/U.S. border. Between March, 1977, and March, 1978, SRC was able to sell at least four shipments of ultra-range 155-mm shells, each the size of a small guided missile, to South Africa. The Armaments Development Production Corporation (ARMSCOR), South Africa's government armaments agency, was able to acquire a 20 per cent interest in SRC. It secured not only the clandestine shipment of Howitzer shells but also the transfer of the relevant technology including, most observers believe, nuclear applicability. South Africa can thus now proceed with the manufacture in South Africa of these shells and export them to other countries.

All this took place after Canada's acceptance of the 1963 voluntary arms embargo and the mandatory arms embargo of 1977. Concerned Canadians ask how these transactions could have escaped the government's attention. As early as October, 1977, it had received information that such shipments were taking place from Canada via the Caribbean. Indeed, in 1977, the RCMP even searched the SRC crates in Saint John, New Brunswick. Why was SRC permitted to export further shells to Spain twice in 1978 without any impediment or government scrutiny about the ultimate recipient of the shipment? Had it not been for an alert media responding to Antiguan dock workers' reports, the arms shipments might never have become public.

It is this case which justifies a concern that the enforcement mechanisms of the arms embargo against South Africa are weak and are carried out with a singular lack of enthusiasm. It raises the question about other possible arms shipments from Canada as yet undetected.

In the spring of 1980, the denominational members of the Taskforce urged that a thorough review of existing legislation and enforcement mechanisms be undertaken by the Canadian government. A cloud of suspicion will remain over Canada's seriousness in preventing resident industries from breaching the arms embargo until the results of such a review are made public.

We ask that a review of existing legislation and enforcement mechanisms relating to the arms embargo against South Africa take place with all possible speed and that tighter enforcement measures be instituted and published.

We further recommend that a Parliamentary Sub-Committee be established and charged with the supervision of all aspects of the enforcement of the mandatory arms embargo. (*Recommendation 7.*)

B. **Dual Purpose Items**: The second category of items on the Export Control List concerns dual purpose equipment, i.e., equipment which may have civilian as well as military uses. Items in this category require individual export permits which are granted or withheld by the Department of Industry, Trade and Commerce. The list of dual purpose items is not published nor are the rules governing the granting of export permits for South Africa entirely clear....

In 1964, the government vetoed the export by Ford Canada of 10,000 four-wheel-drive trucks to the South African government. The then secretary of state for external affairs, the Honourable Paul Martin, stated: "... All trucks capable of being used for military purposes come within the meaning of the resolution.... I am sure the interpretation placed on the Security Council resolution by Canada was the only one we could take, in the light of the clear implication of that resolution."

Since then the Canadian government has retreated from the integrity of this position and ... has interpreted the voluntary and the subsequent mandatory arms embargo as narrowly as possible. The 1964 interpretation given by the Honourable Paul Martin is echoed with some urgency by the Security Council Committee, established by Resolution 421 and charged with making the arms embargo more effective. In its recent report (S/14179) it states:

> States should prohibit the export to South Africa of dual purpose items, i.e. items provided for civilian use but with the potential for diversion or conversion to military use. In particular, they should cease the supply of aircraft, aircraft engines, aircraft parts, electronic and telecommunications equipment, and computers to South Africa...

Canada's defence-sharing agreement with the United States, her own aggressive promotion for the export of military equipment, and her decision subsequent to Mr. Martin's statement to interpret extremely narrowly the South African arms embargo, lead us to fear that Canada might be tempted to abandon her already weak policy commitments in regard to South Africa and to quietly follow whatever policy changes the United States might adopt.

We ask the Canadian government to reaffirm its commitment and to strengthen its adherence to Security Council Resolution 418 by:

(a) enacting effective legislation or by announcing comparable policy directives regarding the arms embargo against South Africa which would include the establishment of stronger monitoring and enforcement mechanisms;

(b) interpreting the terms "arms and related material" as covering the transfer of all technology useful to the military and "dual purpose" equipment, be they undertaken through bilateral, third party or through transshipment via third country arrangements;

(c) refraining scrupulously from any nuclear collaboration with South Africa;

(d) dissociating itself from any act on the part of the United States which would violate or weaken the mandatory arms embargo against South Africa;

(e) protesting any official or unofficial contact between member states or officers of NATO and South Africa.
(*Recommendation 8.*)

CANADA'S VOTING RECORD AT THE UNITED NATIONS

A review of Canada's voting record of UN General Assembly resolutions raises doubts about the seriousness with which the government opposes apartheid even in such public arenas. Between 1978 and 1980, Canada opposed or abstained from practically all resolutions which had the intent of exerting pressure on the apartheid regime in economic, military and nuclear matters.

Canada opposed, for example, a resolution calling for an international conference on sanctions against South Africa, suggesting that the Canadian government does not even consider the subject worthy of public debate and will presumably oppose all international efforts calling for such sanctions against South Africa.

Canada also opposed a resolution calling for an oil embargo against South Africa. Increasingly, oil supplies to South Africa are considered "munitions of war" since oil is indispensable for the functioning of the South African military and police. The South African government is well aware of this and has, in 1970, legislated the National Supplies Procurement Act. Under "conditional selling," oil companies are required to supply the South African military and police and to hold large stocks at their own expense as a condition to build and expand refineries. Support for an oil embargo would therefore place pressure upon the South African police and military in much the same way as does the arms embargo. It is surprising and regrettable that Canada opposed this resolution.

Most astonishing, though, is Canada's abstention from General Assembly resolutions that call for an end to military and nuclear collaboration with South Africa and from a resolution calling for the Implementation of the Declaration on the Denuclearization of Africa. How can such votes be reconciled with a stated support of the mandatory arms embargo? It would seem reasonable that a country that has itself refused to develop and stockpile nuclear weapons would without hesitation support resolutions intended to end the collaboration with the potential of enabling South Africa to develop nuclear weapons.

But for Canada's firm commitment in regard to apartheid in sports, her voting pattern suggests that the only resolutions on which Canada cast an affirmative vote are those that urge non-governmental organizations to continue their research and education but require very little of governments.

In 1977, Canada assumed a major role over Namibia, which is discussed below. However, in most areas Canada has chosen to be a quiet and complacent member of the world community as far as apartheid is concerned. The Canadian government's unwillingness to close the EDC's corporate account for transactions with South Africa excludes from its 1977 policy announcement the one area which would have made a significant difference to the "phasing out of all government-sponsored commercial support activities in South Africa." In its continuing corporate connections through the CDC, the Canadian government manifests a retreat from the position taken in 1971 over Polymer. In its narrow interpretation of the mandatory arms embargo, it is content to retreat even from its 1964 position. The government's unwillingness to support increased United Nations efforts in regard to economic, military and nuclear collaboration with South Africa cannot but lead us to the conclusion that the Canadian government has decided to be as inoffensive as possible to Pretoria, notwithstanding its 1977 new policy announcements.

NAMIBIA

In May 1977, after the five-nation Contact Group had assumed responsibility for bringing about a peaceful and just independence for Namibia, leaders of the churches in Namibia sent a letter to the representatives of these five states. Canada is one of them, together with the U.S.A., Britain, France and West Germany. The letter reads in part:

> The support and sympathy towards SWAPO seems to be increasing, and hatred towards South Africa also, because of the activities of the army and police against civilians.
>
> People here show very little sympathy towards the Turnhalle [the Namibian assembly created by South Africa]. The Turnhalle represen-

tatives are not representative. The proposed interim government is considered a bluff, as are the homeland governments. The blacks have not been asked, nor are they being asked, whether they want the Turnhalle or not.

America and other Western nations are losing the image and prestige they once had as they only try to secure their business interests for a while without any real interest for the people of the country. A radical and practical change in the policies of the Western nations is needed if they want to get an independent and neutral Namibia. Action is needed, not words.

Those were strong words in 1977. Four years later, with Western credibility at an even greater ebb after the failure of the Namibia Conference in January, 1981, the words of Namibia's churches remain pertinent. Hopes for the implementations of Security Council Resolution 435 of 1978 were dashed through years of successful manoeuvres on the part of South Africa to avoid a cease-fire and UN supervised elections in Namibia and finally by her decision to scuttle the Conference on the flimsiest of pretexts.

After years of ritualistic Western protests against South Africa's illegal occupation of Namibia prior to 1977, and unwilling to back armed resistance, the five Western states, in an effort to avoid a Security Council Sanctions resolution, begged for time to seek South Africa's cooperation for a settlement in Namibia. During the ensuing four years, Namibians suffered continuing and increased repression and Angola became the target of repeated South African military incursions. Meanwhile, South Africa was able to:

1. install its own (Democratic Turnhalle) puppet regime as a Constituent Assembly;

2. elevate this unconstitutional body to become the National Assembly;

3. provide for (and force unwilling black Namibians into) the Assembly's own defence and police force;

4. lobby for international recognition, notably (as it did in Geneva) by insisting that negotiations take place with the "internal parties" rather than with South Africa, the occupying power.

In sum, South Africa used the long years of drawn-out negotiations with, what she knew to be, patient partners, to consolidate its hold over Namibia administratively and militarily.

The Canadian government, as one of the negotiating partners, cannot, at this point, abandon its responsibility. It is under a particular obligation now to prove to Namibians and to the rest of Africa that the trust it had solicited in 1977 was well-founded and that its principal concern is Namibia and not the good will of South Africa. Canada must now take the initiative for measures which ought to be less palatable to the South African government than UN supervised elections. There can be little choice for Canada now—and one would hope for the other four contact states—than to support SWAPO, the one negotiating partner which had without reservation supported the final terms for a timetable and for a ceasefire and elections which were agreed upon by the five contact states and the United Nations.

It is a fact, which has probably not escaped other critical observers, that all five contact states have powerful corporate interests in the resource sector in Namibia, especially in the uranium mining industry. Canada played an active role in the efforts during the early 1970s to successfully increase the market price of uranium. There was close collaboration between Britain and France together with South Africa. These historical and ongoing relationships cast a shadow of doubt over the seriousness with which these same states have pursued their role of bringing to an end South Africa's illegal occupation of Namibia. Canadian, U.S., French, British and German, as well as South African companies, have continued to gain from the extraction of depletable resources including substantial uranium deposits over which Namibians have no control and from which they derive no material benefits. This, given Namibia's international legal status, constitutes theft.

In 1974, the UN Council for Namibia, taking cognizance of this fact, issued Decree No. 1, which would forbid the export of Namibian resources by foreign companies. Not surprisingly, no Western nation has adopted Decree No. 1.

Not only has the Canadian government neglected to support Decree No. 1 of the UN Council for Namibia, it has indirectly through tax concessions underwritten the plunder of Namibian resources with Canadian taxpayers' money.

In 1975, the Canadian churches first raised the issue of tax concessions to Canadian companies operating in Namibia (Section 126 of the Income Tax Act). In 1977, as part of the announcement of Canadian policy changes towards South Africa, the Honourable Don Jamieson announced that he had requested "the Department of Finance and others to look into the implications of possible tax concessions which companies obtain for their operations in Namibia under 'what is essentially an illegal regime.' " We submit that such tax concessions should long since have been withdrawn.

We urge the Canadian government to take immediate action to protect Namibian resources from illegal foreign exploitation by adopting Decree No. 1 of 1974 of the United Nations Council for Namibia.

We ask further that tax concessions for Canadian companies operating in Namibia be withdrawn. Any expenditure in Namibia for exploration and development should not be recognized as a legitimate cost for calculations in a company's taxable income. (*Recommendation 9.*)

FURTHER READING

Brewin, Andrew; Duclos, Louis; and MacDonald, David (M.P.'s). *One Gigantic Prison: The Report of the Fact-Finding Mission to Chile, Argentina and Uruguay,* September 30 to October 10, 1976. Toronto: The Inter-Church Committee on Chile, 1976.

Canadian Church Leaders. *Canadian Policy in Central America,* Toronto: ICCHRLA, 1983.

Canadian Church Leaders. *Canadian Policy Towards Southern Africa.* An 'Ecumenical Consensus' paper presented to the secretary of state for external affairs and the minister of industry, trade and commerce on November 12, 1975. Reprinted in *The Chelsea Journal* 3/2 (March/April, 1977): 72-78.

ICCHRLA. *Submission to the Canadian Ambassador to the 37th Session of the United Nations Commission on Human Rights.* Toronto: 1981.

ICCHRLA. *Submission to the Canadian Ambassador to the 38th Session of the United Nations Commission on Human Rights.* Toronto: 1982.

ICCHRLA. *Submission to the Canadian Ambassador to the 39th Session of the United Nations Commission on Human Rights.* Toronto: 1983.

Inter-Church Committee on Human Rights in Latin America. *Canada and Latin America in the 1980s: Alternatives for Development.* Toronto: 1981.

Matthews, Robert, and Pratt, Cranfort, eds. *Church and State: The Christian Churches and Canadian Foreign Policy.* Toronto: Canadian Institute of International Affairs, 1982.

Roche, Douglas. *Justice Not Charity: A New Global Ethic for Canada.* Toronto: McClelland and Stewart, 1976.

Taskforce on the Churches and Corporate Responsibility. *Bread, Peace, and Liberty: Human Rights and Economic Development in Chile.* Toronto: 1979.

TCCR. *Canada and Namibian Uranium.* Toronto: 1982.

TCCR. *Canadian Economic Relations with Countries That Violate Human Rights.* A brief to the Sub-Committee on Latin America and the Caribbean of the Standing Committee on External Affairs and National Defence. Toronto: 1982.

TCCR. *Canadian Policy towards Southern Africa: An Analysis of the Canadian Government Response of 15 June 1982 to the Brief of the TCCR 5 May 1981.* Toronto: 1983.

TCCR. *Investment in Oppression: Canadian Responses to Apartheid.* Toronto: 1979 (revised edition).

The United Church of Canada, Department of Church in Society. *Issue 19-20, One Body: Human Rights, A Global Struggle* (1978).

The United Church of Canada, Department of Church in Society. *Issue 25, Central America: The Moment of Tension between Dying and Birth* (1982).

EPILOGUE

The final selection in this book expresses very well both the general thrust of the Canadian churches' teaching on social justice and the lack of discernible progress towards a more just society in this country. It is a brief presented to the federal Cabinet on March 17, 1978, by representatives of the Canadian Council of Churches and the Anglican, Lutheran, Presbyterian, Roman Catholic and United Churches of Canada. The document is entitled simply *Inter-Church Brief on Economic Outlook.*

Paradoxical as it may seem, the more clearly injustices in Canadian society are identified, the more resistant to change they become. As the Canadian economy stagnates, there is a mad scramble for development at any cost, and such proposals as a guaranteed annual income, a just settlement of Native land claims, and more and better foreign aid are rejected on the grounds that we cannot afford them at this time. Instead, billions of dollars are invested in energy resource projects which are often directly opposed to the welfare of Canadians. Not only are social injustices taking place, but the average Canadian is being forced to pay for them through higher prices and taxes.

It is easy to despair in a situation like this. Perhaps the greatest contribution that the churches can make in times like this is to provide hope that a better Canada is possible, and that we should all continue to work for it.

21 · INTER-CHURCH BRIEF ON ECONOMIC OUTLOOK

CANADIAN CHURCH LEADERS, 1978

Introduction

This brief is the latest in a series of questioning reflections that church representatives have presented to the federal Cabinet in the period since March, 1973. For this occasion, at the invitation of the Cabinet itself, the focus will be the country's economic outlook.

Our approach will be to re-examine two questions (northern development, income distribution) raised in our other briefs, and to pose new questions about two other areas (investment transfers, regional disparities) that also are key factors for the country's economic outlook. These are not the only issues that concern us, as can be seen in our other briefs and the various inter-church projects for research and action; nor have we lost interest in the others, if we have selected four issues for this limited presentation.

In collaborating as Christians to raise these issues, one of our aims is to promote an ethical critique of economic activity. In this we are building once again on our previous submissions to Cabinet. Throughout, we have stressed that our ethical base is the prophetic tradition of God's call for justice and good stewardship. Concerning the economic outlook, then, the basic ethical questions have to do with who will control the earth's resources and who will benefit as they are developed for human use.

While we address the federal level of government on this occasion, we want to stress at the outset our awareness that the dominant institutions forming this country's economic system include the provincial and municipal governments; industry, and especially the large transnational corporations, many foreign owned; financial institutions, such as banks and investment firms; trade unions; the legal system; and professional bodies in the financial and legal fields.

In addition, a vast amount of economic activity takes place informally among families and other support groups of friends and neighbours. Indeed, at the broadest level of analysis, no group or individual is without some responsibility for the present state of the economy and for improvements to it. Therefore it is with an awareness that we are involved and have roles to play that we turn now to matters that are more directly responsibilities of the federal government.

Northern Development

On June 20 last year, in a similar exchange of views with the federal Cabinet, an inter-church delegation especially questioned northern energy policies and your then impending pipeline decision. We still have many of the questions raised at that time, and some new ones:

(a) Why has no real progress been made on Native land claims around the Alcan pipeline route? The Council of Yukon Indians has our support in their insistence that these matters be settled before construction of the pipeline begins. Native leaders perceive that with the latest change of ministers responsible for northern affairs there was a real change in policy.

(b) Why has the government failed to proceed with a second review of the pipeline's environmental and social impact by an independent body as promised?

(c) How will the government guarantee for Canadians the maximum in job benefits from construction across Canadian territory of this line to serve American markets?

(d) In view of public criticism since the pipeline agreement was signed last September, how will Canadians be assured that Canadian public funds will never be spent on the pipeline?

In reiterating these questions, we wish to recall that our concern last June was not just with details of the pipeline settlement. The inter-church brief on that occasion also called for an overall new energy policy and industrial strategy for this country. This was based on the contention that the present model of industrial development tends excessively to be capital intensive, highly technological, energy intensive, export oriented, and foreign controlled. Moreover, it is biased in favour of the larger enterprises, as exemplified by the complaints of smaller exploration firms in Alberta that they have excessive gas reserves and inadequate markets.

Given no discernible progress to date on any new Canadian energy policy or industrial strategy, we conclude that the *economic outlook* forecast by pipeline plans is for continuation of these industrial tendencies questioned last June. This means continued industrial concentration in only a few centres of the country; continued minimizing of job opportunities; continued development of Canadian resources for the gain of a small minority rather than for the basic needs of many people who lack jobs and opportunities for full self-realization; and a continued flow of Canadian wealth into a few hands, many of them foreign.

To sum up on this point, we continue to see in the present pipeline plans a bleak economic outlook for Canadians—whether they be northern residents whose way of life and livelihood will be drastically changed, or southern residents for whom the main outlook seems to be the risk of further staggering increases in public debt. Responsibility for turning this country to development patterns that serve the basic needs of all Canadians rests heavily, though not exclusively, on the federal Cabinet.

Income Distribution

For a decade the question of a guaranteed annual income that could lift people out of poverty without sacrificing their dignity has been discussed by governments, economists, the press and the churches. In 1971 the Special Senate Committee on Poverty saw the guaranteed annual income as the "first firm step in the war against poverty." In 1973 the minister of national health and welfare, Hon. Marc Lalonde, launched a social security review with the provinces that seemed to be making headway towards assistance for individuals and families whose income derived from work, and yet who remained below the poverty level.

The social security review ended in 1976 with improvements in Family Allowances and the Canada Pension Plan, but without agreement between Ottawa and the provinces on establishing a guaranteed annual income, or the semblance of one.

With the bleak prospects faced by a multitude of Canadians in this present crisis of high unemployment, with many former breadwinners moving from unemployment insurance to welfare, the need is greater than ever for Ottawa and the provinces to create "an acceptable basic income for all Canadians."

One social fact that motivates our concern in this regard is the inflexibility of the disparity of income distribution in Canada. While various aid and welfare programs have made occasional short-term changes, the general situation has remained so constant that this country truly has a rigid, if hidden, class structure. Official annual reports group income earners by fifths from lowest to highest, and calculate for each of the five groups the percentage of income that each receives annually. The following table is a way of presenting the situation that has persisted for the past quarter century:

Percentage of Annual Income by Groups

	1951	1961	1971	1975
Top fifth	42.8	41.1	43.3	42.6
Above middle	23.3	24.5	24.9	25.1
Middle fifth	18.3	18.3	17.6	17.6
Below middle	11.2	11.9	10.6	10.6
Bottom fifth	4.4	4.2	3.6	4.0

Final figures for 1976 are not available, but preliminary indications are that the top fifth may have gained 44.0 per cent of the total at the cost of all other groups, the bottom group slipping to 3.9 per cent.

A table of this kind comes alive when the constant figures for the bottom fifth are seen to be the niggardly share of this country's wealth that goes to the poorest individuals and families. The usual rejoinder that other countries have even worse statistics is beside the point. Our view, in the words of the Anglican taskforce on the economy, is "based upon the moral and theological judgment that so far as Canada is concerned at least, the existence of poverty is unjust." Hence the support in our churches for measures to bring the poor into full participation in our society. While there would be support for the idea that priority should be given to creating meaningful work opportunities, it must be added that a very great many of the poor cannot work, for example, the aged and handicapped. Hence the crucial need for continued government leadership towards both dignified employment and a guaranteed annual wage.

Therefore, it is urgent that the federal government either reopen discussions with the provinces or undertake measures within its own competence. The latter course would most readily be achieved, we believe, by amendments to the Income Tax Act, to ensure a more effective redistribution of income.

Investment Transfers

In the past few months there have been some dramatic cases of massive layoffs, especially in the mining industry. Yet, as Canadian operations have been shut down, some of the same companies have been investing their capital in other countries, in some cases giving support there to regimes that violate human rights.

The immediate direct effect in Canada of increased unemployment has aroused much public attention, and rightly so. These examples expose the socially disruptive consequences of an economic system oriented to profit on investment as a primary end in itself. Entire enterprises are moved even though this may be clearly against the wishes and best interests of local people who have organized their entire lives in expectation of a relatively stable livelihood. "The multinational corporations which carve up a large part of the world's wealth seldom acknowledge much responsibility for the elimination of poverty and social injustice," an Anglican taskforce wrote last year.

The political will of peoples and governments count for little in such cases, even though basic human rights are at stake. This was stressed by Bishop A. Carter of Sault Ste. Marie, speaking just before Christmas:

> The massive layoff of workers in Sudbury violates one of the most fundamental rights of life, namely, the right to work and to provide the basic needs of life to one's family. Moreover, the decisions of the companies to cut back production and terminate jobs were announced suddenly and made without consultation. In effect, the workers became victims of market forces and the company's exaggerated concentration on profit.

With the growth of ever larger conglomerates and the decline of smaller local enterprises, the outlook is for decreased local autonomy, and increased powerlessness and impoverishment of more and more people, unless corrective actions are taken. An analysis of corporation taxation statistics for recent years indicates one of the ways in which present government policy favours a few large interlocking enterprises over the many smaller ones.

Tax returns for 1974 show that 300 to 1,000 large firms were the main beneficiaries of current tax deferment provisions. In that

year, the largest 300 firms had about 65 per cent of total deferments, while about 82 per cent went to the largest 1,000. These
1,000 firms represented about one-third of 1 per cent of the nearly
300,000 firms that reported, so that about 99.7 per cent of all firms
had only 18 per cent of deferments. Tax policy can be said to favour
large, capital-intensive firms over small and medium-size labour-
using units. The current pattern of corporate investment and
expansion in Canada is clearly linked to current tax policy. That
pattern, as current layoffs show, does not favour wide distribution
of jobs and other opportunities and advantages. Yet, without these,
people are marginalized, if not reduced to dependence. In this
regard, to cite but one example, a United Church poverty taskforce
recently called for federal and provincial policies

> ... that will provide *meaningful* employment, in industries that rely more
> on the skills and ingenuity of individuals than expensive machinery
> hungry for oil, gas and hydro. This type of industry is built up with an
> eye to maintaining regional self-sufficiency, and in general takes note
> that small *is* beautiful.

Regional Disparities

It is evident in Canada that economic growth, and hence jobs and
all social amenities, have been clustered in the Montreal-Hamilton
area. What is seldom mentioned is the fact that direct policies
contributed a great deal to this concentration, at the expense of
other parts of the country. Yet a 1976 federal government publication for the UN Habitat Conference in Vancouver recorded this
simple fact of history:

> Confederation in 1867 brought a determination to forge a Canadian
> economic unity to match the political union just achieved.... To create
> a national economy, the new government single-mindedly pursued a
> three-part policy: to build a transcontinental railway; to settle the prair-
> ies; and to raise a tariff wall to protect the fledgling manufacturing
> industries of central Canada.... In the Maritime provinces, the effect of
> the tariffs was to increase the cost of goods and, with the exception of
> the Sydney steel industry, this meant that industrial development would
> eventually take place elsewhere. But the policy was successful in Ontario
> and Quebec and confirmed their role as the industrial heartland of
> Canada.

Other presentations of our history add other insights into policies which over time have contributed to today's well-known picture

of regional disparities. Policies concerning parliamentary representation, railway rates, centralized banking and industrial development (such as taxation, as already discussed) all had their impacts. Internal migration figures confirm the pattern: Canada has its own neglected "Third World" areas, from which people migrate to the favoured metropolitan centres. A recent study describes Canada as

... a nation of regions one of which monopolizes most of the capital, manufacturing, employment and political power while others suffer the opposite effect, i.e., lack of capital, low manufacturing output, high unemployment and lack of political clout.... The Atlantic region is a well-defined hinterland sharing similarities with the North and to some extent with the West. The situation is not helped either by the heavy domination of Canada by outside economic interests, in particular the U.S., a situation which makes it very difficult for Canada to correct internal inequalities.

The phenomenon of regional disparities in Canada is thus linked to the problems of unemployment, of poverty, of investment transfers and of inappropriate industrial strategies, all discussed earlier in this brief. Moreover, current policies aimed at correcting regional imbalances, such as by the Department of Regional Economic Expansion, tend to replicate the same metropolitan-hinterland model. The emphasis has been on large-scale industrialization of designated urban "growth centres." Once again, people and resources outside such designated urban centres continue to suffer comparative underdevelopment. So disparities within regions are being added to those between regions.

The Victims of the Economic System

The problems we have been discussing have deep and often tragic consequences in the lives of some of our fellow citizens. By listening to what local people almost everywhere are saying, by taking into account the daily problems that must be faced by poor people and economically weak groups, one gets a clearer picture of the gravity of the situation. The current crisis hits individuals—those who are poor, unemployed, marginalized, aged—and also has an impact on homes, at work, in depressed regions and, indeed, the whole country.

One might be tempted to ignore these difficulties and say that everything is going to turn out in the end. But that would be to have a hand in maintaining the current situation and the present economic system. During the past few years, the churches of this country frequently have called on our governments, as well as all citizens, to bring about a greater degree of justice and equality in our society, as well as a better sharing of our common riches. We intervene once more in that sense today, to place before you the worries of a growing number of people about both present and future.

To many people, those with political power seem incapable of intervening effectively in the economic arena, for real power is in the hands of those who hold the capital. Those who define the Canadian economy are, for the most part, the heads of transnational companies. Their decisions often are taken outside this country, according to long-term and deliberately organized plans. In this sense, the Canadian economic system is not only interdependent with world economies; it is also at the mercy of financial powers who decide the times of crisis and of prosperity. As Wallace Clement notes, the country is gradually losing control of its economy:

> With direct investment, dependency and control increase over time, as in a parasitic relationship; it does not generate a situation where debts are paid off whereby indigenous control increases over time, as in portfolio investment. The parasitic elite gathers in capital and resources from Canada and in turn is able to reallocate this surplus into further control.

In times of growth or prosperity, this model of economic liberalism, taken on a country-wide scale, gives rise to a sense that people are living in comfort. In reality, however, this apparent well-being is not real except in terms of the prosperity of the financial powers. Centred on consumption of goods and the waste of basic energies and resources, this system gives an advantage to some groups of citizens by making them ever richer, and drives deeper into poverty those who cannot get much out of the struggle. The cost of living is the same for everyone, but many do not have equal means to face it. In a study of "The Impoverishment of Low Wage Earners," the Montreal Metropolitan Social Service Centre found the following:

> Over 20 years of work, low-wage earners become poorer and suffer deteriorating health, when not forced into unemployment or welfare, while those higher paid, that is, with more schooling, see their situations improve and reach enviable levels.

Thus we live in a situation that builds up differences between rich and poor. Unshared prosperity causes some to thirst for even more wealth and nourishes personal and collective selfishness, while it plunges others into feelings of frustration, humiliation and inferiority.

In times of crisis, this system engenders the phenomenon of acute social dependence on the part of many of our fellow citizens, who for survival can count only on state handouts. The longer the crisis lasts, the more it works at a deep level of people's outlooks, and ends up by alienating workers, the jobless, and their families. They develop a lack of self-confidence, apathy, a weakened sense of responsibility and family difficulties. Many lose all confidence in public authorities and react more and more against the economic materialism which holds them hostage; others fall into chronic idleness and become parasites of whom society itself disapproves. However, many of these people could make a creative and enriching contribution to their milieu, through neighborhood and cooperative projects.

More and more people are convinced, because of its record of broken promises, that the present economic system cannot bring real solutions to these problems. It seems to them urgent to find another way to live together, to create a setting in which human values take first place over every other consideration.

It is imperative and urgent that there be a radical change in this consumer society that emphasizes *having* things. The change must be in the direction of a society that stresses *being* someone, and which bears within it a global vision of the human person and of humanity. As has been stressed, "we do not believe in separating the economic from the human, nor development from the civilizations in which it exists. What we hold important is man, each man and every group of men, and we even include the whole of humanity."

NOTES

INTRODUCTION

[1] Cf. John R. Williams, "Religion in Newfoundland: The Churches and Social Ethics," *Religion and Culture in Canada*, ed. by Peter Slater (Waterloo: Wilfrid Laurier University Press, 1977), pp. 95-116.

[2] Cf. Richard Allen, *The Social Passion: Religion and Social Reform in Canada 1914-28* (Toronto: University of Toronto Press, 1971); Richard Allen, ed., *The Social Gospel in Canada* (Ottawa: National Museums of Canada, 1975); Gregory Baum, *Catholics and Canadian Socialism: Political Thought in the Thirties and Forties* (Toronto: James Lorimer and Co., 1980).

[3] An example of this is the book co-sponsored by the St. John's, Nfld., Ten Days Committee and the Newfoundland Association for Full Employment, *Work and Technological Change: Case Studies of Longshoremen and Postal Workers in St. John's*, by Brian O'Neill (St. John's: NAFE/Ten Days, 1981).

[4] Cf. GATT-Fly, *Ah-hah! A New Approach to Popular Education*, (Toronto: Between the Lines Press, 1983).

[5] Cf. Gregory Baum, "Economics and Religion," *The Ecumenist* 20/5 (July-August, 1982): 76-78, and Larry Colle, "Religion and Politics: Canada's New Right," *Catholic New Times*, Nov. 14, 1982.

[6] A comprehensive program of "social animation" is outlined in the publication of the Episcopal Commission for Social Affairs of the Canadian Conference of Catholic Bishops, *Witness to Justice* (Ottawa: CCCB, 1979).

CHAPTER 4 • WHO'S IN CONTROL?

[1] W. Clement, *The Canadian Corporate Elite* (Toronto: McClelland and Stewart, 1975), pp. 82-83.

[2] *Ibid.*, p. 82.

[3] Paper presented to Churchperson's Seminar by Eric Kierans, March, 1976.

[4] W. Clement, *The Canadian Corporate Elite*, p. 19.

[5] Ibid., p. 19.

[6] Barnet and Muller, *Global Reach* (New York: Simon and Shuster, 1974), p. 8.

[7] T. Naylor, *The History of Canadian Business* (Toronto: James Lorimer and Co., 1975), p. xviii.

[8] Barnet and Muller, *Global Reach*, p. 8.

[9] R. Ledogar, *Hungry for Profits*, (New York: IDOC, 1976), p. 5.

[10] Barnet and Muller, *Global Reach*, p. 10.

[11] J. Deverell and LAWG, *Falconbridge* (Toronto: James Lorimer and Co., 1975), p. 179.

[12] Statistics Canada, *Income Distribution by Size*, 1974.

[13] Barnet and Muller, *Global Reach* article, *New Yorker* magazine, Dec. 1974.

[14] See for instance *How Much Tax Do You Really Pay?* The Fraser Institute, 1976.

[15] A collection of interviews with corporate leaders published by the Investors Group, Winnipeg.

[16] See *Employment, Growth and Basic Needs* (Geneva: International Labour Organization, 1976).

[17] Sweezy, *Monthly Review*, October, 1976.

[18] *Business Week*, August 9, 1976.

[19] Newman, Peter. *The Canadian Establishment* (Toronto: McClelland and Stewart, 1975), p. 143.

[20] Barnet and Muller, *Global Reach* article.

[21] Barnet and Muller, *Global Reach*, p. 379.

CHAPTER 5 · DECENNIAL REVISION OF THE BANK ACT

[1] The Toronto Dominion Bank, the Royal Bank, the Canadian Imperial Bank of Commerce, the Bank of Nova Scotia, the Bank of Montreal.

[2] *Worlds Apart*, Human Rights and Economic Relations, Canada-Chile, Latin American Working Group, June, 1978.

[3] *Corporate Concentration and the Taskforce on the Churches and Corporate Responsibility*, February, 1976.

[4] See Nesbitt & Thompson, *International Consortium Loans by Canadian Chartered Banks*, 1976.

CHAPTER 6 · TO ESTABLISH A KINGDOM OF JUSTICE

[1] *A Society to be Transformed*, Pastoral Message of the Catholic Bishops of Canada, December 1, 1977, Ottawa, p. 4.

[2] Statistics Canada, *Analysis of Income Distributions by Size in Canada*, 1978. Professor Mike Bradfield of the Department of Economics, Dalhousie University, gives a further explanation of unequal distribution of income through an analysis of Revenue Canada taxation statistics. In 1973, Professor Bradfield points out, the top 3/10 of 1 per cent of the population, those who earned over $50 thousand, earned 28.4 per cent of the taxable dividends paid. Another 1.3 per cent in the income range of $20-50 thousand earned 22.6 per cent. This means that 1.6 percent of the population earned 51 per cent of all taxable shares.

[3] For a popular commentary, on this problem, see Ferdinand Lundberg, *The Rich and The Superrich* (New Jersey: Lyle Stewart, 1968).

[4] David Jay Bercuson, *Canada and the Burden of Unity* (MacMillan Company of Canada, 1977); Social Action Commission, Roman Catholic Diocese of Charlottetown, *Background Document on Atlantic Region Disparity*, September 15, 1977; Tom Naylor, *History of Canadian Business 1867-1914* (Toronto, 1975), c.f. Introduction to vol. 1. by Eric Kierans. *Economic Overview, Review of Selected Trends in the Prince Edward Island Economy, 1971-1977*, Department of Development, P.E.I. Government. C.W. Gonick, *Inflation or Depression, An Analysis of the Continuing Crisis of the Canadian Economy* (Toronto: James Lorimer and Co., 1975).

[5] Social Action Commission, Roman Catholic Diocese of Char-lottetown, *Background Paper on Atlantic Region Disparity*, September 15, 1977.

[6] Pope John Paul II, *Redemptor Hominis*, Canadian Conference of Catholic Bishops, Ottawa, March 1979, no. 15.

[7] *Ibid.*

[8] *Ibid.*, no 16.

[9] *Ibid.*

[10] *From Words to Action*, Pastoral Message, Catholic Bishops of Canada, 1976. Further explanation of Social Sin is found in: *Medellin Documents*, 1968; *Justice in the World*, Report of Third World Synod of Bishops, 1971; Dr. Gregory Baum, "The Theology of Liberation," *New Internationalist*, December, 1978.

In these documents Social Sin is described as oppressive structures and institutions that damage and devour people by enhancing the wealth and power of the rich minority over the poor and destitute. The destructive power is not derived from the malice of the individuals but from the twisted logic of institutions themselves. Colonialism is an institutional evil. It subjugates people, makes them economically and politically subservient and exploits them for the benefit of the political power.

[11] Pope Paul VI, *Populorum Progressio*, St. Paul Editions, Vatican City, 1967, no. 33.

[12] Isaiah 65:21-22 and Amos 9:11-15.

[13] Pope John Paul II, *Redemptor Hominis*, no. 18.

[14] Cardinal George B. Flahiff, *Synod Intervention on Christian Formation For Justice*, Rome, October 1, 1971, p. 2.

[15] Pope John Paul II, *Redemptor Hominis*, no. 17.

[16] Pope Paul VI, *Populorum Progressio*, no. 49.

CHAPTER 7 · ETHICAL REFLECTIONS ON THE ECONOMIC CRISIS

[1] Among the more recent pastoral statements, see: Episcopal Commission for Social Affairs, *Unemployment: The Human Costs*, Canadian Conference of Catholic Bishops, 1980; Comité des

affaires sociales, *Luttes des travailleurs en temps de crise et Les jeunes face à la crise*, Assemblée des évêques du Quebec, 1982. For an ethical reflection on the economic crisis in France, see the recent statement of the Bishops of France: *Pour de nouveaux modes de vie*, Déclaration du Conseil permanent de l'Episcopat sur la conjoncture économique et sociale, 1982.

2   John Paul II, *Laborem Exercens*, nos. 4, 6, 9, 24, 25, 26.

3   *Unemployment: The Human Costs*, no. 5

4   *Laborem Exercens*, no. 26.

5   See for example, John Paul II, *Laborem Exercens*, 1981; John Paul II, *Redemptor Hominis*, 1979; Paul VI, *Octogesima Adveniens*, 1971; Paul VI, *Populorum Progressio*, 1967; World Synod of Bishops, *Justice in the World*, 1971.

6   See, for example, A.G. Frank, *Crisis in the World Economy* (New York: Holmes and Meier, 1980); Samir Amin *et al*, *La crise, quelle crise? Dynamique de la crise mondiale* (Paris: Maspéro, 1982); S. Rousseau, *Capitalism and Catastrophe: A Critical Appraisal of the Limits to Capitalism* (Cambridge: Cambridge University Press, 1979); *Social Analysis Linking Faith and Justice* (Washington, D.C.: Center of Concerns, 1980); *La crise économique et sa gestion*, Actes du colloque de l'Association d'économie politique, tenu à l'université du Québec à Montréal (Montréal: Boréal Express, 1982); Cy Gonick, *Inflation or Depression, An Analysis of the Continuing Crisis of the Canadian Economy* (Toronto: Lorimer, 1975).

7   See, for example, forecasts of the Conference Board of Canada, November, 1982. Their forecasts predict moderate recovery with greater unemployment. (With forecasts of economic recovery for 1983 and 1984, unemployment is forecast at 12.7 per cent for 1983 and 11.4 per cent for 1984.)

8   Observers point out that the highly capital-intensive nature of modern weapons manufacture creates a more rapid rate of technological obsolescence of fixed-capital and thus leads to greater inflationary pressures and higher unemployment. See M. Kaldor, "The Role of Military Technology in Industrial Development," UN Group of Government Experts on the Relationship of Disarmament and Development, May, 1980. For a more extensive analysis of this question, see A. Eide and M. Thee, eds., *Problems of Contemporary Militarism* (London, 1980).

[9] See, for example, *La crise économique et sa gestion*, part I, "La crise actuelle des societés capitalistes."

[10] John Paul II, *Laborem Exercens*, no. 12, on the "priority of labour." For a commentary, see G. Baum, *The Priority of Labour* (New York: Paulist Press, 1982).

[11] John Paul II, *Laborem Exercens*, no. 13, particularly comments on the error of "economism" and "materialism."

[12] *Ibid.*, no. 5.

[13] See CCCB, *A Society to Be Transformed*, 1977; Paul VI, *Populorum Progressio*, nos. 33 and 57.

[14] For analysis of global disparities, see Brandt Commission Report, *North-South: A Program for Survival*, 1980. For data on disparities in Canada, see *Income Distribution by Size in Canada*, Statistics Canada, 1980. For more extended analysis see J. Harp and J.R. Hofley, eds., *Structured Inequality in Canada* (Scarborough: Prentice-Hall, 1980).

[15] See the budget statements of the Hon. Allan MacEachen, November, 1981, and June 28, 1982, plus the recent statement on the economy by the Hon. Marc Lalonde, October 29, 1982.

[16] See budget statement of Hon. Allan MacEachen, June 28, 1982. Finance Department officials have stated that the 6 and 5 program will have the "unintended effect of transferring incomes from wages to profits" (see Toronto *Globe and Mail*, August 28, 1982).

[17] It should be noted, for example, that: (1) people earning $18,000 who can least afford reductions in their incomes below the inflation rate are subjected to the same rate of control as people earning $50,000 salaries or more who could afford an income freeze; (2) it is estimated that approximately 30 per cent of the total Net National Income generated in Canada (1980) came in the form of dividends, interest and other investment income rather than wages and salaries which are subject to controls.

[18] See concerns expressed by the Canadian Labour Congress in their "Statement on Economic Policy," July 8, 1982. For a further perspective see, "Wage Controls Won't Work," *Public Employee*, Fall, 1982. See also the report of the Confédération des syndicats nationaux (CSN), "Du travail pour tout le monde," février 1982.

[19] See *Unemployment: The Human Costs*, no. 12.

[20] *Unemployment: The Human Costs*, nos. 9 and 14.

[21] For examples of proposed industrial strategies, see Canadian Labour Congress, *Economic Policy Statement*, May, 1982. See also the recent proposals of the Confédération des syndicats nationaux, *La Presse*, November 18, 1982.

[22] As an example of thinking about alternative directions, see W. Wagerman, *Christians and the Great Economic Debate*, (London: SCM Press, 1977).

[23] See, for example, the following Science Council of Canada Reports: *The Weakest Link*: A Technological Perspective on Canadian Industrial Underdevelopment; *Forging the Links*: A Technological Policy for Canada; *Hard Times/Hard Choices*: Technology and the Balance of Payments.

[24] For references to "true community" see Rt. Hon. Pierre E. Trudeau, *Statements on the Economy*, parts I and III.

CHAPTER 10 · NORTHERN DEVELOPMENT: AT WHAT COST?

[1] These reflections and judgements are based on a variety of consultations and conversations with people concerned with the future development of the Canadian North. See in particular a recent work by Louis-Edmond Hamelin, *Nordicité canadienne* (Montreal: HMH, 1975).

[2] For example, cf. Eric Gourdeau, "The People of the Canadian North," and "Impressions of the Land," in *Arctic Alternatives* (Ottawa: Canadian Arctic Resources Committee, 1973).

[3] The particular phrase is the title of a documentary produced by the National Film Board and a direct quote from the Cree Indian people of the Mistassini area in Northern Quebec. Variations of this theme are frequently expressed by Native Peoples throughout the North.

[4] Cf. Lloyd Barber, *The Basis for Native Claims in Canada* address to the Rotary Club, Yellowknife, N.W.T., October, 1974. Mr. Barber is the Indian claims commissioner for Canada. See also, René Fumoleau, o.m.i., *As Long as This Land Shall Last* (Toronto: McClelland & Stewart, 1975).

[5] Cf. Wade Rowland, *Fueling Canada's Future*, (Toronto: MacMillan of Canada, 1974), chapter two.

[6] This concern was expressed in a July 11, 1973, letter to Premier Bourassa by Cardinal Maurice Roy of Québec, writing as president of the Assemblée des évêques du Québec.

[7] Cf. two comparative articles: *Whose Development?—The Impact of Development on the Native Peoples of Canada and Brazil; What Price Development? Foreign Investment and Resources Extraction in British Columbia and Jamaica*. Both articles are available from the Inter-Church Committee for World Development Education, 600 Jarvis St., Toronto.

[8] For example, cf. *l'Aménagement de la Baie James: progrès ou désastre?* par le comité pour la défense de la Baie James, Montreal; *The Churchill Diversion—Time Runs out for the Native Peoples of the North*, available from the Canadian Association in Support of Native Peoples, Ottawa; *Northwest Development: What and For Whom*, available from the Northwest B.C. Conference Committee, Terrace, B.C.

[9] This has been the case with most of the major energy projects in the North to date. A land settlement is currently being negotiated with the Native People of the James Bay region, but these negotiations are taking place *after* the basic industrial plans have been established.

[10] For example, the Natives of Nelson House Reserve and South Indian Lake in Northern Manitoba face serious problems of flooding. Cf. "Northern Manitoba: The Project and the People," *Bulletin*, Canadian Association in Support of Native Peoples, December, 1974.

[11] For example, during the construction of the Pointed Mountain Pipeline in the Territories, only 30 Native People were employed for a maximum of three months, while 320 workers were brought in from the South. In 1970, after the federal government had invested $9 million in Panarctic it has employed only 6 natives at $1.75 an hour. Cf. Melville Watkins, "Resources and Underdevelopment," in *(Canada) Ltd.*, ed. by Robert M. Laxer (Toronto: McClelland & Stewart, 1973).

[12] *Gaudium et spes*, no. 69; *Populorum Progressio*, no. 22.

[13] James Wash-shee, President, Indian Brotherhood of the Northwest Territories, cited in the Brotherhood's initial submission to the Berger Inquiry, 1975.

[14] Cf. George Manuel, *The Fourth World* (Toronto: Collier & MacMillan, 1974).

[15] Third Synod of Bishops, 1971, *Justice in the World*, p. 14.

[16] Cf. *An Energy Policy for Canada: Phase I* (Ottawa: Department of Energy, Mines and Resources, 1973).

[17] *Ibid.*, vol. 1, p. 11.

[18] Cf., for example, Wade Rowland, *Fueling Canada's Future*; Canadian Arctic Resources Committee, *Gas From the Mackenzie Delta: Now or Later*; James Laxer, *Canada's Energy Crisis; Background Statement on the Arctic*, Pollution Probe at the University of Toronto, March 28, 1972, revised April 12, 1972.

[19] Cf. Rowland, *Fueling Canada's Future*, p. 44.

[20] Based on statistics provided by Meadows *et al*, *The Limits to Growth*, a Report for the Club of Rome's Project on the Predicament of Mankind, 1972.

[21] Cf. Barbara Ward, and René Dubos, *Only One Earth* (England: Penguin Books, 1972), p. 44.

[22] Cf. Ivan Illich, *Energy and Equity* (New York: Harper-Row, 1974).

[23] Cf. Mihajlo Mesarovic and Eduard Pestel, *Mankind at the Turning Point*, Second Report to the Club of Rome.

[24] *Simplicity and Sharing*, 1972 Labour Day Message, Canadian Conference of Catholic Bishops. Cf. also Thomas S. Derr, *Ecologie et libération humaine* (Genève: Éditions Labour et Fides, 1974).

[25] *Development Demands Justice*, a joint statement by Canadian Church leaders, March, 1973.

[26] Canadian Oblate Conference, *The Religious Situation of the Canadian Native People*, November, 1971.

[27] Third Synod of Bishops, 1971, *Justice in the World*, Introduction.

[28] For detailed information, cf. *Resource Kit on Northern Development*, available at cost, from the Social Affairs Desk, Canadian Catholic Conference, 90 Parent Avenue, Ottawa K1N 7B1.

CHAPTER 15 • BRIEF TO THE SPECIAL JOINT COMMITTEE OF THE SENATE AND OF THE HOUSE OF COMMONS ON IMMIGRATION POLICY

[1] John XXIII, *Pacem in Terris*, Art. 25.

[2] See Vatican II, *The Church in the Modern World*, Art. 29, 60-66.

[3] For example, we disagree with the view that the Green Paper contains "the full range of policy issues which need to be discussed." See Freda Hawkins, "Review of the Green Paper on Immigration," *Social Sciences in Canada*, vol. 3, no. 1-2 (1975), p. 30.

[4] See, "There was a time when strangers were welcome here..." *Canadian News Synthesis Project*, July, 1975.

[5] *Pacem in Terris*, Art. 102.

[6] *Our Sunday Visitor*, December 3, 1972. (For Canadian reactions to this affirmation of Barbara Ward, see, *Public Consultation on Population Questions*, Canadian Institute of International Affairs in Co-operation with the Family Planning Federation of Canada and the Inter-Church Project on Population, Toronto, May, 1974, p. 16, "The Social Justice Approach," pp. 19-21, "Population and Social Justice," pp. 28-29, "The Social Justice View."

ADDRESSES OF GROUPS MENTIONED IN THIS BOOK

The Anglican Church of Canada,
Unit on Public Social Responsibility,
600 Jarvis Street,
Toronto, Ontario M4Y 2J6.

The Baptist Convention of Ontario and Quebec,
Social Action Committee,
217 St. George Street,
Toronto, Ontario M5R 2M2.

The Canadian Conference of Catholic Bishops,
Episcopal Commission for Social Affairs,
90 Parent Avenue,
Ottawa, Ontario K1N 7B1.

The Canadian Council of Churches,
40 St. Clair Avenue East,
Toronto, Ontario M4T 1M9.

Centre for the Study of Economics and Religion,
The Fraser Institute,
626 Bute Street,
Vancouver, B.C. V6E 3M1.

The Church Council on Justice and Corrections,
151 Slater Street, No. 305,
Ottawa, Ontario K1P 5H3.

Citizens for Public Justice,
229 College Street,
Toronto, Ontario M5T 1R4.

Confederation of Church and Business People,
15 Wellington Street West, Suite 14,
Toronto, Ontario M5J 1G7.

GATT-Fly,
11 Madison Avenue,
Toronto, Ontario M5R 2S2

Inter-Church Coalition on Africa
129 St. Clair Avenue West
Toronto, Ontario M4V 1N5.

Inter-Church Coalition on Resource Development in Manitoba,
470 Stella Avenue,
Winnipeg, Manitoba R2W 2V1.

Inter-Church Commission on the Social Impact of Resource Development,
P.O. Box 2097,
St. John's, Newfoundland A1C 6E6.

Inter-Church Committee on Human Rights in Latin America,
40 St. Clair Avenue East,
Toronto, Ontario M4T 1M9.

Inter-Church Committee for Refugees,
40 St. Clair Avenue East,
Toronto, Ontario M4T 1M9.

Inter-Church Project on Population,
c/o Bernard Daly,
90 Parent Avenue,
Ottawa, Ontario K1N 7B1.

Inter-Church Uranium Committee,
P.O. Box 7724,
Saskatoon, Saskatchewan S7K 4R4.

Jesuit Centre for Social Faith and Justice,
947 Queen Street East,
Toronto, Ontario M4M 1J9.

Lutheran Church in America—Canada Section,
Committee on Social Issues and Concerns,
710 Campbell Street,
Winnipeg, Manitoba R3N 1C3.

National Inter-Faith Immigration Committee,
67 Bond Street,
Toronto, Ontario M5B 1X5.

PLURA,
c/o Rev. Robert Lindsay,
85 St. Clair Avenue East,
Toronto, Ontario M4T 1M8.

The Presbyterian Church in Canada,
Board of Congregational Life,
50 Wynford Drive,
Don Mills, Ontario M3C 1J7.

Project North,
80 Sackville Street,
Toronto, Ontario M5A 3E5.

Project Ploughshares,
Institute for Peace and Conflict Studies,
Conrad Grebel College,
University of Waterloo,
Waterloo, Ontario N2L 3G6.

The Salvation Army,
Commission on Moral and Social Standards and Issues,
20 Albert Street,
Toronto, Ontario M5G 1A6.

Taskforce on the Churches and Corporate Responsibility,
129 St. Clair Avenue West,
Toronto, Ontario M4V 1N5.

Ten Days for World Development,
Room 315, 85 St. Clair Avenue East,
Toronto, Ontario M4T 1M8.

The United Church of Canada,
Department of Church in Society,
Division of Mission in Canada,
85 St. Clair Avenue East,
Toronto, Ontario M4T 1M8.

Printed in Canada